30.

D1477500

To
Robert LaVigne
Painter & Lover
& his natural happey eight year old dick

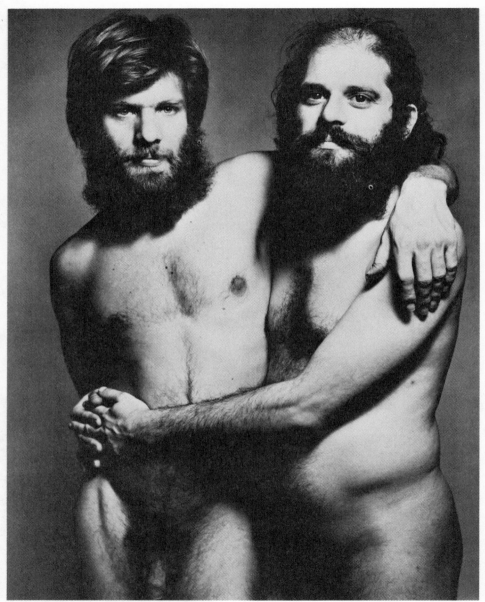

Peter Orlovsky (left) and Allen Ginsberg, NYC, 1963
Photo by Richard Avedon

ALLEN GINSBERG / PETER ORLOVSKY

STRAIGHT HEARTS' DELIGHT

Love Poems and Selected Letters
1947–1980

Edited by Winston Leyland

Sure, if that long-with-love acquainted eyes
Can judge of love, thou feel'st a lover's case . . .
—*Sir Philip Sidney*
from Astrophel and Stella (1591)

Gay Sunshine Press
San Francisco

First Edition 1980

The following Ginsberg poems are reprinted with permission of City Lights Books, San Francisco: "A Supermarket in California", and "Song" from *Howl & Other Poems* © 1956, 1959 by Allen Ginsberg. "The Green Automobile," "Love Poem on Theme by Whitman," and "Malest Cornifici Tuo Catullo" from *Reality Sandwiches* © 1963 by Allen Ginsberg. "Why Is God Love, Jack?" "Morning," "Message II," "Who Be Kind To," "Kral Majales," "Chances 'R'," and "City Midnite Junk Strains" from *Planet News* © 1968 by Allen Ginsberg. "Elegy for Neal Cassady," "Please Master," "On Neal's Ashes," "Over Denver Again," "Rain-wet Asphalt Heat, Garbage Curbed Cans Overflowing," "Graffiti," "After Thoughts," "Kiss Ass," and "Over Laramie" from *The Fall of America* © 1972 by Allen Ginsberg. "I Lay Love on My Knee," "Love Replied," "Come All Ye Brave Boys," and "Drive All Blames into One" from *Mind Breaths* © 1977, 1978 by Allen Ginsberg. "Understand This Is a Dream" from *Airplane Dreams* © 1968 by Allen Ginsberg. "Night Gleam" first appeared in *Angels of the Lyre: A Gay Poetry Anthology*, Panjandrum Press/Gay Sunshine Press, 1975, and was later reprinted in *Mind Breaths*. "Sweet Boy, Gimme Yr Ass" first appeared in *Orgasms of Light: The Gay Sunshine Anthology*, Gay Sunshine Press, 1977, and was later reprinted in *Mind Breaths*. The following Ginsberg poems are reprinted by permission of Grey Fox Press: "A Further Proposal," "Do We Understand Each Other?" "Western Ballad," "Pull My Daisy," and "The Shrouded Stranger" from *The Gates of Wrath, Rhymed Poems 1948-1952* © 1972 by Allen Ginsberg. The following poems are reprinted with permission of Full Court Press: "Jimmy Berman's Rag," "Many Loves," "Troost Street Blues," "The House of the Rising Sun," "Everybody Sing," "2 AM Dirty Jersey Blues," and "Hardon Blues" from *First Blues Rags, Ballads & Harmonium Songs 1971-74* © 1975 by Allen Ginsberg. The following Ginsberg poems are reprinted with permission of Cherry Valley Editions: "Reading French Poetry," "C'mon Jack, turn me on your knees," "Punk Rock Your My Big Crybaby," and "Lack Love" from *Poems All Over the Place* © 1978 by Allen Ginsberg. "In Society" and "I Made Love to Myself" are reprinted with permission from *Empty Mirror*, Totem/Corinth Books, © 1961 by Allen Ginsberg. "The Names" was published in a slightly different version in *As Ever: The Collected Correspondence of Allen Ginsberg and Neal Cassady*, Creative Arts, © 1977 by Allen Ginsberg.

The following Orlovsky poems are reprinted with permission of City Lights Books: "Woe Its Waring Time Again in the Armey," "Me & Allen," and "Some One Liked Me When I Was Twelve" from *Clean Asshole Poems and Smiling Vegetable Songs* © 1978 by Peter Orlovsky. The Orlovsky "Sex Experiments" first appeared in *Fuck You/A Magazine of the Arts*.

The following letters are reprinted with permission of Columbia University, New York, Allen Ginsberg Papers, Rare Book and Manuscript Library: Letters by Ginsberg: 1958—Jan. 20, 28. Feb. 15, 24. April 1. May 30. June 8, 15, 21. 1960—Jan. 24. Feb. 9. June 12. 1961—Aug. 3. 1965—May 10. All letters by Peter Orlovsky. Also reprinted with permission of Columbia: holograph letters and photos/drawings on pages 113-114, 120-122, 209. The following letters are reprinted with permission of Humanities Research Center, The University of Texas at Austin: Letters by Allen Ginsberg: 1956—May. 1961—Aug. 2, Oct. 21. 1963—May 31. Oct. 10. 1965—Feb. 4, 15. May 4.

Frontispiece photo © 1970 by Richard Avedon. The three erotic LaVigne drawings (pp. 14, 31, 90) and photos on p. 135 are from the personal collection of Allen Ginsberg. Drawings of Ginsberg/Orlovsky on pp. 226-227 © 1980 by Robert LaVigne. Reprinted with permission. Ginsberg/Orlovsky photo on p. 180 © 1979 by Elsa Dorfman and The Witkin Gallery Inc.; from the postcard published by The Witkin Gallery, Inc., 41 E. 57 St., NY 10022. Photo of Neal Cassady (p. 57) © by Carolyn Cassady.

Cover design by Frank Holbrook
Publication of this book was made possible in part by a grant from the National Endowment for the Arts, Washington, D.C.

Library of Congress Cataloging in Publication Data:

Ginsberg, Allen, 1926-
    Straight hearts' delight.

    Includes index.
    1. Love poetry, American.   2. Homosexuality - Poetry.   3. Ginsberg, Allen, 1926-   - Correspondence.   4. Orlovsky, Peter, 1933-   - Correspondence.   5. Poets, American - 20th century - Correspondence.   I. Orlovsky, Peter, 1933-   joint author.   II. Leyland, Winston, 1940-
III. Title.

PS595.H65G56   811'.54   80-17216

ISBN 0-917342-64-X
ISBN 0-917342-65-8 (pbk.)

Gay Sunshine Press, PO Box 40397, San Francisco, CA 94140
Write for free catalog of books available.

Contents

POEMS BY PETER ORLOVSKY

SELECTED LETTERS 1956-1965

List of Illustrations

Editor's Note and Acknowledgments

THREE YEARS AGO I conceived the idea of publishing a "lover's hand-book" by Allen Ginsberg and Peter Orlovsky. My intention was to include poems and letters by the two poets in one volume, concentrating on those which related to gay love and consciousness and those with special bearing on their own love relationship. I have known both men for several years and have published their work many times in *Gay Sunshine Journal* during the past decade, including an in-depth interview with each of them. Allen's poems also appear in the two anthologies of gay literature edited by myself: *Angels of the Lyre* (1975) and *Orgasms of Light* (1977).

Both poets reacted with enthusiasm to the idea, and the book took form. It was relatively easy for the three of us to choose the poems, written during a thirty-year period. But a problem arose in choosing letters. In the past twenty-five years hundreds of letters were exchanged between Allen and Peter during their periods of separation (mostly when traveling abroad). There obviously was insufficient space to print their collected correspondence in one modest volume. I therefore decided to select the most interesting letters from a nine-year period of literary and personal accomplishments (1956-1965).

Letters written in the first six months of 1958 when Allen was living in Paris and Peter in New York are especially well represented here. First drafts of several important Ginsberg poems are in these Paris–New York letters along with much material on their own personal interaction and on their friends (Burroughs, Kerouac, Leroy Jones, etc.). Later letters give us an in-depth look at Peter's Indian trip of 1963 and Allen's controversial visits to Cuba and Czechoslovakia in 1965, among other events.

With a few exceptions original spelling and punctuation have been kept throughout the letters. Because of space limitations several letters were edited to a shorter length. Any deletions are indicated by bracketed ellipses. In a handful of cases names have been changed to protect the privacy of living persons. Those footnotes dictated verbatim by Ginsberg and Orlovsky are so indicated; the remainder are by the editor or authors. Both poems and letters are presented in chronological order.

I wish to thank first and foremost Allen and Peter for their kindness and generosity during the three years that this book was in preparation, and especially for their warm hospitality during my 1979 visit to Naropa. Thanks also to David Chura and Jason Shinder who so patiently researched Ginsberg/Orlovsky letters and photos at Columbia University; and to Richard Mills who researched Ginsberg letters at the University of Texas, Austin. Thanks to Kenneth Lohf of the Special Collections Division of Columbia University and to the Humanities Research Center at the University of Texas, Austin, for allowing the use of materials in their archives. Special thanks to Carolyn Cassady for providing the photo of her husband Neal; to Robert LaVigne for his drawings; to Frank Holbrook for his superb cover design; to Matt Lowman and Carse McDaniel for their professional indexing of the book; to City Lights Books, Grey Fox Press, Totem/Corinth Books, Cherry Valley Editions, and Full Court Press for permission to reprint poems; and to all those who encouraged me during its preparation.

WINSTON LEYLAND
San Francisco
Spring 1980

Chronology of Letters and
Explanation of Texts

PETER ORLOVSKY and I lived together in San Francisco till sometime after publication of *Howl* (1956), while I shipped on MSTS (Military Sea Transport Service) boats to the Arctic and Peter drove an ambulance to make money to go to Europe. Then, with Lafcadio Orlovsky (who'd lived with us in Bay Area for a year) and Gregory Corso, we took buses via Los Angeles to Mexico City and joined Kerouac for a month. We all drove together in an old crowded car back to New York (Gregory flew). After several months in Manhattan, Gregory sailed for Paris and Jack (Yugoslavian freighter) to Tangier where Burroughs had been in residence for four years. Peter and I joined them in 1957; soon Jack left for swift trip Paris–London–home. Alan Ansen arrived from Venice and continued work typing *Naked Lunch* begun by Jack and myself in Tanger.

Peter and I stayed on in Morocco with Burroughs and Ansen for several months, then traveled through Spain, summered in Venice with Ansen, visited Vienna, Munich, Paris, and spent a month in Amsterdam with Gregory and then we three settled in Paris at 9 rue Gît-le-Cœur for nearly a year. Peter returned to New York some months before me to rescue his brother Julius from Central Islip State Hospital. Thus the density of the correspondence in that period.

The next period of separation was in 1960; I spent six months in South America. In 1961 we set off together from the U.S. to return to Tangier & spent months there with Burroughs, Corso, Bowles & others, Leary visiting, then Peter went on alone to Athens & Middle East. I followed and we met each other again by appointment on a street in Tel Aviv that fall. Traveling to India via West Africa, we joined Gary Snyder & Joane Kyger in New Delhi early in 1962. I left after a year and a half alone to meet Olson, Creeley, Duncan, Levertov, and others in summer 1963 Vancouver poetry conference. Peter stayed on in Benares & letters went back & forth between us for almost half a year—mine from San Francisco, Peter writing as he moved overland thru Pakistan, Baluchistan, Iran, Turkey & by Oriental express thru Europe to London. Correspondence of 1965 marks a separate trip I took through Cuba, Russia, Poland, Czechoslovakia and London.

The last decades' affairs of the heart are accounted somewhat in the poetry section of this book; more ample epistolary detail awaits the patient labor of some future scholar. Some readers had been baffled by absence of 50's literary life detail in my own *Journals Early Fifties Early Sixties* (Grove Press 1977); I hope this present volume sketches in some missing particulars of those years.

This book isn't a complete record of all correspondence between 1957 and 1965 but a choice emphasizing highlights of romantic love and literary history researched by David Chura (at New York's Columbia University Archives), and by Richard Mills (at the University of Texas Library, Austin), thereafter selected and edited by Winston Leyland in consultation with the authors. Thanks also to Jason Shinder for researching additional Orlovsky letters, and other work. Final text of poems and letters was examined by the authors and editor at the Jack Kerouac School of Disembodied Poetics at Naropa Institute, Boulder, Colorado, in the last days of July, 1979.

ALLEN GINSBERG

Poems by
Allen Ginsberg

Let the mercy of the flower's direction beckon in the eye.
Let the straight flower bespeak its purpose in straightness—
to seek the light.
Let the crooked flower bespeak its purpose in crookedness—
to seek the light.
Let the crookedness and straightness bespeak the light.

> —from "Psalm III" in *Reality Sandwiches*
> (Ginsberg), 1963

Allen Ginsberg (glasses), Peter Orlovsky, and Natalie Jackson
San Francisco, summer 1954
Drawing by Robert LaVigne

14

A FURTHER PROPOSAL

Come live with me and be my love,
And we will some old pleasures prove.
Men like me have paid in verse
This costly courtesy, or curse;

But I would bargain with my art,
(As to the mind, now to the heart)
My symbols, images, and signs
Please me more outside these lines.

For your share and recompense,
You will be taught another sense:
The wisdom of the subtle worm
Will turn most perfect in your form.

Not that your soul need tutored be
By intellectual decree,
But graces that the mind can share
Will make you, as more wise, more fair,

Till all the world's devoted thought
Find all in you it ever sought,
And even I, of skeptic mind,
A Resurrection of a kind.

This compliment, in my own way,
For what I would receive, I pay;
Thus all the wise have writ thereof,
And all the fair have been their love.

1947†

†Those poems devoted to Neal Cassady (marked †) follow chronologically from first
meeting to news of his death and later years' reflections.

IN SOCIETY

I walked into the cocktail party
room and found three or four queers
talking together in queertalk.
I tried to be friendly but heard
myself talking to one in hiptalk.
"I'm glad to see you," he said, and
looked away. "Hmn," I mused. The room
was small and had a double-decker
bed in it, and cooking apparatus:
icebox, cabinet, toasters, stove;
the hosts seemed to live with room
enough only for cooking and sleeping.
My remark on this score was under-
stood but not appreciated. I was
offered refreshments, which I accepted.
I ate a sandwich of pure meat; an
enormous sandwich of human flesh,
I noticed, while I was chewing on it,
it also included a dirty asshole.

More company came, including a
fluffy female who looked like
a princess. She glared at me and
said immediately: "I don't like you,"
turned her head away, and refused
to be introduced. I said, "What!"
in outrage. "Why you shit-faced fool!"
This got everybody's attention.
"Why you narcissistic bitch! How
can you decide when you don't even
know me," I continued in a violent
and messianic voice, inspired at
last, dominating the whole room.

Dream 1947

DO WE UNDERSTAND EACH OTHER?*

My love has come to ride me home
To our room and bed.
I had walked the wide sea path,
For my love would roam
In absence long and glad
All through our land of wrath.
We wandered wondrously,
I, still mild, true and sad,
But merry, mad and free
My love was. Look! yet come love hath.
Is not this great gentility?

I only remembered the ocean's roll,
And islands that I passed,
And, in a vision of death and dread,
A city where my soul
Visited its vast
Passage of the dead.
My love's eternity
I never entered, when, at last
"I blush with love for thee,"
My love, renewed in anger, said.
Is this not great gentility?

Over the road in an automobile
Rode I and my gentle love.
The traffic on our way was wild:
My love was at the wheel,
And in and out we drove.
My own eyes were mild.
How my love merrily
Dared the other cars to rove:
"But if they stop for me,
Why, then, I stop for them, my child."
Is this not great gentility?

East Harlem, 1948†

*[a dream]

A WESTERN BALLAD

When I died, love, when I died
My heart was broken in your care;
I never suffered love so fair
as now I suffer and abide
when I died, love, when I died.

When I died, love, when I died
I wearied in an endless maze
that men have walked for centuries,
as endless as the gate was wide
when I died, love, when I died.

When I died, love, when I died
there was a war in the upper air;
all that happens, happens there;
there was an angel at my side
when I died, love, when I died.

1948†

PULL MY DAISY

Pull my daisy
tip my cup
all my doors are open
Cut my thoughts
for coconuts
all my eggs are broken
Jack my Arden
gate my shades
woe my road is spoken
Silk my garden
rose my days
now my prayers awaken

Bone my shadow
dove my dream
start my halo bleeding
Milk my mind &
make me cream
drink me when you're ready
Hop my heart on
harp my height
seraphs hold me steady
Hip my angel
hype my light
lay it on the needy

Heal the raindrop
sow the eye
bust my dust again
Woe the worm
work the wise
dig my spade the same
Stop the hoax
what's the hex
where's the wake
how's the hicks
take my golden beam

Rob my locker
lick my rocks
leap my cock in school
Rack my lacks
lark my looks
jump right up my hole
Whore my door
beat my boor
eat my snake of fool
Craze my hair
bare my poor
asshole shorn of wool

Say my oops
ope my shell
bite my naked nut
Roll my bones
ring my bell
call my worm to sup
Pope my parts
pop my pot
raise my daisy up
Poke my pap
pit my plum
let my gap be shut

   —*Allen Ginsberg, Jack Kerouac & Neal Cassady*
      ca. 1948

THE SHROUDED STRANGER

Bare skin is my wrinkled sack
When hot Apollo humps my back
When Jack Frost grabs me in these rags
I wrap my legs with burlap bags

My flesh is cinder my face is snow
I walk the railroad to and fro
When city streets are black and dead
The railroad embankment is my bed

I sup my soup from old tin cans
And take my sweets from little hands
In Tiger Alley near the jail
I steal away from the garbage pail

In darkest night where none can see
Down in the bowels of the factory
I sneak barefoot upon stone
Come and hear the old man groan

I hide and wait like a naked child
Under the bridge my heart goes wild
I scream at a fire on the river bank
I give my body to an old gas tank

I dream that I have burning hair
Boiled arms that claw the air
The torso of an iron king
And on my back a broken wing

Who'll go out whoring into the night
On the eyeless road in the skinny moonlight
Maid or dowd or athlete proud
May wanton with me in the shroud

Who'll come lay down in the dark with me
Belly to belly and knee to knee
Who'll look into my hooded eye
Who'll lay down under my darkened thigh?

1949

I made love to myself . . .

I made love to myself
in the mirror, kissing my own lips,
    saying, "I love myself
I love you more than anybody."

ca. 1950

THE GREEN AUTOMOBILE

If I had a Green Automobile
        I'd go find my old companion
        in his house on the Western ocean.
                Ah! Ah! Ah! Ah! Ah!

I'd honk my horn at his manly gate,
        inside his wife and three
        children sprawl naked
                on the living room floor.

He'd come running out
        to my car full of heroic beer
        and jump screaming at the wheel
                for he is the greater driver.

We'd pilgrimage to the highest mount
        of our earlier Rocky Mountain visions
        laughing in each others' arms,
                delight surpassing the highest Rockies.

and after old agony, drunk with new years,
        bounding toward the snowy horizon
        blasting the dashboard with original bop
                hot rod on the mountain

we'd batter up the cloudy highway
        where angels of anxiety
        careen through the trees
                and scream out of the engine.

We'd burn all night on the jackpine peak
        seen from Denver in the summer dark,
        forestlike unnatural radiance
                illuminating the mountaintop:

childhood youthtime age & eternity
        would open like sweet trees
        in the nights of another spring
                and dumbfound us with love,

for we can see together
        the beauty of souls
        hidden like diamonds
                in the clock of the world,

like Chinese magicians can
        confound the immortals
        with our intellectuality
                hidden in the mist,

in the Green Automobile
        which I have invented
        imagined and visioned
                on the roads of the world

more real than the engine
        on a track in the desert
        purer than Greyhound and
                swifter than physical jetplane.

Denver! Denver! we'll return
        roaring across the City & County Building lawn
        which catches the pure emerald flame
                streaming in the wake of our auto.

This time we'll buy up the city!
        I cashed a great check in my skull bank
        to found a miraculous college of the body*
                up on the bus terminal roof.

But first we'll drive the stations of downtown,
        poolhall flophouse jazzjoint jail
        whorehouse down Folsom
                to the darkest alleys of Larimer

paying respects to Denver's father
        lost on the railroad tracks,
        stupor of wine and silence
                hallowing the slum of his decades,

salute him and his saintly suitcase
        of dark muscatel, drink
        and smash the sweet bottles
                on Diesels in allegiance.

Then we go driving drunk on boulevards
        where armies march and still parade
        staggering under the invisible
                banner of Reality—

hurtling through the street
        in the auto of our fate
        we share an archangelic cigarette
                and tell each others' fortunes:

fames of supernatural illumination,
        bleak rainy gaps of time,
        great art learned in desolation
                and we beat apart after six decades. . . .

and on an asphalt crossroad,
        deal with each other in princely
        gentleness once more, recalling
                famous dead talks of other cities.

The windshield's full of tears,
        rain wets our naked breasts,
        we kneel together in the shade
                amid the traffic of night in paradise

and now renew the solitary vow
        we made each other take
        in Texas, once:
                I can't inscribe here. . . .

                    . . . . . .

                    . . . . .

How many Saturday nights will be
        made drunken by this legend?
        How will young Denver come to mourn
                her forgotten sexual angel?

How many boys will strike the black piano
        in imitation of the excess of a native saint?
        Or girls fall wanton under his spectre in the high
            schools of melancholy night?

While all the time in Eternity
        in the wan light of this poem's radio
        we'll sit behind forgotten shades
            hearkening the lost jazz of all Saturdays.

Neal, we'll be real heroes now
        in a war between our cocks and time:
        let's be the angels of the world's desire
            and take the world to bed with us before we die.

Sleeping alone, or with companion,
        girl or fairy sheep or dream,
        I'll fail of lacklove, you, satiety:
            all men fall, our fathers fell before,

but resurrecting that lost flesh
        is but a moment's work of mind:
        an ageless monument to love
            in the imagination:

memorial built out of our own bodies
        consumed by the invisible poem—
        We'll shudder in Denver and endure
            though blood and wrinkles blind our eyes.

So this Green Automobile:
        I give you in flight
        a present, a present
            from my imagination.

We will go riding
        over the Rockies,
        we'll go on riding
            all night long until dawn,

then back to your railroad, the SP
             your house and your children
             and broken leg destiny
                          you'll ride down the plains

in the morning: and back
             to my visions, my office
             and eastern apartment
                          I'll return to New York.

                                     NY 1953†

*Jack Kerouac School of Disembodied Poetics at Naropa Institute, Boulder, Colo.,
founded 1974.

LOVE POEM ON THEME BY WHITMAN *

I'll go into the bedroom silently and lie down between the bridegroom
    and the bride,
those bodies fallen from heaven stretched out waiting naked and restless,
arms resting over their eyes in the darkness,
bury my face in their shoulders and breasts, breathing their skin,
and stroke and kiss neck and mouth and make back be open and known,
legs raised up crook'd to receive, cock in the darkness driven tormented
    and attacking
roused up from hole to itching head,
bodies locked shuddering naked, hot hips and buttocks screwed into each
    other
and eyes, eyes glinting and charming, widening into looks and abandon,
and moans of movement, voices, hands in air, hands between thighs,
hands in moisture on softened lips, throbbing contraction of bellies
till the white come flow in the swirling sheets,
and the bride cry for forgiveness, and the groom be covered with tears of
    passion and compassion,
and I rise up from the bed replenished with last intimate gestures and
    kisses of farewell—
all before the mind wakes, behind shades and closed doors in a darkened
    house
where the inhabitants roam unsatisfied in the night,
nude ghosts seeking each other out in the silence.

1954†

*Written in Neal Cassady's house, San Jose; see *Heartbeat* by Carolyn Cassady for back-
ground of this poem.

SONG

The weight of the world
    is love.
Under the burden
    of solitude,
under the burden
    of dissatisfaction

    the weight,
the weight we carry
    is love.

Who can deny?
    In dreams
it touches
    the body,
in thought
    constructs
a miracle,
    in imagination
anguishes
    till born
in human—

looks out of the heart
    burning with purity—
for the burden of life
    is love,

but we carry the weight
    wearily,
and so must rest
in the arms of love
    at last,
must rest in the arms
    of love.

No rest
    without love,
no sleep
    without dreams

of love—
        be mad or chill
obsessed with angels
        or machines,
the final wish
        is love
—cannot be bitter,
        cannot deny,
cannot withhold
        if denied:

the weight is too heavy

        —must give
for no return
        as thought
is given
        in solitude
in all the excellence
        of its excess.

The warm bodies
        shine together
in the darkness
        the hand moves
to the center
        of the flesh,
the skin trembles
        in happiness
and the soul comes
        joyful to the eye—

yes, yes,
        that's what
I wanted,
        I always wanted,
I always wanted,
        to return
to the body
        where I was born.

1954†

MALEST CORNIFICI TUO CATULLO

I'm happy, Kerouac, your madman Allen's
finally made it: discovered a new young cat,
and my imagination of an eternal boy
walks on the streets of San Francisco,
handsome, and meets me in cafeterias
and loves me. Ah don't think I'm sickening.
You're angry at me. For all of my lovers?
It's hard to eat shit, without having visions;
when they have eyes for me it's like Heaven.

SF 1955‡

‡ Poems in this book marked "‡" are devoted to Peter Orlovsky.

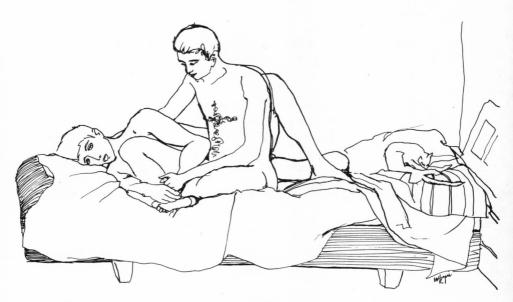

Allen Ginsberg and Peter Orlovsky, San Francisco, summer 1954
Drawing by Robert LaVigne

A SUPERMARKET IN CALIFORNIA

What thoughts I have of you tonight, Walt Whitman, for I walked down the sidestreets under the trees with a headache self-conscious looking at the full moon.

In my hungry fatigue, and shopping for images, I went into the neon fruit supermarket, dreaming of your enumerations!

What peaches and what penumbras! Whole families shopping at night! Aisles full of husbands! Wives in the avocados, babies in the tomatoes!—and you, Garcia Lorca, what were you doing down by the watermelons?

I saw you, Walt Whitman, childless, lonely old grubber, poking among the meats in the refrigerator and eyeing the grocery boys.

I heard you asking questions of each: Who killed the pork chops? What price bananas? Are you my Angel?

I wandered in and out of the brilliant stacks of cans following you, and followed in my imagination by the store detective.

We strode down the open corridors together in our solitary fancy tasting artichokes, possessing every frozen delicacy, and never passing the cashier.

Where are we going, Walt Whitman? The doors close in an hour. Which way does your beard point tonight?

(I touch your book and dream of our odyssey in the supermarket and feel absurd.)

Will we walk all night through solitary streets? The trees add shade to shade, lights out in the houses, we'll both be lonely.

Will we stroll dreaming of the lost America of love past blue automobiles in driveways, home to our silent cottage?

Ah, dear father, graybeard, lonely old courage-teacher, what America did you have when Charon quit poling his ferry and you got out on a smoking bank and stood watching the boat disappear on the black waters of Lethe?

Berkeley 1955

THE NAMES *

Time comes spirit weakens and goes blank apartments shuffled through
    and forgotten
The dead in their cenotaphs locomotive high schools & African cities
    small town motorcycle graves
O America what saints given vision are shrouded in junk their elegy a
    nameless hoodlum elegance leaning against death's military garage
Huncke who first saw the sun revolve in Chicago survived into middle-
    age Times Square
Thief stole hearts of wildcat tractor boys arrived to morphine brilliance
    Bickford table midnight neon to take a fall
arrested 41 times late 40's his acned skin & black spanish hair grown coy
    and old and lip bitten in Rikers Island Jail
as bestial newsprint photograph we shared once busted, me scared of
    black eye cops Manhattan
you blissful nothing to lose digging the live detectives perhaps even
    offering God a cigarette
I'll answer for you Huncke I never could before—admiring your natural
    tact and charm and irony—now sad Sing Sing
whatever inept Queens burglary you goofed again let God judge his
    sacred case
rather than mustached Time Judge steal a dirty photograph of your soul—
    I knew you when—
& you loved me better than my lawyer who wanted a frightened rat for
    official thousand buck mousetrap, no doubt, no doubt—
Shine in Cell free behind bars Immortal soul why not
Hell the machine can't sentence anyone except itself, have I to do that?
It gives jail I give you poem, bars last twenty years rust in a hundred
my handwork remains when prisons fall because the hand is compassion

Brilliant bitter Morphy stalking Los Angeles after his ghost boy
haunting basements in Denver with his Montmartre black beard
Charming ladies' man for gigolo purpose I heard, great cat for Shake-
    spearean sex
first poet suicide I knew we sat on park benches I watched him despair
    his forehead star
my elder asked serious advice, gentle man! international queer pride
    humbled to pre-death cigarette gun fright
His love a young blond demon of broken army, his nemesis his own mad
    cock for the kids sardonic ass

his dream mouthful of white prick trembling in his head—woke a bullet
    in his side days later in Passaic
last moments gasping stricken blood under stars coughing intestines &
    lighted highway cars flowing past his eyes into the dark.

Joe Army's beauty forgotten that night, pain cops nightmare, drunken
    AWOL through Detroit
phonecalls angels backrooms & courtmarshal lawyers trains a kaleido-
    scope of instant change,
shrinkage of soul, bearded dead dreams, all Balzac read in jail,
late disappearance from the city hides metamorphosis to humancy loath-
    ing that deathscene.

Phil Black hung in Tombs, horsefaced junky, dreamy strange murderer,
    forgotten pistol three buck holdup, stoolpigeon suicide I save him
    from the grave

Iroquois his indian head red cock intelligence buried in miserous soli-
    taire politics
his narcissistic blond haired hooknosed pride, I made him once he
    groaned and came
Later stranger chill made me tremble, I loved him hopeless years,
he's hid in Seattle consumed by lesbian hypochondrias' stealthy com-
    munion, green bullfighters envy age,
unless I save him from the grave, but he won't talk no more
much less fall in my arms or any mental bed forgiveness before we climb
    Olympics death,

Leroi returning to bughouse monkishness & drear stinky soupdish his
    fatness fright & suffering mind insult a repetitious void
"I have done my best to make saintliness as uninteresting as possible"
and has succeeded, when did I last write or receive ambiguous message
    jokey hangdog prophetic spade

Joan in dreams bent forward smiling asks news of the living
as in life the same sad tolerance, no skullbone judge of drunks
asking whereabouts sending regards from Mexican paradise garden where
    life & death are one
as if a postcard from eternity sent with human hand, wish I could see you
    now, it's happening as should

whatever we really need, we ought get, don't blame yourself—a photo-
graph on reverse

the rare tomb smile where trees grow crooked energy above grass—

yet died early—old teeth gone, tequila bottle in hand, an infantile paraly-
sis limp, lacklove, the worst—

I dreamed such vision of her secret in my frisco bed, heart can live the
rest by my, or her, best desire—love

Bill King black haired sorry drunken wop lawyer, woke up trembling in
Connecticut DT's among cows

Him there to recover I guess, but made his way back to New York shud-
dering to fuck stiff *Time* girls,

Death charm in person, sexual childlike radiant pain

See his face in old photographs & bandaged naked wrist leaning melan-
choly contemplating the camera

awkward face now calm, kind to me in cafeteria one sober morn looking
for jobs at breakfast,

but mostly smiled at roof edge midnight, all 1920's elegance reincarnate
in black vomit bestriven suit

& screetchy records *Mahagonny* airplane crash, lushed young man of
1940's hated his fairy woe, came on Lizzie's belly or Ansen's sock in
desperate orgies of music canopener

God but I loved his murdered face when he talked with a mouthful of
rain in 14th St subway—

where he fell skull broken underground last, head crushed by the radiant
wheel on iron track at Astor Place

Farewell dear Bill that's done, you're gone, we all go into the ancient
void drunkard mouth

you made it too soon, here was more to say, & more to drink, but now
too late to sit and talk

all night toward the eternity you sought so well so fearlessly in so much
alcoholic pain with so much fire behind eyes with such

sweet manner in your heart that never won a happy fate thru what bleak
years you saw your red skull burning deathshead in the U.S. sun

Mix living dead, Neal Cassady, old hero of travel love alyosha idiot seek-
train poems, what crown you wear at last

what fameless reward for patience & pain, what golden whore come
secret from the clouds, what has god bidden for your coffin and
heart someday,

what will give back your famous arm, your happy catholic boy eye, orphan
    torso shining in poolhall & library, intimate spermworks with old
    girls downtown rockabelly energy,
what Paradise built high enough to hold your desire, deep enough to en-
    compass your cock kindnesses, soft for your children to pray, 10 foot
    iron wheels you fell under?
what American heaven receive you? Christ allow sufferings then will he
    allow you His opening tinbarrel Iowa light as Jerusalem?
O Neal that life end we together on knees know harvest of prayers
    together,
Paradise autos ascend to the moon no illusion, short time earth life
    Bibles bear our eyes, make it dear baby
Stay with me Angel now in Shroud of railroad lost bet racetrack broke
    leg oblivion
till I get the shining Word or you the cockless cock to lay in my ass hope
    mental radiance—
It's all lost we fall without glory to empty tomb comedown to nothing but
    evil thinkless worm, but we know better
merely by old heart hope, or merely Desire, or merely the love whisper
    breathed in your ear on lawns of long gone by Denver,
merely by the night you leaned on my body & held me for All & called me
    to Adore what I wondered at as child age ten I
wandered by hopeless green hedges, when you sat under alley balcony
    garbagestair, ache in our breasts Futurity
meeting Love for Love, so wept as child now man I weep for true end,
Save from the grave! O Neal I love you I bring this Lamb into the middle
    of the world happily—O tenderness—to see you again—O tender-
    ness—to recognize you in the middle of Time.

Paris 1957†

*This poem was later enclosed in a letter to Neal Cassady.

UNDERSTAND THAT THIS IS A DREAM

Real as a dream
What shall I do with this great opportunity to fly?
What is the interpretation of this planet, this moon?
If I can dream that I dream / and dream anything dreamable / can I dream
I am awake / and why do that?
When I dream in a dream that I wake / up what
happens when I try to move?
I dream that I move
and the effort moves and moves
till I move / and my arm hurts
Then I wake up / dismayed / I was dreaming / I was waking
when I was dreaming still / just now.
and try to remember next time in dreams
that I am in dreaming.
And dream anything I want when I'm awaken.
When I'm in awakeness what do I desire?
I desire to fulfill my emotional belly.
My whole body my heart in my fingertips thrill with some old fulfillments.
Arcane parchments my own and the universe the answer.
Belly to Belly and knee to knee.
The hot spurt of my body to thee to thee
old boy / dreamy Earl / you Prince of Paterson / now king of me / lost
    Haledon
first dream that made me take down my pants
urgently to show the cars / auto trucks / rolling down avenue hill.
That far back what do I remember / but the face of the leader of the gang
was blond / that loved me / one day on the steps of his house blocks away
all afternoon I told him about my magic Spell
I can do anything I want / palaces millions / chemistry sets / chicken coops /
    white horses
stables and torture basements / I inspect my naked victims
chained upside down / my fingertips thrill approval on their thighs
white hairless cheeks I may kiss all I want
at my mercy. on the racks.
I pass with my strong attendants / I am myself naked
bending down with my buttocks out
for their smacks of reproval / o the heat of desire
like shit in my asshole. The strange gang
across the street / thru the grocerystore / in the wood alley / out in the
    open on the corner /

Because I lied to the Dentist about the chickencoop roofing / slate stolen
     off his garage *
by me and the boy I loved who would punish me if he knew
what I loved him.
That now I have had that boy back in another blond form
Peter Orlovsky a Chinese teen-ager in Bangkok ten years twenty years
Joe Army on the campus / white blond loins / my mouth hath kisses /
full of his cock / my ass burning / full of his cock
all that I do desire. In dream and awake
this handsome body mine / answered
all I desired / intimate loves / open eyed / revealed at last / clothes on the
     floor
Underwear the most revealing stripped off below the belly button in bed.
That's that / yes yes / the flat cocks the red pricks the gentle pubic hair /
     alone with me
my magic spell. My power / what I desire alone / what after thirty years /
I got forever / after thirty years / satisfied enough with Peter / with all I
     wanted /
with many men I knew one generation / our sperm passing
into our mouths and bellies / beautiful when love / given.
Now the dream oldens / I olden / my hair a year long / my thirtyeight birth-
     day approaching.
I dream I
am bald / am disappearing / the campus unrecognisable / Haledon Avenue
will be covered with neon / motels / Supermarkets / iron
the porches and woods changed when I go back / to see Earl again
He'll be a bald / flesh father / I could pursue him further in the garage
If there's still a garage on the hill / on the planet / when I get back. From
     Asia.
If I could even remember his name or his face / or find him /
When I was ten / perhaps he exists in some form.
With a belly and a belt and an auto
What ever his last name / I never knew / in the phonebook / the Akashic
     records.
I'll write my Inspiration for all Mankind to remember,
My Idea, the secret cave / in the clothes closet / that house probably down /
Nothing to go back to / everything's gone / only my idea
that's disappearing / even in dreams / grey dust piles / instant annihilation
of World War II and all its stainless steel shining-mouthed cannons
much less me and my grammar school kisses / I never kissed in time /
and go on kissing in dream and out on the street / as if it were for ever.

38

No forever left! Even my oldest forever gone, in Bangkok, in Benares,
swept up with words and bodies / all into the brown Ganges /
passing the burning grounds and / into the police state.
My mind, my mind / you had six feet of Earth to hoe /
Why didnt you remember and plant the seed of Law and gather the sprouts
   of What?
the golden blossoms of what idea? If I dream that I dream / what dream
should I dream next? Motorcycle rickshaws / parting lamp shine / little
   taxis / horses hoofs
on this Saigon midnight street. Ankor Wat ahead and the ruined citys old
   Hindu faces
and there was a dream about Eternity. What should I dream when I wake?
What's left to dream, more Chinese meat? More magic Spells? More
   youths to love before I change & disappear?
More dream words? This can't go on forever. Now that I know it all /
goes whither? For now that I know I am dreaming /
What next for you Allen? Run down to the Presidents Palace full of Mor-
   phine /
the cocks crowing in the street. / Dawn trucks / What is the question?
Do I need sleep, now that there's light in the window?
I'll go to sleep. Signing off until / the next idea / the moving van arrives
   empty
at the Doctors house full of Chinese furniture.

Saigon May 31 –June 1, '63

*Cf. "Drive All Blames into One," page 80.

WHY IS GOD LOVE, JACK?*

Because I lay my
        head on pillows,
Because I weep in the
        tombed studio
Because my heart
        sinks below my navel
because I have an
        old airy belly
    filled with soft
        sighing, and
    remembered breast
        sobs—or
    a hands touch makes
        tender—
Because I get scared—
Because I raise my
        voice singing to
            my beloved self—
Because I do love thee
        my darling, my
        other, my living
            bride
my friend, my old lord
        of soft tender eyes—
Because I am in the
        Power of life & can
        do no more than
        submit to the feeling
        that I am the One
            Lost
Seeking still seeking the
        thrill—delicious
        bliss in the
            heart abdomen loins
                & thighs
Not refusing this
        38 yr. 145 lb. head
        arms & feet of meat

Nor one single Whitmanic
    toenail condemn
nor hair prophetic banish
    to remorseless Hell,
Because wrapped with machinery
I confess my ashamed desire.

                    1963

*Addressed to the poet Kerouac.

MORNING

Ugh! the planet screams
Doves in rusty cornice-
        castles peer
down on auto crossroads,
        a junkey in white jacket
wavers in yellow light on
        way to a negro in bed
Black smoke flowing on roofs, terrific
        city coughing—
garbage can lids music over
        truck whine on E. 5th St.
Ugh! I'm awake again—
        dreary day ahead
what to do? —Dull letters
        to be answered
an epistle to M. Duchamp
more me all day the same
clearly

        Q. "Do you want to live or die?"
        A. "I don't know"
        said Julius after 12 years
                State Hospital

Ugh! cry negros in Harlem
Ugh! cry License Inspectors, Building
        Inspectors, Police Congressmen.
        Undersecretaries of Defense.
Ugh! Cries Texas Mississippi!
Ugh! Cries India
Ugh! Cries US
                Well, who knows?

O flowing copious!
        total Freedom! To
Do what? to blap! to
        embarrass! to conjoin
Locomotive blossoms to Leafy
        purple vaginas.

To be dull! ashamed! shot!
    Finished! Flopped!
To say Ugh absolutely mean-
    ingless here
To be a big bore! even to
    myself! Fulla shit!

Paper words! Fblup! Fizzle! Droop!
Shut your big fat mouth!
Go take a flying crap in the
    rain!
Wipe your own ass! Bullshit!
You big creep! Fairy! Dopey
    Daffodil! Stinky Jew!
Mr Professor! Dirty Rat! Fart!

Honey! Darling! Sweetie pie!
Baby! Lovey! Dovey! Dearest!
My own! Buttercup! O Beautiful!
Doll! Snookums! Go fuck
        yourself,
    everybody Ginsberg!
And when you've exhausted
    that, go forward?
Where? kiss my ass!

O Love, my mouth against
    a black policeman's breast.

        NY 1963

MESSAGE II *

Long since the years
letters songs Mantras
eyes apartments bellies
kissed and grey bridges
walked across in mist
Now your brother's Welfare's
paid by State now Lafcadio's
home with Mama, now you're
in NY beds with big poetic
girls & go picket on the street
I clang my finger-cymbals in Havana, I lie
with teenage boys afraid of the red police,
I jack off in Cuban modern bathrooms, I ascend
over blue oceans in a jet plane, the mist hides
the black synagogue, I will look for the Golem,
I hide under the clock near my hotel, its intermission
for Tales of Hoffman, nostalgia for the 19th century
rides through my heart like the music of Die Moldau,
I'm still alone with long black beard and shining eyes
walking down black smokey tramcar streets at night
past royal muscular statues on an old stone bridge,
Over the river again today in Breughel's wintery city,
the snow is white on all the rooftops of Prague,
Salute beloved comrade I'll send you my tears from Moscow.

March 1965 ‡

*Ginsberg's earlier poem "Message I," also dedicated to Peter Orlovsky, can be read in
its first, previously unpublished draft on page 168.

44

KRAL MAJALES

And the Communists have nothing to offer but fat cheeks and eyeglasses
and lying policemen
and the Capitalists proffer Napalm and money in green suitcases to the
Naked,
and the Communists create heavy industry but the heart is also heavy
and the beautiful engineers are all dead, the secret technicians conspire
for their own glamor
in the Future, in the Future, but now drink vodka and lament the Secu-
rity Forces,
and the Capitalists drink gin and whiskey on airplanes but let Indian
brown millions starve
and when Communist and Capitalist assholes tangle the Just man is ar-
rested or robbed or had his head cut off,
But not like Kabir, and the cigarette cough of the Just man above the
clouds
in the bright sunshine is a salute to the health of the blue sky.
For I was arrested thrice in Prague, once for singing drunk on Narodni
street,
once knocked down on the midnight pavement by a mustached agent
who screamed out BOUZERANT,*
once for losing my notebooks of unusual sex politics dream opinions,
and I was sent from Havana by plane by detectives in green uniform,
and I was sent from Prague by plane by detectives in Czechoslovakian
business suits,
Cardplayers out of Cezanne, the two strange dolls that entered Joseph K's
room at morn
also entered mine, and ate at my table, and examined my scribbles,
and followed me night and morn from the houses of lovers to the cafés
of Centrum—
And I am the King of May, which is the power of sexual youth,
And I am the King of May, which is industry in eloquence and action in
amour,
and I am the King of May, which is long hair of Adam and the Beard of
my own body
and I am the King of May, which is Kral Majales in the Czechoslovakian
tongue,
And I am the King of May, which is old Human poesy, and 100,000
people chose my name,
and I am the King of May, and in a few minutes I will land at London
Airport,

And I am the King of May, naturally, for I am of Slavic parentage and a
    Buddhist Jew
who worships the Sacred Heart of Christ the blue body of Krishna the
    straight back of Ram
the beads of Chango the Nigerian singing Shiva Shiva in a manner which
    I have invented,
and the King of May is a middleeuropean honor, mine in the XX century
despite space and the Time Machine, because I heard the voice of Blake
    in a vision,
and repeat that voice. And I am King of May that sleeps with teenagers
    laughing.
And I am the King of May, that I may be expelled from my Kingdom
    with Honor, as of old,
To shew the difference between Caesar's Kingdom and the Kingdom of
    the May of Man—
and I am the King of May, tho paranoid, for the Kingdom of May is too
    beautiful to last for more than a month—
and I am the King of May because I touched my finger to my forehead
    saluting
a luminous heavy girl trembling hands who said "one moment Mr. Gins-
    berg"
before a fat young Plainclothesman stepped between our bodies—I was
    going to England—
and I am the King of May, returning to see Bunhill Fields and walk on
    Hampstead Heath,
and I am the King of May, in a giant jetplane touching Albion's airfield
    trembling in fear
as the plane roars to a landing on the grey concrete, shakes & expells air,
and rolls slowly to a stop under the clouds with part of blue heaven still
    visible.
And *tho* I am the King of May, the Marxists have beat me upon the
    street, kept me up all night in Police Station, followed me thru
    Springtime Prague, detained me in secret and deported me from our
    kingdom by airplane.
Thus I have written this poem on a jet seat in mid Heaven.

May 7, 1965

*Czech expletive for fairy-faggot.
See pp. 223–229 for letters on Ginsberg's Prague experiences.

WHO BE KIND TO

Be kind to your self, it is only one
    and perishable
of many on the planet, thou art that
one that wishes a soft finger tracing the
    line of feeling from nipple to pubes—
one that wishes a tongue to kiss your armpit,
    a lip to kiss your cheek inside your
    whiteness thigh—
Be kind to yourself Harry, because unkindness
    comes when the body explodes
napalm cancer and the deathbed in Vietnam
is a strange place to dream of   trees
    leaning over and angry American faces
grinning with sleepwalk terror over your
    last eye—
Be kind to yourself, because the bliss of your own
    kindness will flood the police tomorrow,
because the cow weeps in the field and the
    mouse weeps in the cat hole—
Be kind to this place, which is your present
    habitation, with derrick and radar tower
    and flower in the ancient brook—
Be kind to your neighbor who weeps
    solid tears on the television sofa,
he has no other home, and hears nothing
    but the hard voice of telephones
Click, buzz, switch channel and the inspired
    melodrama disappears
and he's left alone for the night, he disappears
    in bed—
Be kind to your disappearing mother and
    father gazing out the terrace window
    as milk truck and hearse turn the corner
Be kind to the politician weeping in the galleries
    of Whitehall, Kremlin, White House
    Louvre and Phoenix City
aged, large nosed, angry, nervously dialing
    the bald voice box connected to

electrodes underground converging thru
        wires vaster than a kitten's eye can see
on the mushroom shaped fear-lobe under
        the ear of Sleeping Dr. Einstein
crawling with worms, crawling with worms, crawling
        with worms the hour has come—
Sick, dissatisfied, unloved, the bulky
        foreheads of Captain Premier President
        Sir Comrade Fear!
Be kind to the fearful one at your side
        Who's remembering the Lamentations
        of the bible
the prophesies of the Crucified Adam   Son
        of all the porters and char men of
                    Bell   gravia—
Be kind to your self who weep under
        the Moscow moon and hide your bliss hairs
        under raincoat and suede Levis—
For this is the joy to be born, the kindness
        received thru strange eyeglasses on
        a bus thru Kensington,
the finger touch of the Londoner on your thumb,
        that borrows light from your cigarette,
the morning smile at Newcastle Central
        station, when longhair Tom blond husband
        greets the bearded stranger of telephones—
the boom bom that bounces in the joyful
        bowels as the Liverpool Minstrels of
        CavernSink
raise up their joyful voices and guitars
        in electric Afric hurrah
        for Jerusalem—
The saints come marching in, Twist &
        Shout, and Gates of Eden are named
        in Albion again
Hope sings a black psalm from Nigeria,
        and a white psalm echoes in Detroit
        and reechoes amplified from Nottingham to Prague
and a Chinese psalm will be heard, if we all
        live our lives for the next 6 decades—
Be kind to the Chinese psalm in the red transistor
        in your breast—

Be kind to the Monk in the 5 Spot who plays
        lone chord-bangs on his vast piano
lost in space on a bench and hearing himself
        in the nightclub universe—
Be kind to the heroes that have lost their
        names in the newspaper
and hear only their own supplications for
        the peaceful kiss of sex in the giant
        auditoriums of the planet,
nameless voices crying for kindness in the orchestra,
screaming in anguish that bliss come true
        and sparrows sing another hundred years
        to white haired babes
and poets be fools of their own desire—O Anacreon
        and angelic Shelley!
Guide these new-nippled generations on space
        ships to Mars' next universe
The prayer is to man and girl, the only
        gods, the only lords of Kingdoms of
        Feeling, Christs of their own
        living ribs—
Bicycle chain and machine gun, fear sneer
        & smell cold logic of the Dream Bomb
have come to Saigon, Johannesberg,
        Dominica City, Pnom Penh, Pentagon
        Paris and Lhasa—
Be kind to the universe of Self that
        trembles and shudders and thrills
        in XX Century,
that opens its eyes and belly and breast
        chained with flesh to feel
        the myriad flowers of bliss
        that I Am to Thee—
A dream! a Dream! I don't want to be alone!
        I want to know that I am loved!
I want the orgy of our flesh, orgy
        of all eyes happy, orgy of the soul
        kissing and blessing its mortal-grown
        body,
orgy of tenderness beneath the neck, orgy of
        kindness to thigh and vagina

Desire given with meat hand
    and cock, desire taken with
    mouth and ass, desire returned
    to the last sigh!
Tonite let's all make love in London
    as if it were 2001 the years
    of thrilling god—
And be kind to the poor soul that cries in
    a crack of the pavement because he
    has no body—
Prayers to the ghosts and demons, the
    lackloves of Capitals & Congresses
    who make sadistic noises
    on the radio—
Statue destroyers & tank captains, unhappy
    murderers in Mekong & Stanleyville,
That a new kind of man has come to his bliss
    to end the cold war he has borne
    against his own kind flesh
    since the days of the snake.

June 8, 1965

CHANCES "R"

Nymph and shepherd raise electric tridents
      glowing red against the plaster wall,
The jukebox beating out magic syllables,
A line of painted boys snapping fingers
      & shaking thin Italian trouserlegs
            or rough dungarees on big asses
               bumping and dipping
ritually, with no religion but the
      old one of cocksuckers
naturally, in Kansas center of America
      the farmboys in Diabolic bar light
      alone stiff necked or lined up
      dancing row on row like Afric husbands
& the music's sad here, whereas Sunset Trip or
Jukebox Corner it's ecstatic pinball machines—
Religiously, with concentration and free
         prayer; fairy boys of the plains
         and their gay sisters of the city
step together to the center of the floor
      illumined by machine eyes, screaming drumbeats,
        passionate voices of Oklahoma City
           chanting No Satisfaction
Suspended from Heaven the Chances R
      Club floats rayed by stars
        along a Wichita tree avenue
      traversed with streetlights on the plain.

February 1966

CITY MIDNIGHT JUNK STRAINS

for Frank O'Hara

Switch on lights yellow as the sun
                              in the bedroom . . .
The gaudy poet dead   Frank O'Hara's bones
                              under cemetery grass
An emptiness at 8PM in the Cedar Bar
          Throngs of drunken
                    guys talking about paint
          & lofts, and Pennsylvania youth.
                    Kline attacked by his heart
& chattering Frank
                    stopped forever—
          Faithful drunken adorers, mourn.
                    The busfare's a nickle more
          past his old apartment 9th Street by the park.
Delicate Peter loved his praise,
          I wait for the things he says
                              about me—
          Did he think me an Angel
              as angel I am still talking into earth's microphone
                              willy nilly
              —to come back as words ghostly hued by early death
              but written so bodied
                        mature in another decade.
Chatty prophet
                    of yr own loves, personal
                    memory feeling fellow
          Poet of building-glass
I see you walking you said with your tie
          flopped over your shoulder   in the wind down 5th Ave
              under the handsome breasted workmen
                    on their scaffolds ascending Time
                        & washing the windows of Life
—off to a date with Martinis & a blond
              beloved poet far from home
                    —with thee and Thy sacred Metropolis
          in the enormous bliss   of a long afternoon
          where death is the shadow
                    cast by Rockefeller Center
                        over your intimate street.

Who were you, black suited, hurrying to meet,
    Unsatisfied one?
               Unmistakable,
                   Darling date
for the charming solitary   young poet with a big cock
         who could fuck you all night long
              till you never came,
    trying your torture on his   obliging fond body
    eager to satisfy god's whim that made you
            Innocent,   as you are.
I tried   your boys and found them ready
    sweet and amiable
        collected gentlemen
           with large sofa apartments
    lonesome to please   for pure language;
and you mixed with money
        because you knew enough language to be rich
          if you wanted your walls to be empty—
Deep philosophical terms dear Edwin Denby serious as Herbert Read
    with silvery hair   announcing your dead gift
to the grave crowd   whose historic op art   frisson was
the new sculpture your big blue wounded body made in the Universe
    when you went away   to Fire Island for the weekend
  tipsy with a family of decade-olden friends

Peter stares out the window   at robbers
    the Lower East Side   distracted in Amphetamine
I stare into my head   & look for your/ broken roman nose
    your wet mouth-smell of martinis
        & a big artistic tipsy kiss.
  40's only half a life   to have filled
    with so many fine parties and evenings'
    interesting drinks together with one
        faded friend or new
        understanding social cat . . .
I want to be there in your garden party in the clouds
        all of us naked
strumming our harps and reading each other   new poetry
    in the boring celestial
        friendship Committee Museum.
You're in a bad mood?

Take an Asprin.
In the Dumps?
I'm falling asleep
safe in your thoughtful arms.
Someone uncontrolled by History would have to own Heaven,
on earth as it is.
I hope you satisfied your childhood love
Your puberty fantasy   your sailor punishment on your knees
your mouth-suck
Elegant insistency
on the honking self-prophetic Personal
as Curator of funny emotions to the mob,
Trembling One, whenever possible. I see New York thru your eyes
and hear of one funeral a year nowadays—
From Billie Holiday's time
appreciated more and more
a common ear
for our deep gossip.

July 29, 1966

KISS ASS

Kissass is the Part of Peace
America will have to Kissass Mother Earth
Whites have to Kissass Blacks, for Peace & Pleasure,
Only Pathway to Peace, Kissass.

Houston, Texas '67

ELEGY FOR NEAL CASSADY

OK Neal
        aethereal Spirit
                bright as moving air
                        blue as city dawn
happy as light   released by the Day
        over the city's new buildings—

Maya's Giant bricks rise rebuilt
                        in Lower East Side
        windows shine in milky smog,
                Appearance unnecessary now.

Peter sleeps alone next room, sad.
Are you reincarnate? Can ya hear me talkin?
If anyone had strength to hear the invisible,
And drive thru Maya Wall
        you *had* it—
                        What're you now, Spirit?
That were spirit in body—

The body's cremate
                by Railroad track
        San Miguel Allende Desert,
                outside town,
        Spirit become spirit,
                or robot reduced to Ashes.

Tender Spirit, thank you for touching me with tender hands
When you were young, in a beautiful body,
        Such a pure touch it was Hope beyond Maya-meat,
        What you are now,
                Impersonal, tender—
you showed me your muscle/warmth/over twenty years ago
when I lay trembling at your breast
                put your arm around my neck,
—we stood together in a bare room on 103'd St.
Listening to a wooden Radio,
                                with our eyes closed
Eternal redness of Shabda
                        lamped in our brains

at Illinois Jacquet's Saxophone Shuddering,
prophetic Honk of Louis Jordan,
Honeydrippers, Open The Door Richard
To Christ's Apocalypse—
The buildings're insubstantial—
That's my New York Vision
outside eastern apartment offices
where telephone rang last night
and stranger's friendly Denver Voice
asked me, had I heard the news from the West?

Some gathering Bust, Eugene Oregon or Hollywood Impends
I had premonition.
"No" I said—"been away all week,"
"you haven't heard the News from the West,
Neal Cassady is dead—"
Peter's dove-voic'd Oh! on the other line, listening.

Your picture stares cheerful, tearful, strain'd,
a candle burns,
green stick incense by household gods.
Military Tyranny overtakes Universities, your Prophecy
approaching its kindest sense brings us
Down
to the Great Year's awakening.
Kesey's in Oregon writing novel language
family farm alone.
Hadja no more to do? Was your work all done?
Had ya seen your first son?
Why'dja leave us all here?
Has the battle been won?

I'm a phantom skeleton with teeth, skull
resting on a pillow
calling your spirit
god echo consciousness, murmuring
sadly to myself.

Lament in dawnlight's not needed,
the world is released,
desire fulfilled, your history over,

Neal Cassady, San Francisco 1952
Photo by Carolyn Cassady

story told, Karma resolved,
                                    prayers completed
vision manifest, new consciousness fulfilled,
                            spirit returned in a circle,
world left standing empty, buses roaring through streets—
            garbage scattered on pavements galore—
Grandeur solidified, phantom-familiar fate
                            returned to Auto-dawn,
                                    your destiny fallen on RR track
My body breathes easy,
                    I lie alone,
                                    living
After friendship fades from flesh forms—
heavy happiness hangs in heart,
                    I could talk to you forever,
                            The pleasure inexhaustible,
                                    discourse of spirit to spirit,
                                                O Spirit.
Sir spirit, forgive me my sins,
Sir spirit give me your blessing again,
Sir Spirit forgive my phantom body's demands,
Sir Spirit thanks for your kindness past,
Sir Spirit in Heaven, What difference was yr mortal form,
            What further this great show of Space?
            Speedy passions generations of
                    Question? agonic Texas Nightrides?
                    psychedelic bus hejira-jazz,
            Green auto poetries, inspired roads?
Sad, Jack in Lowell saw the phantom most—
            lonelier than all, except your noble Self.
Sir Spirit, an' I drift alone:
                    Oh deep sigh.

                                    10 *Feb.* 1968, 5–5:30 A.M.†

PLEASE MASTER

Please master can I touch your cheek
please master can I kneel at your feet
please master can I loosen your blue pants
please master can I gaze at your golden haired belly
please master can I gently take down your shorts
please master can I have your thighs bare to my eyes
please master can I take off my clothes below your chair
please master can I kiss your ankles and soul
please master can I touch lips to your hard muscle hairless thigh
please master can I lay my ear pressed to your stomach
please master can I wrap my arms around your white ass
please master can I lick your groin curled with blond soft fur
please master can I touch my tongue to your rosy asshole
please master may I pass my face to your balls,
please master, please look into my eyes,
please master order me down on the floor,
please master tell me to lick your thick shaft
please master put your rough hands on my bald hairy skull
please master press my mouth to your prick-heart
please master press my face into your belly, pull me slowly strong thumbed
till your dumb hardness fills my throat to the base
till I swallow & taste your delicate flesh-hot prick barrel veined Please
Master push my shoulders away and stare in my eye, & make me bend over
        the table
please master grab my thighs and lift my ass to your waist
please master your hand's rough stroke on my neck your palm down my
        backside
please master push me up, my feet on chairs, till my hole feels the breath
        of your spit and your thumb stroke
please master make me say Please Master Fuck me now Please
Master grease my balls and hairmouth with sweet vaselines
please master stroke your shaft with white creams
please master touch your cock head to my wrinkled self-hole
please master push it in gently, your elbows enwrapped round my breast
your arms passing down to my belly, my penis you touch w/ your fingers
please master shove it in me a little, a little, a little,
please master sink your droor thing down my behind
& please master make me wiggle my rear to eat up the prick trunk
till my asshalfs cuddle your thighs, my back bent over,

till I'm alone sticking out, your sword stuck throbbing in me
please master pull out and slowly roll into the bottom
please master lunge it again, and withdraw to the tip
please please master fuck me again with your self, please fuck me Please
Master drive down till it hurts me the softness the
Softness please master make love to my ass, give body to center, & fuck
     me for good like a girl,
tenderly clasp me please master I take me to thee,
& drive in my belly your selfsame sweet heat-rood
you fingered in solitude Denver or Brooklyn or fucked in a maiden in
     Paris carlots
please master drive me thy vehicle, body of love drops, sweat fuck
body of tenderness, Give me your dog fuck faster
please master make me go moan on the table
Go moan O please master do fuck me like that
in your rhythm thrill-plunge & pull-back-bounce & push down
till I loosen my asshole a dog on the table yelping with terror delight to be
     loved
Please master call me a dog, an ass beast, a wet asshole,
& fuck me more violent, my eyes hid with your palms round my skull
& plunge down in a brutal hard lash thru soft drip-flesh
& throb thru five seconds to spurt out your semen heat
over & over, bamming it in while I cry out your name I do love you
please Master.

May 1968†

ON NEAL'S ASHES

Delicate eyes that blinked blue Rockies all ash
nipples,Ribs I touched w/ my thumb are ash
mouth my tongue touched once or twice all ash
bony cheeks soft on my belly are cinder, ash
earlobes & eyelids, youthful cock tip, curly pubis
breast warmth, man palm, high school thigh,
baseball bicept arm, asshole anneal'd to silken skin
                    all ashes, all ashes again.

August 1968†

OVER DENVER AGAIN

Grey clouds blot sunglare, mountains float west, plane
softly roaring over Denver—Neal dead a year—clean suburb yards,
fit boardinghouse for the homosexual messenger's
alleyway Lila a decade back before the Atombomb.
Denver without Neal, eh? Denver with orange sunsets
& giant airplanes winging silvery to San Francisco—
watchtowers thru red cold planet light, when the Earth Angel's dead
the dead material planet'll revolve robotlike
& insects hop back and forth between metallic cities.

Feb. 13, 1969†

RAIN-WET ASPHALT HEAT,
GARBAGE CURBED CANS OVERFLOWING

I hauled down lifeless mattresses to sidewalk refuse-piles,
old rugs stept on from Paterson to Lower East Side filled with bed-bugs,
grey pillows, couch seats treasured from the street laid back on the street
— out, to hear Murder-tale, 3rd Street cyclists attacked tonite—
Bopping along in rain, Chaos fallen over City roofs,
shrouds of chemical vapour drifting over building-tops—
Get the *Times,* Nixon says peace reflected from the Moon,
but I found no boy body to sleep with all night on pavements 3 AM home
    in sweating drizzle—
Those mattresses soggy lying by full five garbagepails—
Barbara, Maretta, Peter Steven Rosebud slept on these Pillows years ago,
forgotten names, also made love to me, I had these mattresses four years
    on my floor—
Gerard, Jimmy many months, even blond Gordon later,
Paul with the beautiful big cock, that teenage boy that lived in Pennsyl-
    vania,
forgotten numbers, young dream loves and lovers, earthly bellies—
many strong youths with eyes closed, come sighing and helping me
    come—
Desires already forgotten, tender persons used and kissed goodbye
and all the times I came to myself alone in the dark dreaming of Neal or
    Billy Budd
— nameless angels of half-life— heart beating & eyes weeping for lovely
    phantoms—
Back from the Gem Spa, into the hallway, a glance behind
and sudden farewell to the bedbug-ridden mattresses piled soggy in dark
    rain.

August 2, 1969

GRAFFITI 12TH CUBICLE MEN'S ROOM SYRACUSE AIRPORT

11 November 1969

I am married and would like to fuck someone else
Have a strange piece (Go Home)
USN '69
I want to suck a big cock Make Date
Support Third World Struggle Against US Imperialism
I fucked Mom and got VD
All power to the Viet Cong!
Yeah! Max Voltage up the Ass!! Ω
Perhaps Man needs—But to kill is only brown butter Wax
April 20, 1965   Mike Heck & Salena Bennett
Keep on Chugglin
Eat prunes and be a regular guy.
I would like to suck a big cock.
So would I.
War is good business Invest your son.
Help me J.P.
John Wayne flunked basic training.
Pat Miller '69 Home on Leave
My wife sucks cock.
Chickenman Lives Yes somewhere in Argentina
Peace & Love Sucks
I want a blow job Who do I call
What if someone gave a war & Nobody came?
Life would ring the bells of Ecstasy and Forever be Itself again.
J. Edgar Hoover F.B.I. is a Voyeur.
Man, I'm really stoned out of my skull really O-Zoned—good old LSD
the colors in here are so nice really fine colors and the floor tile is
really outasight if you haven't tried it you ought to since it is the only
way to really get your head together by first getting it apart LSD
Forever.

$CH2CH2N(CH3)2$

AFTER THOUGHTS

When he kissed my nipple
    I felt elbow bone thrill—
When lips touched my belly
    tickle ran up to my ear
When he took my cock head to tongue
    a tremor shrunk sphincter, joy
        shuddered my reins
I breathed deep sighing ahh!

— — — — — — — — — — — —

Mirror looking, combing
    grey glistening beard
Were I found sharp eyed
    attractive to the young?
Bad magic or something—
Foolish magic most likely.

November 1969, *to J. G.*

64

OVER LARAMIE

Western Air boat bouncing
　　under rainclouds stippled
　　　　down grey Rockies
　　　　　　　Springtime dusk,
Look out on Denver, Allen,
　　　　mourn Neal no more,
　　　Old ghost bone loves departed
　　　New lives whelm the plains, rains
　　　　wash Rocky mountainsides
World turns under sun eye
　　　Man flies a moment Cheyenne's
　　　　dry upland highways
A tiny fossil brachiopod in pocket
　　　Precambrian limestone clam
　　　　　　fingernail small
four hundred fifty million years old

Brain gone, flesh passed thru myriad
　　　phantom reincarnations,
the tiny-ridged shell's delicate
　　　　as hardened thought.

— over Laramie, Front Range
　　　pine gully snow pockets,
Monolith Cement plume smoke
　　　casting dust gas over
　　　　the red plateau
　　　into the New World.

April 12, 1971†

JIMMY BERMAN RAG *

Whozat Jimmie Berman
I heard you drop his name?
Whadd'ze got to say
what papers is he sellin?
I dont know if he's the guy
I met or aint the same—
Well that Jimmie Berman was
a boy that is worth tellin':

Jimmie Berman on the corner
Sold the New York Times
Jimmie Berman in New York
He had a long long Climb—

Started as a shoeshine boy
Ended on Times Square—
Jimmie Berman whatzat rose
You got settin' in your hair?

Jimmie Berman what's your sex
Why ya hang round here all day?
Jimmie Berman What Love Next
O What (God) do you pray?

Who you wanna sleep with tonite Jimmie Boy
Would'ya like—Come with me?
Jimmy Berman—O my love,
Oh what misery—

Jimmie Berman do you feel
the same as what I do
Jimmy Berman wont you come home
And make love with me too?

Jimmie Berman I'll take my clothes off
Lay me down in bed
Jimmy Berman drop your pants
I'll give you some good head

Eighteen year old Jimmie!
The Boy is my delight!
Eighteen year old Jimmy
I'll love him day and night!

Now I know I'm getting kinda old
To chase poor Jimmy's tail
But I wont tell your other loves—
It be too long a tale.

Jimmy Berman please love me
I'll throw myself at your feet—
Jimmy Berman I'll give you money O
Wont that be neat!

Jimmie Berman just give me
your heart and yeah your soul
Jimmy Berman please come home
With me I would be whole

Jimmie Berman on the street
Waitin for his god!
Jimmy Berman as I pass
Gives me a holy nod.

Jimmy Berman he has watched
And seen the Strangers pass—
Jimmy Berman he gave up—
He wants no more of ass.

Jimmy Berman does yoga
He smokes a little grass,
Jimmie Berman's back is straight,
He knows what to bypass—

Jimmy Berman dont take Junk
He dont shoot speed neither
Jimmie Berman's got a healthy mind
And Jimmy Berman is Ours—

Jimmy Berman, Jimmy Berman
I will say Goodbye
Jimmy Berman Jimmy Berman
Love you till I die—

Jimmy Berman Jimmy Berman
Wave to me as well—
Jimmy Berman Jimmy Berman
We've abolished Hell!

Nov. 17, 1971

*Improvised to "Jimmy Brown Newsboy," tune strummed by Bob Dylan and Happy Traum after Dylan'd replied, "Go as far as you want" to question "How dirty should I get?" at recording session.

MANY LOVES

Old rumors . . .

Many people I know are dead
Many people with whom I was in bed
Many souls I know underground
Many heroes I'll— never found

My first love Neal Cassady
He ran away from me
Second love Kerouac
He began to drink, alack

Peter the third
        took Speed quite long
    (quite long quite long quite long)
He's back in the World now
        doing no wrong
    (food growing food growing food)

Many loves are underground
Many loves make no more sound
Many loves are gone to the sky
Many loves have said goodbye

Nov. 20, 1971

TROOST STREET BLUES

You can teach me baby,
                        you can touch my soul
You can have my mouth,
                        you can have my jellyroll
Gimmie your heart baby
                        fuck me up my asshole

You can kiss my lips in Kansas
                        Belly naked on mine
You can suck my tongue
                        or suck my cock so fine
I love to put my tongue up in
                        your sweet behind

There's frightened deafed white folks
                        in Kansas City
Walter's Crescendo Lounge here
                        is my place to be
I have a bed on Troost Street,
                        back in Eternity

I can't find my words,
                        my feelings are unreal
I used to sit by your bedside
                        your prick I love to steal
Your belly's in an ash urn
                        Now how do I feel?*

Kansas City, got the blues
                        Early midnight Walter's bar
Years later sitting by the jukebox
                        how funky people are
But O them black musicians make me
                        feel like a soul star

I'm back in Kansas City
                        with my old time used-to-be
Alone with my Alone
                        that's the story you and me

I once met Lester Young
                    and got down on my knees

Bodies rot and faces vanish
                    Lips turn white
I had my dreams my love is dead
                    O Heaven it's all right
Here I am in Kansas City
                    I think I'll spend an empty night

                                        1972†

*See "On Neal's Ashes," page 61.

THE HOUSE OF THE RISING SUN

There's been a house in New Orleans
               they call the Rising Sun
And it's been the ruin of many a poor boy
               and God I know I'm one

I sailed down there in '45
               tryin to get my body laid
I could not get my pecker up
               and Lord I felt betrayed

It was my first time on a ship
               w/ Puerto Rican men
I'll smoke their marijuana but
               never go to their whorehouse again

That girl was pretty young & cold
               I lay down on her in bed
She waited naked for my act
               lay there like a corpse new dead

And since that day I sucked the cocks
               of a couple hundred boys
The Rising Sun has set on me
               the man in the moon's my joys

Yeh since that day I sucked the cocks
               of a hundred teenage souls
Lord I'll trade the House of the Rising Sun
               for a Peghouse w/ a Hundred Holes.

Dec. 23, 1972

EVERYBODY SING

Everybody's just   a little
            bit homo   sexual
                        whether they like it or not
Everybody feels   a little bit
                of love for the boys
                        even if   they almost forgot

Everybody goes   a little
            bit sweet hearted
                        for a poor freckled sun faced lad
Y'all give him   a little
            bit of your soul
                        like a girl that's never been had

Now everybody everybody
                everybody knows
                        how thrilling a kiss can be
right on the mouth
                no thought no doubt
                        from that singing boy from Tennessee—

Everybody knows   what it
            is to fall in love
                        with the football hero bold
But so everybody's thought
                never do get lost
                        God remembers when you're growing old.

Everybody's born   just a
            little bit gay
                        a little bit fairy, and a dog
Everybody's born a lordly
                King of May and a
                        little bit even of a hawg.

So if you can't get with your
                natural human
                        and dont want no part queer

You line yourself up against
              the wall with your ghosts
                    and shoot to kill your fear.

You can empty your revolver
              in any woman's cunt
                    or any man's mouth you despise
You can call whore names
              or play fairy games
                    plutonium burning in your eyes,

But you'll never get laid
              by a lady or a maid
                    who won't be scared of your thighs
No you'll never get laid
              but with the money you paid
                    to buy off your woman with lies,
No you'll never get laid
              and see freely displayed
                    the Goddess that comes in disguise—

So if you're in trouble
              and y'dont like your double
                    why dontcha come see me?
I'll take you by the hand
              and love you through the land
                    and ease your tender misery.

Feb. 4, 1973

For lead sheet music to this song see *First Blues,* Full Court Press, 1975, p. 48.

NIGHT GLEAM

Over and over thru the dull material world the call is made
over and over thru the dull material world I make the call
O English folk, in Sussex night, thru black beech tree branches
the full moon shone at three AM, I stood in under wear on the lawn—
I saw a mustached English man I loved, athlete's breast and farmer's arms,
I lay in bed that night   many loves beating in my heart
sleepless hearing songs of generations electric returning intelligent
        memory
to my frame, and so went to dwell again in my heart
and worship the Lovers there, love's teachers, youths and poets who live
        forever
in the secret heart, in the dark night, in the full moon, year after year
over & over thru the dull material world the call is made.

11 *July* 1973

SWEET BOY, GIMME YR ASS

lemme kiss your face, lick your neck
touch your lips, tongue tickle tongue end
nose to nose, quiet questions
ever slept with a man before?
hand stroking your back slowly down to the cheeks' moist hair soft asshole
eyes to eyes blur, a tear strained from seeing—

Come on boy, fingers thru my hair
Pull my beard, kiss my eyelids, tongue my ear, lips light on my forehead
—met you in the street you carried my package—
Put your hand down to my legs,
touch if it's there, the prick shaft delicate
hot in your rounded palm, soft thumb on cockhead—

Come on come on kiss my full lipped, wet tongue, eyes open—
animal in the zoo looking out of skull cage—you
smile, I'm here so are you, hand tracing your abdomen
from nipple down rib cage smooth skinn'd past belly veins, along muscle
    to your silk-shiny groin
across the long prick down your right thigh
up the smooth road muscle wall to titty again—
Come on go down on me your throat
swallowing my shaft to the base tongue
cock solid suck—
I'll do the same your stiff prick's soft skin, lick your ass—

Come on Come on, open up, legs apart here this pillow
under your buttock
Come on take it here's vaseline the hard on here's
your old ass lying easy up in the air—here's
a hot prick at yr soft mouthed asshole—just relax and let it in—
Yeah just relax hey Carlos lemme in, I love you, yeah how come
you came here anyway except this kiss this hug this mouth these
    two eyes looking up, this hard slow thrust this
        softness this relaxed sweet sigh?

3 January 1974, *to* C. R.

2 AM DIRTY JERSEY BLUES

I come from New Jersey and I love to suck your prick
I come from New Jersey   you're the boy I surely pick
'F I were walking round Jersey City   Looking for sumpen quick

I come from Paterson New Jersey & I like to make love fast
But the love I like to make is love that Forever'll last
That's why ever time I see you   I bend down & kiss your ass.

I love them Jersey City boys   Their bellies are so ruddy fine
Yeah them Jersey City boys have asses   like sweet wine
Sucken Jersey City Cock's like   sucken on a joint with my mind

Love your Jersey City Belly love your   Jersey City breast
& in yr Jersey City arms O honey   I take my sweetest rest
When I look into your Jersey City eyes   all New Jersey is expressed

Do you love me a little Jersey City? Yeah you   love me a lot!
O Jersey City boy I love you   all I got
Gimme your Jersey City come   I'll swallow on the spot

When I lie on your Jersey City   heart taste your Jersey City kiss
I know sweet 21 year old boy   New Jerseys of pure bliss
And if you dont believe me   you dont know the fun you miss.

Feb. 10, 1974, *to C. R.*
(1-4-1-5-1 Chord Changes)

HARDON BLUES

Blues is like a hardon   comes right in your mouth
Blues is like a hardon,   it comes in your mouth
never know when its coming   in your North or in yr South

Yea Blues like a hardon, leads you down the road
Blues like a hardon, your standing on the road
Lord I gotta stop here, get rid of my weary load

Blues is like a hardon, it takes you far from home
Go outin night time, in streets & subways roam
looking for a lover like the blues who won't let you alone

Blues is like a hardon, it takes you far from home
Go out in the night time, streets & subways roam
looking for a lover like the blues who won't let you alone

Blues is like a hardon, I can't leave it alone
Sitting in my bed in Boulder, all I can do is groan
If I dont get it off right now, someday it'll all be gone.

Aug. 16, 1974, *with R. M.*

COME ALL YE BRAVE BOYS

Come all you young men that proudly display
Your torsos to the Sun on upper Broadway
Come sweet hearties mighty with girls
So lithe and naked to kiss their gold curls
Come beautiful boys with breasts bright gold
Lie down in bed with me ere ye grow old,
Take down your blue jeans, we'll have some raw fun
Lie down on your bellies I'll fuck your soft bun.

Come heroic half naked young studs
That drive automobiles through vaginal blood
Come thin breasted boys and fat muscled kids
With sturdy cocks you deal out green lids
Turn over spread your strong legs like a lass
I'll show you the thrill to be jived up the ass
Come sweet delicate strong minded men
I'll take you thru graveyards & kiss you again

You'll die in your life, wake up in my arms
Sobbing and hugging & showing your charms
Come strong darlings tough children hard boys
Transformed with new tenderness, taught new joys
We'll lie embrac'd in full moonlight till dawn
Whiteness shows sky high over the wet lawn
Lay yr head on my shoulder kiss my lined brow
& belly to belly kiss my neck now

Yeah come on tight assed & strong cocked young fools
& shove up my belly your hard tender tools,
Suck my dick, lick my arm pit and breast
Lie back & sigh in the dawn for a rest,
Come in my arms, groan your sweet will
Come again in my mouth, lie silent & still,
Let me come in your butt, hold my head on your leg,
Let's come together, & tremble & beg

                                    25 *Aug* '75 4 AM, *to* R.W.

READING FRENCH POETRY

Poems rise in my brain
like Woolworth's 5 & 10¢ Store perfume
O my love with thin breasts
17 year old boy with smooth ass
O my father with white hands
specks on your feet & foul breath bespeak tumor
O myself with my romance
fading but fat bodies remain
in bed with me warm passionless
unless I exercise myself like a dumbbell
O my Fiftieth year approaching
like Tennessee like Andy a big failure, big nothing—
very satisfactory subjects for Poetry.

Jan. 12, 1976

C'mon Jack, turn me on your knees . . .

C'mon Jack
Turn me on your knees
Spank me & Fuck me
Hit my ass with your hand
Spank me and Fuck me
Hit my hole with your fingers
Hit my ass with your hand
Spank me and fuck me
Turn me on your knees
Ah Robertson it's you
Yes hit my ass with your hand
real hard, ass on your knees
sticking up hard harder slap
Spank me and Fuck me
Ah I'm coming fuck fuck me
Got a hard on Spank me
When you get a hard on Fuck me.

March 29, 1976, *to J.R.*

"DRIVE ALL BLAMES INTO ONE"*

It's everybody's fault but me.
I didn't do it. I didn't start the universe.
I didn't steal Dr. Mahler's tiles from his garage roof for my chicken coop
where I had six baby chicks I paid for so I could attract
my grammar school boyfriends to play with me in my backyard
They stole the tiles I'm going across the street to the candystore
and tell the old uncle behind the glass counter I'm mad at my boyfriends
for stealing that slate I took all the blame—
Last night I dreamt they blamed me again on the streetcorner
They got me bent over with my pants down and spanked my behind I was
      ashamed
I was red faced my self was naked I got hot I had a hard on.

October 25, 1976

*Cf. also "Understand That This Is a Dream," page 37.

PUNK ROCK YOUR MY BIG CRYBABY

I'll tell my deaf mother on you! Fall on the floor
and eat your grandmother's diapers! Drums,
Whatta lotta Noise you want a Revolution?
Wanna Apocalypse? Blow up in Dynamite Sound?
I can't get excited, Louder! Viciouser!
Fuck me in the ass! Suck me! Come in my ears!
I want those pink Abdominal bellybuttons!
Promise you'll murder me in the gutter with Orgasms!
I'll buy a ticket to your nightclub, I wanna get busted!
50 years old I wanna Go! with whips & chains & leather!
Spank me! Kiss me in the eye! Suck me all over
from Mabuhay Gardens to CBGB's coast to coast
Skull to toe Gimme yr electric guitar naked,
Punk President, eat up the FBI w/ yr big mouth.

Mabuhay Gardens, S.F., May 1977

I LAY LOVE ON MY KNEE

I nurs'd love where he lay
I let love get away
I let love lie low
I let my love go
I let love go along
I knew love was strong
so I let love go stray
I told love go away

I called love come home
my tongue wasn't dumb
I kissed love on the neck
& told love to come back
I told love come stay
Down by me love lay
I told love lay down
Love made a fine sound

I told love to Work
as musician or clerk
I sent love to the farm
He could do earth no harm
I told love get married
With children be harried
I said love settle down
with the worms in the ground
I told love have pity
Build me a good city

I taught love to sit
to sharpen his wit
I taught love to breathe
mindful of death
I showed love a straight spine
energetic as mine
I told love take it easy
Manners more breezy
Thoughts full of light
make love last all night

I kissed love on the brow
Where he lay like a cow
moaning and pleasured
his happy heart treasured
I kissed love's own lips
I lay love on his hips
I kissed love on his breast
When he lay down to rest
I kissed love on his thigh
Up rose his cock high

I bid Love leave me now
rest my feverish brow
I'm sick love goodbye
I must close my eye
No love you're not dead
Go find a new bed
for a day for a night
& come back for delight
after thought with new health
For all time is our wealth.

February 21, 1977, *to G.B.*

LOVE REPLIED

Love came up to me
& got down on his knee
& said I am here to serve
you what you deserve
All that you wish
as on a gold dish
eyes tongue and heart
your most private part.

Why do you eat
my behind & my feet
Why do you kiss
my belly like this
Why do you go down
& suck my cock crown
when I bare you the best
that is inside my breast

I lay there reproved
aching my prick moved
But Love kissed my ear
& said nothing to fear
Put your head on my breast
There let your skull rest
Yes hug my breast, this
is my heart you can kiss

Then Love put his face
in my tenderest place
where throbbed my breast sweet
with red hot heart's heat
There, love is our bed
There, love lay your head
There you'll never regret
all the love you can get.

From the hair to the toes
neck & knees in repose
Take the heart that I give

Give heart that you live
Forget my sweet cock
my buttock like a rock
Come up from my thighs
Hear my heart's own straight sighs

I myself am not queer
Tho I hold your heart dear
Tho I lie with you naked
tho my own heart has ached
breast to breast with your bare
body,   yes tho I dare
hug & kiss you all night
this is straight heart's delight.

So bring your head up
from my loins or the cup
of my knees and behind
where you touch your lips blind
Put your lips to my heart
That is my public part
Hold me close and receive
All the love I can give

June 18 1977 5 AM, *for P.F.*

LACK LOVE

Love wears down to bare truth
My heart hurt me much in youth
Now I hear my real heart beat
Strong and hollow deep and neat

I felt my heart wrong as an ache
Took all heart pain I could take
Then took more, my heart did break
Sore in dreams and raw awake

Feeling blood flowing with heat
Each new lover's heart I'd meet
I'd run my hands upon his chest
Trembling hug him breast to breast

Kiss his belly, kiss his eye
Kiss his ruddy boyish thigh
Kiss his feet kiss his pink cheek
Kiss behind him naked meek

Now I lie alone, and a youth
Stalks my house, he won't in truth
Come to bed with me, instead
Loves the thoughts inside my head

Though he knows I think of him
Hold my heart his painful whim
Looks thru me with mocking eyes
Steals my feelings, drinks & lies

Till I look at Love with Truth
Think back on my heart full youth
Hear my heart beat red in bed
Thick and living, love rejected.

                3 AM *Feb* 8, 1978, *on J.R.*

LOVE RETURNED

Love returned with smiles
three thousand miles
to keep a year's promise
Anonymous, honest
studious, beauteous
learned and childlike
earnest and mild like
a student of truth,
a serious youth.

Whatever our ends
young and old we were friends
on the coast a few weeks
In New York now he seeks
scholarly manuscripts
old writs, haunted notes
Antique anecdotes,
rare libraries lain
back of the brain.

Now we are in bed
he kisses my head
his hand on my arm
holds my side warm
He presses my leg
I don't have to beg
his sweet penis heat
enlarged at my hip,
kiss his neck with my lip.

Small as a kid
his ass is not hid
I can touch, I can play
with his thighs any way
My cheek to his chest
his body's my guest
he offers his breast
his belly, the rest
hug and kiss to my bliss

Come twice at last
he offers his ass
first time for him
to be entered at whim
of my bare used cock—
his cheeks do unlock
tongue & hand at soft gland
Alas for my dreams
my part's feeble it seems

Familiar with lust
heartening the dust
of 50 years' boys'
abandoned love joys
Not to queer my idea
he's willing & trembles
& his body's nimble
where I want my hard skin
I can't get it on in.

Well another day comes
Church bells have rung
dawn blue in New York
I eat vegetables raw
Sun flowers, cole slaw
Age shortens my years
yet brings these good cheers
Some nights're left free
& Love's patient with me.

December 16, 1978 6 AM, to R.F.

LOVE FORGIVEN

Straight and slender
Youthful tender
Love shows the way
And never says nay

Light & gentle-
Hearted mental
Tones sing & play
Guitar in bright day

Chanting always
Poetries, please
Speak sweetly, say
Hello, for you may

Voicing always
Melodies, please
Sing sad, & say
Farewell if you may

Righteous   honest
Heart's forgiveness
Woos woes away,
Gives Love to cold clay

10 *March* 80 *for* S.T.

Poems by
Peter Orlovsky

Et le printemps m'a apporté l'affreux rire de l'idiot.
And springtime brought me the idiot's frightful laughter.

—Rimbaud, *Season in Hell*

"because I've been laughing a lot lately" —P.O. '79

Peter Orlovsky (reclining),
Allen Ginsberg, and Natalie Jackson
San Francisco, summer 1954
Drawing by Robert LaVigne

90

WOE—ITS WARING TIME AGAIN IN THE ARMEY

WOE—its Waring time again in the Armey
       and the sargent sees
           that far away look in my eye—
My 18teen yr old pop beef musle curve
           with soft guilty babey brain eyes
is trying to follow Korean War reporting in NY Times
wile sitting in Queens resturantes
     licking 1952 creem cheese counter
& cafeteria music speaker filters down to me
                a coded message
    to jump in orange bus to body exam center.
I could lift 1,000 lbs of invisible neurotic dust cleanleness
      hung-up
    but when sargent confined me to
Letterman Army Hosp. Frisco base barracks
           for failing Sat. morning inspection
       showing 10 dandrif flakes
       & 2 shreds of crew-cut hair
             on a black comb
Sargeant & Major took away my weekend pass They did.
I couldent go see long weekend walks artist boyfriend
             lover big cock painter
& thank you Byron Hunt you talking painter tabol hopping
in Polk & Sutter Streets Forsters Cafateria
             for introducing me to
       fine pen drawing face
& morning Glorey trumpet flowers leaf curl outlines
& my bottom lip findly sweetened by the
      persistent trailing eye of Robert La Vigne
& our year romance at 1403 Gough St.
     My oh My what a big healthey cock he had
     but I was young & strong
     & could take it.

                · 1958 NYC

ME & ALLEN

Realize big difference between me & Allen—he
has such far verbal poetry image—
connecting images getting sap
realization that leads up
ladder to highness of realization—
     I get high thro feeling
& feelings to more purer
feelings or some thing
like it. —it all takes
place in my torso stomache
& up to chest—got by
long talks with myself—
but based not on deep
realization on verbal level
but I get realization on
emotions pull—pull of
emotion—emotional sap
juce spreding thro out
body & makes me wigle in
joy—but the set back on
stage of my mind picture
big drips of sadness—sadness
drips—sadness comes forward
& pours buckets from
joints of connecting bone
brain drops into chest
void—chest void passes
it to it into stomache
stage void—tears
flow—bloody tears
flow in to void—
void of tears of Peters
tears based on knowing
void expanding in my
family members that
I've watched over years
but only come to feel
more sharply now—
death in rage handing out

rage to each member heart
face of my famiely—
my famiely disapears cause
heart turns hard & cant
expand into universe
of all time heart—all
big time heart (everybody)
thumping—thumping sadness
into my heart sadness—
no ladder accross the heart
no ladder comming out of heart
just a nedle out
of heart jabing rib—
crying pain voice alive—
all day on all days—

September 10, 1958 NYC

PETER JERKING ALLEN OFF (FIRST SEX EXPERIMENT)

AG: I feel horney. Ya better close the windows & the door otherwise it will be chilley & put on a robe. How are you going to jerk me off & do that typeing at the same time or lay next to my body?

PO: That's a problem, we did it once already, we have all the time in the world, no rush, I'll use my right hand frist & type with left hand as best I can. OK?

AG: Uhha, Allen gives a sigh of pleasure. Thats not if you can keep that up.

PO: I continue jerking him off, his cock has a slight bend, as if a little warped—got that way when allen was fucking a spadechick, the girl moved her box just when allen was going to come so that his cock came out of her cunt and ramed up against some bone above or below her cunt, when it happened it wasent too painful because—I am jerking him off all this time, he puts his hand to mine to make it go faster and puts his other hand into under my robe lays that hand atop my cock—lifts his legs like woman getting screwed and spreads them—takes the ashtrey from little tabol next to bed with my cig drags a puff—puts it out fast—it was

AG: Keep going pettey, dont break the rythum

PO: he will be comming soon—he lifts his legs—lifts his body off bed ass behind part—i keep jerking him off & try to go faster— with rythum—sexey hotter that way

AG: ouch,

PO: am i herting you?

AG: yeaha, yr doing it so irregurlly—hold my balls

PO: he goes to grab my left hand, wants me to hold his balls—so I do

AG: I keep getting hot then all of a sudden it stops—its all so irregularr—

PO: I go to stick my finger in his ass hole, figgureing that this will get him hot—on the tip of his cock—the lips start to usher up a little due drops of pre-expecting joy that seems about to come—I took my left hand now to jerk him off & with right hand fingered his ass hole—the due started to get more deweer, the cock harder—he raised his legs higher into the air as I started to go faster with my hand over his cock now—figureing if he dident come now he might not come because his cock might be getting sore by all this irregular jerking on his cock—starting to come—the come comes & flies out between wet lips like silver dragon flies & lands on white sheet—some come falls on his cock & some on my knuckles, as hes comming I say "at a boy" & he says in responce to that—a few seconds latter "thats great" & hugs me with both arms & gives maney a sigh. All over & wiped up come. It took 5:45 am to 6:10 am—calender to keep track of how maney cigs I smoke in a day & just before putting my hand to Allens cock I lit a cig & noted it & time when took. End of jerkoff secsson.

Tangers 1961

SECOND SEX EXPERIMENT

PO: Allen is going to blow me till I get a good hard-on so that I can screw him get it in him & —he takes my pants down wile I'm typeing

AG: I'll take yr pants down wile yr typeing—

PO: ready?

AG: him him

PO: Allen puts his head against my back & arms me around the tummey, kisses my back, starts to finger my cock—I get the slight tickle— slightley thrilled—slight thrill, slight—in my cock—almost could say blow me

AG: I love you, & I dig the fact yr more independant—but I feel more afraid, the contact will be broken between us—do you love me? As long as we love each other I dont care what happens—but I dont want to be no contact between us—

PO: I love you—he starts to go for my between legs, lays there with his head—& breathes breaths—starts to suck my breast—my hard-on thrill comes back—will tell him to blow me now—hope he starts to blow me without me haveing to tell him—more sexier that way— he will see my hard-on & start—yes thats what hes doing—I like this a lot—he starts to move in on my cock—wants more leaway between my legs & arm that are slightly in his way—goes up to my tits again after makeing it on my cock again—gets up & lifts his head—on my other tit now & breathing more fulley & sucking more deeper—down to my cock again—lifts his head to my other side, my left to get at my breast & now my cock—his knees on the bed, his ass up in the air facing the celing—hear the sucking noise of his mouth on my cock—would like to come now but—dont realey care unless I get that certain screem of thrill love hot stream piek flow spark—my hard-on going slightly down—he starts kiss-ing my leg—whats he doing now—going for my ass—I hope not I just took a crap a few minutes ago—& he came down to same bathroom whear I was taking a crap & jerking off but dident finish the jerkoff because he came along—now hes on my tit—& looks with his eyes to my face, I see him out corner of my eyes

AG: Kiss me?

PO: I do for a short wile & then get back to

AG: Why dont you put the typewritter on my back then I can blow you directly?

PO: He now is in my ear—& has his hand on my head

AG: Does that feel good or am I just bugging you?

PO: No everything is fine.

AG: Feels very good, I never did this before—aneything ya want me to do?

PO: Keep blowing me

AG: Which side do you like better?

PO: Aney side thats convient for you or you like. He gets knees on the floor & tackles my cock that way—am getting hot—me think I am GOING TO FEEL HOT MORE—hard-on coming back—will I be able to come wile I am typeing—hope to god I can—come get hot pete—up & down he moves—think about girls now—who—fuck me babey—come on you spread yr cunt—allen should be bloweing harder & FASTER—a rythum—I need hes doing it now—his hand there—hes doing that now—I need—now hes after my balls with his tung—my hard-on gone down somewhat—I need faster man-power from him & suck-pull—I dont think I'll be able to come—hes got the rythum back—the beds vibratting a little—he stops I see his back & round buttocks sticking up from the floor—he gets up

AG: I get back upon the bed. Ya got a hankerchief?

PO: Yeha—I go up to my coat on the wall & get into pocket there one for him—he on bed now with mouth on my cock—but before he did that he brought his mouth to my ass on bed—his fingers trying to work there way into my ass hole—his mouth on my tit now—deep suck—back to my cock—he puls a hair out from between his lips—my cock hairs hes back sucking again & kinda quite down there—he moves about again

AG: Ya want to do something—

PO: Whats that?

AG: Stand over bend over the typewritter, & I'll show you something & Extradoranarry—

PO: He goes for my neck & fingers my tummey & licks his tung into my face

AG: You can type standing up a little cant ya?

PO: Sure. What ya want to do. Its dirty

AG: Are you sure?

PO: I just took a crap a cuple of minutes ago

AG: just keep typeing—I'll take care of it.

PO: He goes for water bottle & towel & after he does that wants me to sit on his face—I do

AG: I do but its too much weight for him—hes breathing too hard & has to figure how to support my weight on his face—he usses his arms—hes strugleing a little bit

AG: That feels very strange—

PO: I move my possison to sit on his chest & then he wips my cock into his mouth—hes rubbing my breasts—& streaches his legs apart, one against the wall one up near my head beside it—hes milking my tits—my hard-on slightly comming back—I realey want to come wile at typewritter

AG: Does this possission hert you?

PO: No, keep blowing me as I would like to come at type(writter)—for thats what I want to do & so you just keep blowing & not worrey about what I do but keep yr self going bloweing & not worrey about what I do but keep yr self going bloweing me & I'll take care of this part—I would realey like to come wile at this typewritter—

AG: I would realey like you to screw me—

PO: But that would—I dont think I'll be able to come &

AG: That feels good—I dreamed a lot about that in Mareekiesh—

PO: His cock falls out of my mouth as he passing infrunt of me—

AG: But whats the realey best way to blow you—lift up—thats better

PO: He fixes the bed mattress—bends down again on bed & head on my lap starts continueing to blow me—my hard-on gone down—he cops my balls & sucks my cock with his mouth & his other arm is around my hip & hugs it—other right arm down to my foot on

floor—noise of his mouth—my cock feels funney sensation—
slightly annoyeing feeling—typewritter cover falls over—

AG: can you put yr feet there?

PO: ya, I can do that.

AG: okay?

PO: ya, i am still typeing—it hearts a little bit—

AG: Is there aney way to stop it?

PO: I dont know, its prittey far in.

PO: hes comming—grabs my waist & huggs me—lifts my shirt up to get
to my breast—fingers my cock with his right hand—jerking me
off—he came, thats good—& so fast—he must of liked it—hes
holding on to my balls now & pressing his head-nose against my
back—& he sighs & I feel no pain now that its over & hes still,
relaxed—he coughs & says You know what, Peter—you kow that
possition is like this scene—its like a Bregual*—what you think—?

PO: Yeah. He takes his cock out of my ass, gently—a ball of shit falls
out on the pillow—looks like shape of chicken heart—Allen
thought it was come—but no—he puts it on white paper & carries
it—gets behing me & wipes my ass with underpants & krinckles my
shit up to throw away—my ass feels free—& easey relaxed—now
I go to bathroom—like I always do when he screws me & wash—
he goes for cig—& says that felt very good—

AG: did you like it?

PO: in the beggining no—but when it was all over & the pain was gone
OK & glad to see you likeing it with a smile on yr face

AG: Yeah—it was very luggoubrious & Bregual like.

1961, *Tangers*

*Peter Bruegel (1525-1569), Flemish painter.

ALLEN JERKING OFF ON BED
(SEX EXPERIMENT #3)

AG: Already? Get going.

PO: Hands me his cig.

AG: ya want me to do it fast or slow, give me instructions.

PO: Do aneything ya want.

AG: Its got to be a little 2 way, what kind of sex is that.

AG: Do aneything ya want ya say, how about blowing me

PO: I got a cold saw.

AG: Will ye take it when I am ready to come.

PO: No, Because I dont like to take come.

AG: I dont like to jack off eather, except I do.

PO: I go for cig., Allen gives me his.

AG: Here.

PO: Powerful hand on cock

AG: Come on Peter, you'r condemning me to something awful dont ya realize.

PO: I look to see if hes come, I thought so by the soapeingness, we smile at eachother & wink eye, he with other hand tuches holds my thigh from under neath

AG: Babey dont let yr dog bight me.

PO: Allen gets up from bed, sits up to wipe come off his leg, puts his glasses on & starts to clean the white sheet.

PO: I go for my cig & drop it.

AG: Hay is yr cock alright.

PO: yeaha. Allen reads over my shoulder. I say "I guess thats about it hua."

AG: It felt mych more trajic than that. I thought that you were going to write down something awful that was going to look like a straining grasping fish on the bed.

AG: Did you type when you jerked off?

PO: No.

AG: Ya ought to try it done it some time man, its a gas.

AG: Well ya think we ought to go to bed.

PO: him him.

PO: Thats it, no added things to say.

AG: Ya got aney edatorial comments.

PO: Yes, but sleep best I guess.

July 16, 61
Tangiers

Note: Blow-jobs delore since then. —P.O. Boulder 1980

THANK GOD... I WASN'T A WHORE BOY
(from a conversation between P.O. & A.G., written down by P.O.)

PETER ORLOVSKY: Hold it, hold it, I'm trying, I'm concentrating—just give it a second more—I'm doing my best—December 31! On that day—or whenever they think lovely day—everyone in this big small world will have a dream to start and vote no atom bomb's gonna fall on my little head—no—on everyone's little head. I don't know it's going to happen but it's certain there's no harm to say it. And it would be nice if true.

ALLEN GINSBERG: Well I can just see Pravda & Time both affirming that it's harmful to have pretty wishy dreams just so you won't have to face the reality and do something about it. Whattya think of that?

PO: The dream force is more powerful than Pravda force—than anyone's force. Is more important, powerful's the wrong word.

AG: In other words you think you can get away with being a lamb, and that's all you got to do.

PO: Well that's a little strike against your soul Allen if you think the dream force won't win. Already on the page you got Kruschev winning and me losing. I mean he's right about Russia but can't I be right about just a little atombomb? Well so far we've talked about the atombomb and about dreams and about Germany, and mothers and so much life left on earth that now we got to think about the expanding universe. Everybody taking big trips everywhere else free. carrying briefcases of free food. That takes care of the Starving Problem. I guess the problem is just getting to know everybody on earth. And after you get to know everybody on earth you want to know everybody on the next earth—People like to take walks—so we all got a lot to do. Have big sexual accordoans seranade everyone's heartbeat, so there's no tears of woe from out of the cock. Nothing but a big family of happy come. That's the earth called Street, and what lovely beds we're all going to visit.

AG: Ah, I ain't seen none in a long time.

PO: Whaddya mean didn't I screw you up the ass like a little 13 year old girl recently? and you were on a bed. No thirteen is too young. Well some girls mature early.

AG: Yeah but I haven't even come with you to you in a month.

PO: Well I tried jerking you off the other day.

AG: After I begged you—and you rushed out to get the mail before I even came.

PO: That's not true—no mail—I rushed out to get the pictures before the store closed—I did a lot of things—and it takes so long to jerk you off—and you wanted to relax and have a good time and that takes a longtime—and I was begging you to hurry up—so what really happened then—

AG: I wound up jerking off before you came back.

PO: What you think about when you came?

AG: You fucking me—and how exquisite the pain desolation of lying in bed solitary hopeless ended in Onan-wilderness, here ten years later in Tanger, after all the tender lovings we've given to each other.

PO: Well thank God I didn't charge you anything—that is, I wasn't—I wasn't a whore boy.

AG: Yeh, well, I guess it's all lost now, I'm getting older and creepy middleage looking—I guess you get disgusted when you realize what male bald potbellied being you wound up with for Wife. But that's inevitable, I guess it's time we started out toward Female, or me, started, —and see how that feels again—I still have that nightmare emptiness from Someday when I'm dying and I've left no Me behind, or Child—whole sisters & full sons to futurity, perpetuate this Being—Awful if we didn't even have a chance to settle down and get married & issue new Ginsbergs & Orlovskys before— Wham the bomb falls & ends that whole ecstatic story—That's the last moment fantasy I was telling Gregory about—I had it in Peru when I was high on Ayahuasca—it was so real it made me vow to get married & die Papa—not even thinking of Bomb.

PO: Boy what a dumpy paragraph.

AG: But that's what I mean—specific example, of widening area of consciousness—the druge-trance oped my soul and made me aware of the whole void side of my life & tenderized me to all the girls I'd ever had romance with & denied—so I'm talking about something real now that general men and women can dig—that was just *my* scene—everybody got their own, none shamefull unless mine be called so—So More Soul of this kind is the Answer to the World Problem because there is no other answer except Soul.

PO: Un-hum. Now, you want me to say something?

AG: Yup.

PO: I didn't want to do it, You made me queer, it had to be you Big
Cocky you, but you pulled me so and then I knew
I tried hard to fight it
I'm looking over a four leaf clover the one you
adore all the time, I'm looking over your big sexy soul

AG: That's right you did, you always did keep telling me at the beginning you just wanted to be friends and you were afraid I was just acting nice so I could get in your ass—and now look at us—.

PO: But now I'm a bonafide queer on the witness stand.

AG: Did I make that come true?

PO: Make it? You hipnotized it true.

AG: And now the dehypnotixation is begun, I'm getting old and you're realizing you're no longer in my Power.

PO: That's why I wrote Howl for you, so as to get you off being queer—give you something to do besides queer. I'm making a cigarette for us. But then you started writing poetry going after your mother and left me in the dust. No wonder Kerouac don't love you any more you made him go chase his mother too. And try to get me after my mother—but I was smart and took my brother. My three brothers. Besides You don't love me any more I brood too much. At least that's the big General Tag you think I do all the time, nothing but a hoody brooder. Permanent depressed brooder. Bill keep away from him, he broods. "I know what you mean man" and I think to myself, Bill says to Allen when they talk about me. And I visualize Bill immediately launches on to the vast underworld dream sperit of the russan people (that Orlovsky's russian—him—)—a brood rase, man, thats what—ya can always tell—you see his long hair that he tries to keep back all the time—you can always tell—its a sure sign—they, them russian people I mean Orlovskys just like them—they dont want to go aneywhear—but in their room's & think their create'en something with their hair floweing over there head like it was the HOLEY MOP thats going to clean the world of sins. After a wile Bill fineally says to Allen whos silent & & hopeing Bill will understand him—"yeah man, its best for you to be away from him now—I mean now—pop, bam—Bill knowcks his chair over as he swings his shoulders to get up & when so doing knowcks his two knee-capes togeather that make the sound of "come here Allen"—

AG: Oh, realey Bill, dont wimper like that to me—I mean I'm feeling something right now—dont you realize I have to sooner or later find a girl & get married so I got a Jr!

BB: Take a tip from me kid & steer clear of e'm—they got poisen-juces dripping all over with e'm—fishey smell too—down right phonoragraphic up a streached ass hole—theys whear they make ya look—wise up Allen & picture ya self right—for once in a wile, —cant ya—?

AG: Gee, Bill—if ya onely let me do a collage, a cut-up-collage with ya I be so—aneything Bill—come on Bill, just this one time at yr place—let me bend over with ya and put in pictures of things ya got here to—so we could work togeather—?

BB: Allen my boy, ya alright—now what I'm doing here is—Oh by the way have ya ever knowticed the bass of a babboon—well, I came to the amazeing discovery the other day as I was bending—well you see, —quite frankley Allen you got you got babboon marks one on each ass-hole—I mean er—cheeks—ya butts—& I just got to have a picture of that. It will have jush amazeing effects when the blue hits it—tho I'll try the grey first—dont worry Allen you'll have no baboon markes when I get thru with ya—so dont worry—in fact I'll try to take yr ass away—pronto, just like that—you'll see man, I'm not fooling around—this is strickly straight———& with one mighty dearing sweep that can can be made only once between 2 men in a room together & fingers becomeing rings—does Bill tear up the cut-up for the last time—the picture of them both in a room & disapear they both into the invisible to stay—

AG: Well then Peter Orlovsky now can understand the relation between public questions and private affairs and how you can't separate the two areas of personal activity—as they are so much in the world today, that's what's causing all the trouble, this big schizophrenia between what a man knows he is, and the Front he puts up to the world before a microphone TV Camera or notebook. Is that why we came back to this scene here in Tanger? Because one thing, I don't see how we can solve our world problems if we can't make heaven in our own room land. Can you comment on this?

PO: I know theres a lot of love to go around—& a lot of people are missing the ball—for me, I want to stop smokeing & breathe some starey-air in—?

AG: Well lets go in the room & make love again, is that the answer to the World Question?

PO: Yup. No because I can't give you a baby.

AG: I didn't want to stop coming with you just on account of that—

Tangers 1961 *July*

BB = Bill Burroughs, i.e., novelist William Burroughs.

TANGER SURPRISE

Come on and do iiee it
The music seems to be saying—2 boys dancing as
girls—with red bands around hipps & asses—
one came up to me & asking for what? I guess money
& I pull out arab money— 20 of a laff &
give him 50 franks—hes glad & dances away from me
on matts 20 feet away
to whear mussicans are
playing—young arab who's a waitter in this small
Dance Caffey—throws a bottle top into area
out side this caffey & throws it into the air & still
looks in that direction as if expecting something back—
loveley feminnen girley like dancers

1961 —*Tangers*

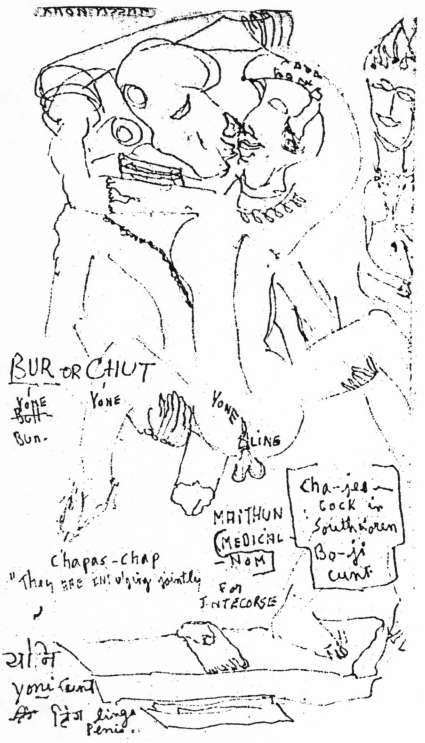

Drawing by Peter Orlovsky, India, 1963. ''From Karjuraho Love Sex Embrace show how to make love this way also known as KHON ASSAN or love hold body just the right movement—young kids gave me the names of different parts of the body.''

SOME ONE LIKED ME WHEN I WAS TWELVE

When I was a kid in summer camp,
around 13teen & one night I lay asleep
in bunglow bed with 13teen other boys,
when in comes one of the camp councilors
who is nice fellow that likes ya, comeing to
my bed, sits down & starts to say: now you
will be leaving soon back to Flushing & I may never see you
again—but if theres ever aneything I

can to do help ya let me know, my farther is
a lawyer & I live at such & such a place
& this is my adress—I like you very much—
& if yr ever alone in the world come to me.
So I loked at him getting sad & tuched &
then years latter like now, 28, laying on
bed, my hunney-due mellon Allen sleeping next to me
—I realize he was quear & wanted my
flesh meat & my sweetness of that age—
that we just might of given each other.

April 1962 Bombay

DILDO SONG SUNG NOTE FOR NOTE ON GUITAR

you are my dildo
dildo
ha ha ha ho
my sweet dildo
Petey love to feel you strong
You are so strong to me
my sweet little
dil-do

You are my strong dildo
ha ha ha ho
my strong dildo
Petey love to fill you strong
You are so strong to me
my sweet little
dil-do

July 29, '79
Naropa, Boulder, Colo.

ALLEN GINSBERG
ON HIS RELATIONSHIP
WITH PETER ORLOVSKY

The best account of the relationship between Allen Ginsberg and Peter Orlovsky is that given by Ginsberg himself in his 1972 interview with Allen Young. It is reprinted here as a preface to the letters. (Excerpted from *Gay Sunshine Interviews,* vol. I, edited by Winston Leyland; Gay Sunshine Press, San Francisco, 1978, pp. 109-113.) Peter Orlovsky's view of the relationship is summed up well in his poem "Me and Allen," page 92 of this book.

ALLEN GINSBERG: We [Peter and I] met in San Francisco. He was living with a painter named Robert LaVigne in '54. I was having a very straight life, just trying it out, working in an advertising company, wearing suits, living up on Nob Hill in a nice big apartment with Sheila, who was a jazz singer and worked in advertising. Things were somewhat unsatisfactory between us. We'd been taking a little peyote, so we were into a psychedelic scene, too.

We got into an argument, so I wandered down one night into an area of San Francisco I'd never noticed then called Polk Gulch, now known as a notorious gay area with lots of gay bars. It was then more of a bohemian section, somewhat gay, artistic. Hotel Wentley was there, right on the corner of Sutter and Polk, and a Foster's cafeteria. I went and sat in the Foster's, late at night. I ran into Robert LaVigne and got into a big, interesting, artistic conversation about the New York painters I knew— Larry Rivers, de Kooning, and Kline. LaVigne was a provincial San Francisco painter, so I was bringing all sorts of fresh poetry, art news from New York.

He took me up to see his place and his paintings, about four blocks away on Gough Street in an apartment that I subsequently lived in for many seasons and still use now. I walked into the apartment and there was this enormous, beautiful, lyrical, seven-by-seven-foot-square painting of a naked boy with his legs spread, and some onions at his feet, with a little Greek embroider on the couch. He had a nice, clean-looking pecker, yellow hair, a youthful teeny little face, and a beautiful frank expression looking right out of the canvas at me. And I felt a heart throb immediately. So I asked who that was, and Robert said, "Oh, that's

Peter; he's here, he's home." And then Peter walked in the room with the same look on his face, a little shyer.

Within a week Robert said that he was going out of town or breaking up with Peter, or Peter was breaking up with him. He asked me if I was interested in Peter, and he'd see what he could arrange. I said, "Ooh, don't mock me." I'd already given up. I already had had a historic love affair with Neal Cassady a decade earlier. So I was already a tired old dog, in the sense of the defeats of love, not having made it, not having found a permanent life companion. And, in 1955, I was already twenty-nine. I wasn't a twenty-year-old kid with romantic notions. That night we were in Vesuvio's bar. Robert had a big conversation with Peter, asking Peter if he was interested, sort of like a *shachun,* a matrimonial arranger.

Then I went home one night. I went to Peter's room. We were to sleep together that night on a huge mattress he had on the floor. I took off my clothes and got into bed. I hadn't slept with too many people. Never openly, completely giving and taking. With Jack or Neal, with people who were primarily heterosexual and who didn't fully accept the sexual-ization of our tenderness, I felt I was forcing it on them; so I was always timid about them making love back to me, and they very rarely did very much. When they did, it was like blessings from heaven. If you get into it, there's a funny kind of pleasure/pain, absolute loss/hope. When you blow someone like that and they come, it's great! And if they touch you once, it's enough to melt the entire life structure, as well as the heart, the genitals and the earth. And it'll make you cry.

So . . . Peter turned around (he was in his big Japanese robe), opened up the bathrobe—he was naked—and put it around me and pulled me into him; and we got close, belly to belly, face to face. That was so frank, so free and so open that I think it was one of the first times that I felt open with a boy. Then, emboldened, I screwed Peter. He wept after-wards, and I got frightened, not knowing what I'd done to make him cry, but completely moved by the fact that he was so involved as to weep. At the same time the domineering, sadism part of me was flattered and erotically aroused.

The reason he wept was that he realized how much he was giving me and how much I was demanding, asking and taking. I think he wept looking at himself in that position not knowing how he'd gotten there; not feeling it was wrong, but wondering at the strangeness of it. The most raw meat of reasons, for weeping.

Then Robert hearing, seeing the situation, came in to comfort Peter a little bit. I was very possessive and I pushed Robert away. That got me and Robert into a funny kind of distrust that lasted for a year or two

Peter Orlovsky
Drawing by Robert LaVigne, 1955

Allen Ginsberg
Drawing by Robert LaVigne, 1956

before our karmas finally resolved. He then realized he was well off on his own; and I was burdened with the karma of love.

Peter was primarily heterosexual, and always was. I guess that was another reason he was shocked—the heaviness of my sadistic possessiveness in screwing him. For the first time in my life I really had an opportunity to screw somebody else! I think that wounded him and thrilled me a little bit. So we still had to work out all that in our relationship over many, many years. It's painful sometimes.

We slept together perhaps one more time. Then I had to go to New York for my brother's wedding at Christmas, '54. I came back and moved into that apartment where they were living, at their invitation. And then there was a triangle of Robert, me and Peter. Peter had not made up his mind whether or not he wanted to make a more permanent relationship with me. I had my eyes on Peter for life-long love; [I was] completely enamored and intoxicated—just the right person for me, I thought. Robert was not sure he hadn't made a mistake, seeing the flow and the vitality that was rising up in both me and Peter. And Peter began withdrawing. He was caught in this rivalry between me and Robert, and, at the same time, there was his unsurety of me and his relation to me. Basically he liked girls anyway, so what was he doing lying there being screwed by me?

So I moved across from the Hotel Wentley and got a room. I was working in a market research job. I had the brilliant inspiration that all the categorizing and market research I was doing could be fed into a machine, and I wouldn't have to add all those columns anymore. So I supervised the transfer for the company, and that left me out of a job just nicely, like a seamless occlusion. Then I got unemployment compensation.

I was being psychoanalyzed at Langley Porter Clinic, an elite extension of U.C. Berkeley Medical School. He was a very good doctor, and I said: "You know, I'm very hesitant to get into a deep thing with Peter, because where can it ever lead. Maybe I'll grow old and then Peter probably won't love me—just a transient relationship. Besides, shouldn't I be heterosexual?" He said, "Why don't you do what you want. What would you like to do?" And I answered, "Well, I really would just love to get an apartment on Montgomery Street, stop working and live with Peter and write poems!" He said, "Why don't you do that?" So I said, "What happens if I get old or something?" And he replied, "Oh, you're a nice person; there's always people who will like you"—which really amazed me. So, in a sense he gave me permission to be free, not to worry about consequences.

So then I waited for Peter, and Peter stayed up at the Gough Street apartment and went to school. I got this room and started writing a lot and waited and waited for Peter. Neal Cassady came by a couple of times. I made it with Neal. I can remember one of the last really wild times I made it with him, because I had a room of my own and there was privacy, finally. He was lying there naked, and I was sitting on his cock, jumping up and down trying to make him come.

And I just waited and waited [for Peter]. There was nothing I could run after or pursue, because I couldn't claim anything by force. Things got too difficult where Peter was living, so he got a room himself in the Wentley, across the street from where I was. And there was embarrassment, coldness—not knowing where each other was, what we would do. I was waiting for him to make some sort of decision. A couple of times we drank a little to see if we could get over the low. We didn't sleep together at all, though I was longing to.

Then one day he was lying in bed, and he started crying again. He said, "Come on and take me." I was too overwhelmed and frightened to even get a hard-on. I didn't know what to do. We both had our clothes on. I was afraid he was interpreting it as me screwing him again, rather than really just having each other. But that soon got resolved, and we moved in together, into an apartment in North Beach. We found an apartment, and it had a room for him, a room for me, and a hall between us; and a kitchen together. So that gave us both a little privacy, and, at the same time, we could make it when we wanted.

He was very moody, very sweet, tender, gentle and open. But every month or two months he'd go into a very dark, Russian, Dostoevskian black mood and lock himself in his room and weep for days; and then he'd come out totally cheerful and friendly. I found after a while it was best not to interrupt him, not to hang round like a vulture; let him go through his own yoga.

The key thing was when we decided on the terms of our marriage—I think it was in Foster's cafeteria downtown about three in the morning. We were sitting and talking about each other, with each other, trying to figure out what we were going to do, who we were to each other, and what we wanted out of each other, how much I loved him, and how much did he love me. We arrived at what we both really desired.

I'd already had a visionary experience: an illumined audition of Blake's voice and a sense of epiphany about the universe. He had had an experience, weeping and lonesome, walking up the hill to his college, and having a sense of an apparition of the trees bowing to him. So we both had some kind of psychedelic, transcendental, mystical image in our brains and hearts.

We made a vow to each other that he could own me, my mind and everything I knew, and my body, and I could own him and all he knew and all his body; and that we would give each other ourselves, so that we possessed each other as property, to do everything we wanted to, sexually or intellectually, and in a sense explore each other until we reached the mystical "X" together, emerging two merged souls. We had the understanding that when our (my particularly) erotic desire was ultimately satisfied by being satiated (rather than denied), there would be a lessening of desire, grasp, holding on, craving and attachment; and that ultimately we would both be delivered free in heaven together. And so the vow was that neither of us would go into heaven unless we could get the other one in—like a mutual Bodhisattva's vow.

That's actually the Bodhisattva's vow—"Sentient beings are numberless, I vow to enlighten them all. Passions are numberless, I vow to quench them all, cut them all down. The nature of the dharma, the doors of nature are endless, I vow to enter every single one of them. Buddha path very high and long and endless—vow to follow through all the way—Buddha path, infinite, limitless, vow to go all the way through." Sentient beings, numberless, unnumbered—countless, vow to count every one, enlighten every single one of them. Basically a vow to be reborn as everybody, one after another, every stone, every leaf blade, vow to be every individual part of the universe at one time or another, and accept the fate of that particle, so to speak.

Well, this is like a limited version of that, almost intuitive, the vow to stay with each other to whatever eternal consciousness: him with his trees bowing, me with Blake eternity vision. I was more intellectual, so I was offering my mind, my intellect; he was more athletic and physical and was offering his body. So we held hands, took a vow: I do, I do, you promise? yes, I do. At that instant we looked in each other's eyes and there was a kind of celestial fire that crept over us and blazed up and illuminated the entire cafeteria and made it an eternal place.

I found somebody who'd accept my devotion, and he found somebody who'd accept his devotion and who was devoted to him. It was really a fulfillment of fantasy, to a point where fantasy and reality finally merged. Desire illuminated the room, because it was a fulfillment of all my fantasies since I was nine, when I began to have erotic love fantasies. And that vow has stuck as the primary core of our relationship. That's the mutual consciousness; it's the celestial social contact, valid because it was an expression of the desire of that time, and it was workable. It's really the basic human relationship—you give yourself to each other, help each other and don't go to heaven without each other.

There's this mythology of Arjuna, from the *Bhagavad Gita,* getting to the door of heaven. He's got this little dog following him, and they say, you can come in but you can't bring your dog. And he says, well, no, if I can't go in with my dog, I won't go. And then they say, Oh, come on, you can go in, just leave him behind, it's only a dog. And he says, no, I love my dog, and I trust that love, and if I can't bring that trust in, then what kind of heaven is this? And the third time, he says, no, no, no, I'll stay out and put the dog in heaven but I won't go in without the dog. I vowed to tears with my dog, I can't leave my dog alone. And so, finally, after the third time, the dog turns out to be Krishna, the supreme lord of the universe and heaven itself. He was only trying to get heaven into heaven. And his instinct was right. And our instinct was right. It was enough to bring us through very difficult times—all through the change of status, beat generation and fame, the alteration of social identity that fame entails.

Our relationship has lasted from 1954 on. The terms have changed tremendously. Peter's gone through a lot of changes, and we've separated for a year at a time. And always come back. We've gone through a lot of phases of sleeping with people together, doing orgies together, sleeping alone together. Now Peter sleeps with a girl. I very rarely sleep with him.* But the origin of our relationship is a fond affection. I wouldn't want to go to heaven and leave Peter alone on earth; and he wouldn't leave me alone if I was sick in bed, dying, gray-haired, wormy, rheumatic. He'd have pity on me. We've maintained our relationship so long that at this point we could separate and it would be all right. I think the karma has resolved and worn out in a sense.

The original premise was to have each other and possess each other until the karma was worn out, until the desire, the neurotic attachment, was satisfied by satiation. And there's been satiation, disappointment and madness, because he went through a long period of speed freakery in the mid-sixties which really strained things. We had times of hostile screaming at each other such as happens in the worst of homo- and heterosexual marriages, where people have murder in their hearts toward each other. That burned out a lot of the false emotion of youth, and the unrealistic graspings, cravings, attachments and dependencies. So he's now independent, and I'm independent of him. And yet there's an independent curiosity between us.

*Oh, we started sleeping with each other again years ago. These things go in phases.
—P.O. & A.G. 1980

118

Selected Letters
between
Allen Ginsberg
and Peter Orlovsky

But if the while I think on thee, dear friend,
All losses are restor'd, and sorrows end.

—Shakespeare, Sonnet XXX

While recording for BBC I realized I was speaking to England, & so spoke well - a great relief - like your TV Fantasy - write a poem you can read on TV & we'll do it in US too. I didn't know about Isadora Duncan & America with Esenin? I can read your writing. Merims wrote me he would be glad to loan you money so if you need it, get from him it's so K. Seen Lucien? Jack should be in N.Y.C. soon. Don Allen has Howard's new address I guess. Poor Henry No I didn't dream you'd fuck up - don't & be so worried what I judge you, I don't judge you Peter - I love you - I was worried you'd be lonesome without me - as I'm beginning to long for you - but glad you feel on your feet, that makes everything Greer for us, between us.

Peter's Poem:

O Blake! Blake! Blake! The yellow sun spanning the green blind
       Channel

How sad you'd be to see endless human fog ~~so~~ over London now.

          Green water, Dover's cliffs, Silence, squeal of gulls afar
              as if the Cliffs Squeaked —

          The Long green dusty 2'nd Class Train at Dover —

I am not these properties: Howling Allen Ginsberg arriving enchanted
       in England

Weeping at the Foggy earth of England's Blake:

But a body's Consciousness with the Roar of Babel

and groan of Armor round my head and thighs

Clanking in the railroad car   amphibrachs of Misery
                                        (a greek jump meter)

Destined for London — where my bliss in the Smoke

may shine brightly like a sudden Mexic Sun.

Allen Ginsberg holograph, from letter of February 15, 1958. (See pages 138–139.)

Dear bloodey teary angel allen. God your ① March 20, 58
Thurresday 4:3.0 PM
last letter 2 poems of mine 2 your every thin poem-
so more just called "Ginsbrug on the street" — yes I
am sorry for not writing you 2 throwing my face
across the sea to you but here goes now - sit
on the bed and relax - smile - I'm near you -
the tears come now to me now and the alli not
well I am feeling good - yesterday as I was
walking on Village street I began talking to myself
" I take all this ugly world in on my breat - let
it all come in and I dont know what I am
going to do with it — things like Taff not in
clean mind - the old lady who I'll never talk to -
ect — for warm hands is the main thing to give 2
try to touch every bodys heart harb cords — —"
dont remember all I said but any way I feel good
and go straight ahead and do the next thing I want
to do and all's that happens to me you want to
know now Dear allen? but I will answer your
questions frist that you have in your last letter -
good that Bill off another of yours - go around Paris
with him - take him to the Cato combs - no - no

Peter Orlovsky (left) and Allen Ginsberg, Paris 1957
Photo by Harold Chapman

Allen Ginsberg in Alaska to Peter Orlovsky in San Francisco

[May?, 1956]
USNS Sgt. Jack J. Pendleton (T-AKV-5)
c/o Fleet Post Office
San Francisco, California

Dear Peter:

Fast note before the mail arrives and is taken off in half hour. Anchored up in place called Icy Cape, Alaska, midnight sun, dead pallor all night long, clouds and now some rainy wind, no ice or icebergs, no land, a radio antenna sticking up out of an invisible beach on the horizon, 40 other ships gathered here, waiting for ice to break up further north to continue. Am in the Arctic Circle but it's not very cold at all, out on deck in Teashirt the other nite for a few minutes. Maybe later more spectacular sights.[1]

Spending time mimeographing 22 page poem I wrote in Mexico as small booklet, about 50 copies may finish it, but not yet.[2] Who do you see? Did Tom Tagalong get down to S.F.? If so take care of him till he can get a job. Spent week drinking with him in Seattle, nice fellow, rather like Neal tho perhaps not so fast & intelligent, but same type of body & orphan soul experiences.

Days calm my mind calm in fact asleep, notating in journal the weather and appearance of the sea but no visions or prayers, just 7¢ I threw into the Bering Straits which is a short body of water separating Russia & Alaska, but couldn't see either it being too foggy.

Berkeley student on ship here studies optometry explained to me all about the mechanics of the eyeball, people are nearsighted because their eyeballs are too long, thus the lens in the front of the eye focusses sharp clear images in the middle of the eyeball not on the rear where it should be for the brain to pick it up.

Never forget how clean and neat you look and pure all dressed in ambulance white coming from work. What's happening? Lafcadio [Orlovsky] working too again? I bet not. Read biography of poet François Villon, 15th century French criminal-poet, laments for the death of beauty, youth, life. Sings the old whore, what's happened to my

petiz tetins, hanches charnues,	*little tits, hips plump*
eslevees; propres, faictissises	*raised, right & ready*
a tenir amoreuses lises,	*to hold amorous combats*
ces larges rains, ce sadinet	*those broad loins, that jewel*

assis sur grosses fermes cuisses   *set in large firm thighs*
dedans son joly jardinet?   *in her pretty little garden?*

Read the French aloud, particularly the next to last line, such lip-smacking cuntlike sounds. —sadinet, assis etc. Real sensual writing.
　Love, write me, will write again when I get mail.

As ever,
Allen

　1 Ship north in military sea transport service, Dew Line stations.
　2 Ginsberg's mimeo *Siesta in Xbalba and Return to the States* is dated July, 1956 (22 numbered pages and dedicated to Karena Shields).

Allen Ginsberg in Paris to Peter Orlovsky in New York

Dear Peter: I concur in everything   Chambre 25
Allen says here. All the best   Paris 6, France
Love, Bill [Burroughs]   January 20, 1958

Dear Petey:

　O Heart O Love everything is suddenly turned to gold! Don't be afraid don't worry the most astounding beautiful thing has happened here! I don't know where to begin but the most important. When Bill [Burroughs] came I, we, thought it was the same old Bill mad, but something had happened to Bill in the meantime since we last saw him.[1] I did not realize it that first evening and day, nor for another day after you'd left, but last night we stayed up till 3 AM talking, like you and I talk, clearing up everything—first we started arguing & misunderstanding as usual, I afraid he had come to claim me now you'd left, he still sherlock-holmes poker-faced impassive, I thought he was tormenting cats still, was worried, felt depressed, I sat on bed cried realizing you were gone & I was alone in this miserable situation, I even got hi on T [marijuana] which made it worse, Francine came in too and leered at me & tried to climb all over me, I was at my wits end, I fell silent terrified on the bed— then a knock on the door—this is 2 nights ago, Saturday nite—and Gregory walked in with great publishing news from Germany (about that, later)[2]—I was so glad to see him, he seemed so familiar & reassuring, only one left from when we were together here, when you were still here, I thought he would save me from sordid sorrows with Satanic Bill—but last night finally Bill & I sat down facing each other across the kitchen table and looked eye to eye and talked, I confessed all my doubt and misery—and in front of my eyes he turned into an Angel!

What happened to him in Tangiers this last few months? It seems he stopped writing and sat on his bed all afternoons thinking and meditating alone & stopped drinking—and finally dawned on his consciousness, slowly and repeatedly, every day, for several months—awareness of "a benevolent sentient (feeling) center to the whole Creation"—he had apparently, in his own way, what I have been so hung up on in myself and you, a vision of big peaceful Lovebrain—said it gave him (came sort of like a revelation slowly) courage to look at his whole life, me, him more dispassionately—he had been doing a lot of self-analysis. Said his whole trip to Paris not to claim me but visit me now & also see an analyst to clear up psychoanalytic blocks left etc. We talked a long time got into tremendous rapport, very delicate, I almost trembled, a rapport much like yours and mine, but not sexual, he even began to dig my feelings about that, my willingness but really I don't want to, has stopped entirely putting pressure on me for bed—the whole nightmare's cleared up over-night, I woke this morning with great bliss of freedom & joy in my heart, Bill's saved, I'm saved, you're saved, we're all saved, everything has been all rapturous ever since—I only feel sad that perhaps you left as worried when we waved goodby and kissed so awkwardly—I wish I could have that over to say goodby to you happier & without the worries & doubts I had that dusty dusk when you left—that you could have heard the conversation, taken part—I'm sure now henceforth when you meet again there'll be no more anxiety between you and Bill, all this is gone from him—the first day there, between us here, when we 3 were together— Bill was still very hesitant & unsure of himself, still hadn't come out— still doubting perhaps but knew inside, as we did not yet, that everything was OK, but still too withdrawn to know to clear it all up—but I know for sure now he's OK & consequently I feel like a million doves—Bill is changed nature, I even feel much changed, great clouds rolled away, as I feel when you and I were in rapport, well our rapport has remained in me, with me, rather than losing it, I'm feeling to everyone, something of the same as between us. And you? What's happening inside Dear Pete? I read Bill your poems, I'll type them & send them soon, everything is happening so fast. I feel like I can write even. Are you OK? Write me happy letter, don't be sad, I love you, nothing can change love, beautiful love, once we have it. I cried the other night realizing you'd gone, thinking that love would go away with you & I'd be alone without connection—but now I see Bill is really on same connection as we are—and I begin to feel connected with everything & everyone, the universe seems so happy. I made it with him the other night, to be good, on junk, before he and I talked, treated him sweetly, as you once treated me, but after our talk & new understanding, there's not even any more need for that, we get along on nonsexual level—maybe occasionally later an overflow we make it—but he no longer needs me like he used to, doesn't think of me as permanent future intimate sex schlupp lover, thinks even he'll wind up maybe after difficulties, with women, we slept apart in different rooms last night, both happy, first time I was alone in bed, I was happy, I missed you (jacked off even), Bill woke me up in the morning, had happy breakfast, talked more, the rapport real, Bill's change real, I changed too no longer suspicious & worried of him, he doesn't even bother the cat—I'm continuing to keep your calender—Bill will accept you—have no more fear, remember Nature is really kind, loves you, he's getting to be as kindly feeling as you & I do at our best when we're not worried—he said he was still sunk & irritable when we were all together in Tangiers—the doubt and uncommunication still hungover unresolved your last day here maybe,—but absolutely it's really now gone, have big peacy happy slumber dreams—Life is so great, & best of all Bill completely aware of this. So we took long walk, it was a blue fine unfoggy day, downtown. Jack wrote nice letter from Florida, sent me all the money, arrived this morning ($225), so we walked downtown to the Opera to Amer Express, cashed it into Travellers checks, now I got Plenty money & Bill has, I repaid him what he loaned us.[3] Don't send me money, I have all I need—maybe later in a few months I be poorer, but right now I have plenty plenty & small expenses, shared with Bill, he no longer lives high anyway so we live cheap henceforth—don't send me the $10, keep it now you'll need it, in fact if you really get in hole tell me I'll send you some. So Jack says he's in Fla. and movies look like they'll buy his book now and he asks where you are, so write him a card (Enclosed find Lafcadio's letter to you arrived 2 days ago).

Also Gregory [Corso]: he came back, happy, he & Bill got along great, Bill likes him, and Alan Ansen wrote Gregory great warmhearted letter saying don't worry about money, come to Venice & stay happy there & safe awhile, let me know if you need money for RR fare there.[4] How strange, Alan suddenly woke up too? I don't know, but it was a great letter from him to Greg. Meanwhile in Germany, Gregory made arrangement for Gregory (not me, it's better this way leaves me free in fact. good deal) to put together one small anthology of me Bill Jack Greg, expensive, and to help in a larger volume of Amer & SF poetry to be published in a few months. So he's going to work on that now in Venice. Furthermore the Germans offered him an apartment in old university town of Heidelberg, for 6 months after Venice, thru the summer, so now he knows where he can go next. He also sending another long Coit-Tower type madpoem to fill out his book for City Lites, so that's going to be good too.

Meanwhile also, a letter arrived from America saying Bill's *Junky* had been finally sold & published in England and Bill is due some more money (under a hundred) from that.

Got on big discussion with Bill of means of extending Love-Bliss to others & spreading the connection between us (told him we had intended that in Tangiers with him, even if it didn't work) without sacrificing intimacy. We'll solve that problem too before we're done. I feel so good today it don't seem hard. It's just that there arent many people who've experienced the freedom that we have. Jack's letter today was nice, and more friendly—but I think he still is doubtful & secret—or doesn't know that we know, or something. But that'll turn to gold later and we'll all get straight with Jack next time we see him too.

So money's rolling in, honey, & love's rolling in. I'll see you in 6 months like I said. Are you alright? Write me as fast as you can. I'm worried you're unhappy & got too much trouble in front of you in NY. Julius will be hard to help.[5] We'll see what we can do. But don't let your own sweet tender knowing Pete be eat by worry. I'll always be with you, & so will the trees & all the rainbows & angels in Heaven be singing last happy cowboy songs with shiney eyes at us.

Tell Lafcadio to stop being Christ of Mars & I'll stop being unhappy christ of poetry. No more Crucifictions! Regards to your momma & Marie.

XXXXXXX How's the ship? Dont take too much horse. I've quit T entirely it's a bringdown & I doan want no more bum kicks. Bill smokes less too. But it varies with everyone. *Black Mt Review* Came out, Creeley editor.[6] —get it at 8th St. Bookstore—send me a copy maybe. Love Allen (with your green pen)

[The next three paragraphs were written on the top and sides of the letter. The second one was written by Gregory Corso.]

No other mail for you except Lafcadio's Letter. Gregory gave Bill big leather German coat & we're paying Gregory's fare to Venice—he leaves Tues nite (tomorrow)

Dear Peter—I'm back from Frankfurt on way to Venice—Hope all is well, beautiful in NY. Love Gregory. I'll write soon from Venice.

We walked into the Bourse again today & also, bright blue sunny day, went to St. Chapelle for 15 minutes on the way home from changing money with Pierre.[7]

1 William S. Burroughs (b. 1914), American Beat writer, novelist, author of *Naked Lunch, The Wild Boys, Exterminator!* etc., a friend of Ginsberg since the 1940s. His name will occur often in subsequent letters, as will those of Corso and Kerouac (below).

2 Gregory Corso (b. 1930), American Beat writer, author of *The Vestal Lady on Brattle Street, Gasoline,* etc.

3 Jack Kerouac (1922–1969), American Beat writer, author of *On the Road, The Subterraneans,* etc., friend of Ginsberg from 1940s New York days.

4 Alan Ansen, scholar, poet, author of *Disorderly Houses* etc., friend-secretary to W. H. Auden, typed *Age of Anxiety* and in the year of this letter typed preliminary *Naked Lunch* in Tangiers.

5 Peter had returned to New York before me to take care of his brother Julius, who had been for the last 12 years in Central Islip State Hospital in Long Island, N.Y. —A.G. '79.

6 *Black Mountain Review* 7, the last issue, which included "Interzone"—a prose passage by Burroughs, "Elsie"—story by Herbert Huncke, first printing of "America," poetry by Philip Whalen, Kerouac's "Brakeman in the Railroad Earth," among other texts, assembled by Creeley in San Francisco in his mid-50s visit.

7 Pierre—black market: 8.5 francs to a dollar.

Peter Orlovsky on board ship returning to New York to Allen Ginsberg in Paris

Jan 22, 58

Dear Allen:

On the ship, close to home, at night, full turky stomache sadness on my face but finally read through the brothers K[aramazov] & see the same madness in my famiely. Have been very quite, sick half the time from the bellybutton waves but eating marvously & to boot havent smoked much at all & to boot have this nice typewritter to type to yo & by odd chance Lary is on same boat with me & so are many orangers that I have eaten but cant seem to find any milk. I know I goofed with Bill [Burroughs] being so silent as if crying in side my throught, yes I gess I am meek, like you say. But at the end of eternity theres nothing to be imbarresed about. I still feel delighted Balf kissed me & I remember Joyce's smile & Bill talking to me when you were out of the room I was crying when on the train & am now cause it was like living in a mansion in a bunch of graps on a vine with the sunset around each window. Love Bill like I love you, be a chair for him to sit on and for him to talk prouldy from—Bill seems more like a brother now then a farther with stern eyes in Tangers. Bill got roses in his teeth. I took a one hour shower yesterday & used to much water that the hall was soken wet twenty people nocked on my door in fright but I kept singing along till cleaned & wash all dirty clothes. Have had two wet dreams so far, did not masterbate once & feel good about that for I must stop that habit for its insulting to my cock. I lay in bed at night than hear crakes all the time & one night lissoning intently & thinking about Jack [Kerouac], the phrase—Jack is a crack in the wall—came into my mind & I laughted to myself a few penies. No storms to tell you about at sea, the ship rocks the most at night & thats when I get sick & my tommy feels like a barrel making icecream & get chills all over. I never thought I would ever be scared looking at the sea from the side of a ship but now I am, tho it was just one time a few days ago in afternoon when looking over the rail and the waves so close & I dont remember what was going thro my mind now but all of a sudden & began to think about how Heart Crain might of felt when he was about to jump he must have been very lonely painfully lonely & that pain from lonelyness was cutting his chest up before he jumped, for a moment I thought I was going to have an hullusination of his body floting in the water & then I through my self back and ran into door shrivering & then a picture of Cranes face with bumps on it ran through my mind. This ship is very big & all togeather different then the ship we took over sea, the food is duble, white tubs for everyone, animal hospitals for dogs, gimnasium's for fat men and women, tea in afternoon with cake, childern playgrounds & all these people so clean it scares me. Did you know Alyoucha [in *The Brothers Karamazov*] has a vision of Christ but is afraid to look at him. I had a dream of Frankinstine & you & Bill were standing on a corner, I was twenty feet from you two, you both had a look of death at me, I yelled with my eyes scremming out of my socites (joints) reciting Myockoffickys poem "then die my verse like my ranke & file of my army"[1] & keept it up to a fanatic point whare I felt so much tension on my face that I might of died at that moment if I had keept yelling at you both. Frankinstine dident scare me he was running after some young girl. And then somewhere along the line Perfume like a log floting in the sea—I felt sad & lonely when I saw your picture in *Evergreen* & then I realized I know your face better than my owne for that one moment.[2] —drink toast to Peter out at sea. I hate to be away from Paris, began to enjoy it there very much. The more dreams of you the better. What time is it? ? ? I forgot to ask you to write a letter to take to Bob Merims to borrow some money from him incase I get broke, it sliped my mind. When I get ashore I will find his adress and send it in this letter. You can write him or me noterizing a lone. Tho the fifty dollars I get will help me along for awile tho when I get a job I dont know when I will get my frist pay check & also I still dont know if I will get Feb. V.A. check, for the Government may start taking that from me to pay this ship trip I owe them so I dont know exactly where I stand so that borrowing money from Bob may be essential so send me a letter OK, ing it soon as can. Sorry I forgot about it before. Big party on ship, last night abord. Have newyears cap on, trying to rob drinks but cant, everybody not drunk enough yet. Oh yes On the frist day out I saw land in the sky & thought it was real. It was only till I left you & Bill to get on train did I feel lonely sadness pains and crying in my throught but now I feel better. tho when I left you I felt our friendship was like sunset dust floating & seperating away—young young young saw flying fish with red boots on. May I ask what color are your viens, hows yourn chimminy throught? The sea is real alright & its full of bellybuttons & mirrors. May I hafe this walse on this wave. Someone wants the typewritter so must move on off. I feel very good & confident things will work out well. Stomache upset at so much expectiency when I get home.

[*At the bottom of this letter was a handwritten note from Peter after he arrived home in New York, dated Jan. 24, 58.*]

Home at last—everything alright—Lafcadio very mad looking—hes very calm an talkative about everything an has presision of Space planet knowledge[3]—my mother apprehensive an nervous. Have lot of things to do; I must get a job as soon as possible. I will need about $50.00 to get started untill frist paycheck so write letter to me or Bob Merims (144 West 16 St. N.Y.C.) as soon as you can. Nick ok, he has good room in city, went to see him when I landed but he no home.[4] Laff [Lafcadio] told me he is working polishing floors & has side job delivering telegrams and has money saved up to help Julius.[5] Laff also said he (Nick) wants to go back to college for one year to study chemistry to complete B.S. degree & get chemistry work.

1 From the Poem "At the Top of My Voice" by Mayakovsky, Marshall tr. Correct wording is: "Then die, my verse, die like the rank & file . . ."
2 *Evergreen Review* No. 2 (1958), the San Francisco Renaissance issue.
3 Lafcadio Orlovsky (b. 1940), younger brother of Peter. "He was reading a lot of mechanical science and was zero-ing in on the idea of taking the best things on earth into outer space on a rocket ship for us all, but he settled for doing a lot of interesting drawings/paintings, like working 9 hours on one little drawing" —P.O. '79.
4 Nicholas Orlovsky (b. 1929), older brother of Peter.
5 Julius Orlovsky (b. 1931), older brother of Peter. "Peter left me in Paris with tears in his eyes thinking of his brother Julius who was locked up many years on the back wards of gigantic mental hospital buildings on Long Island." —A.G. '79.

Allen Ginsberg in Paris to Peter Orlovsky in New York

9 Rue Git Le Coeur
Paris, France
Jan. 28, 1958

Dear Peter:

Got your letter yesterday, glad you are feeling ok, mad that Laf [Lafcadio Orlovsky] burned your books (any of mine—better Get that Genet to Paterson & my papers[1]—reason I am afraid of storing stuff with you is instability of Lafcadio type bookburnings.) I'll answer your letters after I receive them, that way we exchange a letter each 8 days (unless big upsurges & emotional crises require extras), you do same? I write letter to Bob Merims about money today, asking him to loan what you need, he will I'm sure do it if he has it (& he probably has it) so you can see him as soon as you get this letter—he'll have mine. Nick Chemistry college news encouraging. I guess explain to Laff his Hollywood idea fine IF he has connections how to do it (like Jack). No word from Gregory in Venice yet. I saw French anthologist Alain Bosquet, he had my name on list to translate my poetry for his anthology already, asked me for further info on other US poets, so I'm getting it for him. Received advanced paperback copy of Jack's *Subterraneans* from Grove press & read it last nite, it's very intimate & funny—tho Jack seems to reveal unconsciously that he avoids deep final relations with women on account of tie & fear with his mother, & doesn't completely understand it in the end of the book, & so suffers & turns to writing Buddhism on account of self-frustration of human love-possibilities. Get it from Don Allen, the book. (59 W 9 Street—or look up Grove Press in Village phonebook & buy copy for a buck & 25¢.) You found *On The Road* yet? Mail me one if you get money enough.

Scene with Burroughs deepens, I've been to bed with him a few times & there's been great intimacy and relaxation, which will soon I think result in not making it with him no more, he really doesn't need it any more & we have big deep talks without it. He explained his method of meditation to me, how he clears his mind to stillness so he sees his important benevolent sentient soul emerge (he said he in Tangiers in Despair gave up finally & prayed to God & was answered). The way he does it is this. He sits and thinks. Rather than trying to combat & still & shut up his fantasies which fill his mind & shut out Bliss, he plunges into his fantasies, fills them out & feels them as much as he can. If he has a mean hostile fantasy, like killing me or you say or his Nurse, he accepts it as really a part of himself & feels it—rather than rejecting it as unwholesome, or not really him. It is really him, he says he realized. All our fantasies—like yours of being drowned by me, or of suffering lonely death or living sordid maybe, all our anxieties—are really parts of us which are TRUE. Rather than shut them out suppress them let them come on in all force no matter how painful they are, accepting their reality. So we will have a flood of contradictory fantasies, like with me some sadistic some masochistic. Meanwhile he, himself, inside, is watching these feelings take over, change disappear, be replaced. The watcher just sits there. When the fantasies and feelings (no matter how painful) are accepted & felt as true, they finally lose their horror—& you see all these parts of yourself unafraid finally, they lose their horrible force—force which comes from trying to deny them. The watcher sits aside & watches them finally, parts of itself (tho not the whole story. The watcher is the whole story) Finally the impersonal benevolent watcher takes over when the air is clear, looking around at yourself objectively without fear. My fear of T [marijuana] for instance was caused by my unwillingness to accept the paranoid sordid perceptions I got as real, I tried to shut them out rather than feeling them. So I tried it the other night. Pretty soon I get sexual masochistic fantasies, of being screwed by you, soon these turned into fantasy more horrible, of being screwed by Bill, then by my brother, then by my father. Then I realized that this masochistic dream of being screwed by my father had always been with me but had been too ugly before for me to accept. Finally I ran thru it fully consciously in my mind—& wound up with a great feeling of new knowledge & liberation from it—instead of having passed it off as unreal. As I used to do. So I think I will start meditating now. You try same. The feeling of the impersonal watcher benevolent clear & pure is same or similar to the feeling you & I have together in bed when we're closest. Just as between us, we cleared up hostility & doubts by bringing them out in the open, so inside myself I have been continuing the same process. The trick is the same. Might try this with regard to your fear & doubts about Julius project—let the full force of anxiety overwhelm you. To see what happens & what you discover, what your real feelings are in full force. Maybe you have already?

Well, so something very interesting happened the other nite, we were discussing all this, & Bill said, that he had gone very far in this process & could still his mind at will now, but that there was some feeling he had underneath that was so horrible to him he could not get at it (having to do with his early trauma with his nurse). And that though he had tried to bring it up, in the past, and more so recently since last sessions in Tangiers on Majoun [marijuana leaf] with himself, it couldn't come—he'd

William Burroughs on beach, Tangier 1957
Photo by Jack Kerouac

Jack Kerouac on beach, Tangier, 1957
Photo by Allen Ginsberg

get near it, it would begin, but he had then such a feeling of fright (as if the universe were turning into nightmare like with us at Assisi with Black door I guess) that prickles went up his neck & he was afraid of the Unknown—and realized it was real, in him, but afraid to continue. He says he's come up to Paris to go to an Analyst & bring it out altogether—in fact he has an analyst, made arrangements to see him twice a week at $10 per & has appointment today. Well we were playing with this feeling 2 nights ago, he tried to feel it, in my presence, I tried to watch and listen, he stood there by the bed looking at me, silence for ten minutes, the air deepened and thickened, the walls of the room closed down, he looked blank-eyed and strange to me, I began to get fear myself, he looked as if he was an unknown robot (like we looked to each other on Peyote—mask faces with what unknown inside us & you with insane universe-laugh staring at me) suddenly I realized he might—the impossible might happen & turn the room into a nightmare, he might turn into monster in a Kafka dream & kill me, I was really beginning to sense something frightening, started to fight back staring, then thought to relax, he relaxed, we both relaxed came back to normal—he explained that that's just what was bugging him, always had bugged him (same fear we felt when he was lushed & hi on Majoun in Tangiers insane waving the machete at us)—that he himself was afraid of—a ghost breaking into consciousness & reality—an early emotion—he said it might be the memory of something so horrible he'd suppressed it all his life—as if perhaps he had as child murdered someone & blanked it out since—so he goes to Analyst this afternoon. It's all coming to a head, he says he feels strong enough now (after religious blisses felt) to combat the Evil & survive its appearance—is not really worried or afraid, but knows he must go thru some temporary Hell soon. Well I'll let you know what happens. (He says, of Analysis, also: the analyst must be someone whose unconscious mind is clear enough, no conflicts, so that when evil universe appears in his mind, the Analyst is unfrightened & unaffected—as I was frightened & insecure at the moment of the breakthru effort described above.)

Well let me know how all sounds. I wrote Parkinson & will go to England the end of this week it's Tuesday now, we'll leave Friday perhaps. Bill will stay there a week. I'll stay two perhaps & dig scene. Unless I hear from you before I leave I'll write you from England. . . . Saw Joy, had lone ball with her 2 nites ago, she came I didn't she wasn't in right period. Talked Francine out of idealizing me, told her not come by except Fridays, hah that's over. Ate chicken at Whitman's the other nite bookstore party.[2] Supper tomorrow with Frechtman. OK Pete write me

big detailed letter about home events & NY scene, & what you think.
xxxxxxxx send poem Cant wait to
see you to try out new
ideas for Love

Love Allen

1 Copy of *Our Lady of the Flowers;* signed by Genet to Ginsberg.
2 George Whitman's Shakespeare & Co. Bookstore on left bank facing Notre Dame,
celebrated radical bohemian meeting place, crash pad, browsing room & site of first
"Beat" poetry reading in Paris. The name was appropriated from the famous & elegant
1920s bookstore frequented by Stein, Joyce, Pound, etc.

Peter Orlovsky in New York City to Allen Ginsberg in Paris

Feb 10, 58

Dear Allen: Great piece of news this morning; got job in Psychiatric MST
—start work Thursday—all dressed in white again—felt great relief
when found out I could work there—of course its a far cry from dream
ambulance attendant job I said I would get on pay—but $60 is ok—40
h. wk. & all benifrets & things—give more attention to patients who are
mostly young: like they have male & female wards combined. [. . .]
    Laff in Npt. [Northpoint]—he ok—dident get much sleep last night
—laying in bed fantasizing about T.V. show & speeching to America—I
feel very good & optomistic and not sad & rejected feeling tho somewhat
confussed & started smoking again—Have been looking up everything
on Vladimir Mayakovski that could get hands on—and will do so about
Essienne[1] —Essienne committed sciwcide—he stayed in room 4 days
alone—wanted to write but no ink so cut rists & wrote sciewcide poem
on wall. [. . .] He said there was nothing to live for no life in life—and
ended the small poem telling future young men to push forward and fight
for love—Essienne married Isadora Duncan—she traveled thru Amer-
ica—Yes I saw that Wallace [interview] in NY *Times* but it was small
wilty fooling about how is responsalble for SF renauccauncce but thro it
away before I knew you wanted—it was short & no whare—it said that
Jack [Kerouac] only lasted a week in NYC reading—but in SF poetry &
jazz is hitting it up—Keenth Patchen says hes responsible,[2] ect, ect.—I
have to get bite to eat honney—I cant continue write now—can you
read my handwritting—no patience—darn coffee at apt—?? go go go
go—help—tea with limon—but I do feel good and so dont worry dear
Allen things are going ok—we'll change the world yet to our dessire—

135

even if we got to die—but OH the world's got 25 rainbows on my window sill. [. . .]

Yes I know Turner,[3] remember when we landed in Venice, [Alan] Ansen stayed up all night & into morning on our frist day there & as we were looking at island cemetry where De-agileff is buried[4] the sun bottom was tuching sea waves & all the water in that direction was yellow-white & I said "Turner's painting"?—Will look up his work in Art Library. Allen, being I got this job & used you as a refference the bestway to work this out when they send you character form of questions about me is what? [. . .]

1 Vladimir Mayakovsky (1893-1930), Russian poet and dramatist; chief poet of the Revolution. Sergei Esenin (1895-1925), Russian poet, bisexual. See essay on Esenin's love affair with Nikolai Klyuev in *Gay Sunshine* 29/30 (1976), pp. 4-5.
2 Kenneth Patchen (1911-1972), West Coast poet.
3 J. M. W. Turner (1775-1851), English landscape painter.
4 Sergei Diaghilev (1872-1929), Russian ballet impresario and art critic.

Allen Ginsberg in London to Peter Orlovsky in New York

Feb. 15, 1958
London

Dear Peter:

Got your letter yesterday, was so happy to receive it and your sweet sex talk. I had been running around with mad mean poets & world-eaters here & was longing for kind words from heaven which you wrote, came as fresh as a summer breeze & "when I think on thee dear friend/ all losses are restored & sorrows end," came over & over in my mind—it's the end of a Shakespeare Sonnet—he must have been happy in love too. I had never realized that before.

Since I wrote you I went to Worcester, visited poet Gael Turnbull, dull nice doctor, but I was agitated & he so calm [. . .] left with a strange uncertainty & depression & went to Oxford University & stayed with fellow we once met in Paris—he was fine, good to see an american face honest again—the first morning out of his window I saw a huge green cow meadow & took a long walk in almost Springtime nature with him by quiet English streams with bells and towers of colleges thru the trees all around—stayed there met & talked to young students, gave small fine reading for about 20 of them, read Creeley Whalen Levertov & "Howl," they dug it all completely. I felt great again, communicating & crying in public—in front of the mild withdrawn English (Blake is right dreaming

136

about Jerusalem to come to England someday)—Came back to London, & drove with the Parkinsons to Stonehenge, & Salisbury a big sweet cathedral looks so calm on a green huge lawn, big as daytime, I sent you postcard of 3000 year old Stonehenge (means stone hangings)—then saw Seymour Wyse old friend of me & Jack & talked all nite with him he owns a record shop here—Hell we could have stayed at his pad if you'd come here—and also have seen Simon[1]—but first, great news, I went to make 5 minute record to fit into Parkinson's broadcast talk on American poetry[2]—and as soon as they heard me read they stopped the show & asked me to record "Howl" & "Supermarket" complete for huge mad broadcast to all England—So I started & gave slow sorrowful reading, built up, almost broke down in tears again, dreaming I was talking thru microphone to the Soul in the Fog, read to Blake himself—even Parkinson saw it was great—so I'll probably get paid almost a hundred dollars for that & maybe they'll broadcast it (still has to be arranged officially)— I left & went out & got drunk. I'd been nervous before—with the Program Director—& he promised to record Gregory & Jack & everybody & read up on U.S. Poetry—seems they are waiting for us here too—all English poets afraid to be real & expose themselves. I started, anyway— have new Faith in something great can be done, moaned, wept, sung, save civilization by Eternal Music, write for the heart of mankind. I felt sad and lonely & got drunk & went to Simon's house, drunkenly following subway signs from station to station, got there 7 o'clock at nite & went out on his Vespa Motor scooter weaving fast around corners flying and balancing behind him ready to scrape my skull on the road for Death if it came to that—went into Big Bars & Pubs & I talked to everybody beautiful all nite & came home with Simon drunk, he invited me to sleep with him, he was drunk too, so we got naked & fell asleep in each others arms without doing anything sexy except kiss in a big warm comfortable house bed—he has a great house, an apartment he shares with a Mad Blues shouting jazz musician who has a lot of money[3]—he has a real Klee drawing (a man with furry lines on his skin) and a Max Ernst and lots of surrealist paintings strange Dadaist pipes & stones and stuffed, miniature dogs in his house, a clean house with music and books—we could also have stayed with him free. I bought a new edition of that Mayakovsky book (printed this time in India)[4]—with more poems, including his great Elegy on Esenin's Death. I'll read the book a week more, show Bill, and send it to you soon.

Good job at Psychedelic Institute[5]—that's where I was a patient you know. I'll write straightforward neat reply when I get their inquiry on you, don't worry—I've had jobs & know how letters of reference should sound. I've stopped masturbating all this 2 weeks in London too—and feel sadness. I can't see you, I wish we were together again, I want to cry in your arms—I sent you Blake's [painting] *Glad Day*—Yes we'll make it again—I'll be back to NYC soon. Parkinson thinks I'll get the Guggenheim & hear from them early next month—he says, I don't know.[6] I got *Black Mt. Review* here already. Michael Rumaker's review [of *Howl*] is o.k., at least it's serious so I don't mind. He's right maybe about overgenerality of images—but misses a lot of the structure and point & is too proud of his own strength, he's a little to worried & cool—but not bad. I didn't mind, anyway. Real Criticism which means something is useful and don't hurt my feelings—I don't feel that attached & identified with the poetry—I feel more identified with you in fact than *Howl*. It was like reading somebody else's work. By the way *Saturday Review of Literature* has note (in Trade Winds column) about us in Brentanos—seems the manager complained to Grove (who thought it was funny). Feb. 1 issue page 8. Also article on Jack in Jan. 11 issue page 75. By the way if it's too much trouble to go to Paterson you can leave my stuff with my brother in L. Island. I didn't get hardon from your letter I got wave of bright joy from vision of us naked on the rocks of the sun, and my heart laughed I was happy, a bolt of sunshine in Fog here—I been in Fog. I already also have *Evergreen* #3. Poem by me in the *Partisan* is "Ready to Roll." Ariel paints same here, I told her to put a cock on Christ on Cross she has, it's dull otherwise.[7] [. . .]

While recording for BBC I realized I was speaking to England, & so spoke well—a great relief—like your TV Fantasy—write a poem you can read on TV and we'll do it in US too. I didn't know about Isadora Duncan & America with Essenin! I can read your writing. [Bob] Merims wrote me he would be glad to loan you money so if you need it, get from him it's ok. Seen Lucien? Jack should be in NYC soon. Don Allen has Howard's new address I guess. Poor Henry.[8] No I didnt dream you'd fuck up— don't be so worried what I judge you, I don't judge you Peter—I love you—I was worried you'd be lonesome without me—as I'm beginning to long for you—but glad you feel on your feet, that makes everything freer for us, between us.

Here's poem:

O Blake! Blake! Blake! The yellow sun spanning the green blind Channel. How sad you'd be to see the dense human fog over London now.
    Green water, Dover's cliffs, silence, squeal of gulls afar
        as if the cliffs squeaked—
    The long green dusty 2'nd class Train at Dover—

I am not these properties: Howling Allen Ginsberg arriving enchanted
in England.
Weeping at the Foggy earth of England's Blake.
But a body & Consciousness with the Roar of Babel
and groan of Armor around my head and thighs
clanking in the railroad car   amphibrachs of Misery
(a greek jump meter)
Destined for London—where my bliss in the Smoke
May shine brightly like a sudden Mexic Sun
If I walk naked mind in the yellow hornless traffic
Forgotten of the cankered Gods & geniuses of sidewalk history
as one with Shakespeare and dead Shelley & Bright Blake
Mortal & Mindless in the maze of ancient cranes & girders
and faces glaring with the broken consciousness
of rooves, smoke, chimneys, churches, rays of lights,
and the great bleak acrid fog of lack love mind strain
rusting the eyes with tears and twisting soft mouths into iron.

(continued but I'll leave this out later)

I don't feel myself (ah relief in my belly) dependent on poetry for
glory and excuse to thrive
No, better, the Ambition and Great Magic Property is Sanctity
— but, bah!, why strain the dream, dependent on that bleak skyscraper,
— why latch on to anything for grand Universal Comet in Society—
— even the winking Lion knows better than that
World Smasher, Smash Yourself!

[previously unpublished]

I'll write you soon from Paris—news of Bill then—he sees Joy he says.[9] Gregory's book is *out* (write Ferlinghetti for copies)—I haven't seen it—Gregory making out with Guggenheim, she loves him & tried to lay him—he's upset, we gave him junk to bring to Alan [Ansen] & he used it all up. Alan was mad at him. Gregory thought he'd come to Paris, angry, but it's more straight now—anyway I hope. O.K. I'll wrap this up. Write me soon baby, I'll write you big long poem I feel as if you were god that I pray to—

Love
Allen

ELGIN MARBLES NAKED LOVE
in British Museum greatest thing in Europe

1 S. W. Taylor, Pata-physician, translator of Alfred Jarry.
2 Thomas Parkinson, Professor of English at U.C. Berkeley, poet, member of Rexroth anarchist circle in Bay Area in 40's, editor of A Case Book of the Beat.
3 George Melly, British "trad" musician, cartoonist and essayist.
4 A translation by Herbert Marshall, first recommended to Peter Orlovsky by Frank O'Hara.
5 Peter applied successfully for job as attendant, New York State Psychiatric Institute.
6 "I didn't till six years later." —A.G. '79.
7 Ariel Parkinson, painter, wife of Thomas Parkinson.
8 Henry Schlachtner, student friend of Peter Orlovsky. Henry please contact Peter. —P.O. '80.
9 Indonesian girl friend (Paris) of Ginsberg and Orlovsky.

Allen Ginsberg in London to Peter Orlovsky in New York

Feb. 24, 1958

Dear Peter:

Hello. Quiet night in Paris, Sunday, Bill [Burroughs] just went downstairs. Harloff & his girl been laughing & calm next door.[1] Well, I'm back from England. I guess I wrote you most of what happened there, though I had two good experiences with the sun the last days, the first: I climbed high dome of St. Paul's Church (where Donne used to preach) to over look London (as in a dream a year ago I had of standing on tower in mid London and looking down on the fog, factories, huge factory with four giant smokestacks, and old red towers of London Bridges)— (and river Thames gutted with coalbarges & industry winding in the middle)— when I got on the dome, open place (a balcony round the topmost egg-tip part)— looked down all over London, saw the dream scene— a clear day over the iron burn river, Tower Bridge black and small below me with white crowned tower-tops, a flag floating over the low Towers of London, red and white cars creeping down Fleet Street, holes in the floor of the city where the bombs 15 years ago, rattle of construction hammers in the air, one clear hammer far below repeating its blows in a hole in the earth near stacks of toothpick-like lumber, miniature railroad cars passing over the bridge slowly with shrieks of brakes faraway & whistle of boats, train crawling like a worm into a hole in the side of the buildings across the glassy river, bonk & crack of hollow wood by skeleton building, girders iron half finished symmetrical sundial concrete monument walks, barges on the river, collections of docks jutting irregular profile against Thames, Houses of Parliament, the little baby british flag flying above it & graduated higher spires clustered nearby, millions of miniature spires, peaks, roofs, churches, flats, chimneys, vast smokestack across the river from Westminster-Parliament piles, a square huge smokestack reaching up over the city with a head of white steam boiling out and flooding the sky, haze, fading into haze, carpet of fog settling down like dust on the low town, clouds above, blue sky, a star reflected gleaming off the top of a spire, worst last, vast, the clear sun above the blue smoke overlaying the crystalwork myriad black roofs, the sun above glimpsed over the whole spreading city, a burst of the clock bells of St Pauls deep & hollow in the air the sound, the sun raying down, the whole landscape lighted up, sunrays slanting all the way down against the faraway flat front of a modern white newspaper building leaning out of Fleet Street, way down below a mile away. Great glimpse, I stayed up there & took notes—which notes here copied above.[2] Crossing back to France on the English Channel, pulling out of Dover on a cold clear day, huge glimpse of the sun again, a great dreamcloud floating over the sky, the sun moving behind it raying down vast aereal halo streams of light on the sea & against the white faraway cliffs (which would otherwise stand there desolate in void nite w dark death landscape against cold black sea)—but now all the great Vast lighted up, rays from the cloud, and way below on the sea beneath the cloud I saw a cargo boat the size of an ant picking its way thru the water, diminished by the vast sea & vast cloud & vaster rays of sun—and suddenly out of the cloud & sun raying over the whole creation full of live boats & ants in fields & birds in trees & passengers & cities full of bodies, I saw a winged live seagull flying out of the cloudy glory & imagined all the dolphins streaming thru the sea, creation streaming all over the universe. So that was two big mad shots of immensity I photo'd in my brain on the trip. Show Jack. Hey! Big kiss Pete.

Back in Paris that night, Bill gloomy, he been drinking paregoric (new kick for me I tried it, you can buy it in drugstores cheap free—opium drink, like Elixir Terpinhydrate & Codeine, but this is elixir of opium, feels like black O we had in Tangiers.) & so has light habit—I got him to doc here & he has his kicking medicine apomorphine & is coming off now, I guess will be alright. He was glooming about state of the world, all them armies & armories & closing down of soul maybe forever, in oncoming civilization. Letters, letters, arriving, heard from Denise Levertov (she called L. but he was rather abrupt & cold so never saw him) she was waiting to hear from you & she had 2 poems & her picture in *Mademoiselle,* Jan. Saw Holmes' article in *Esq.*[3] very good, & Jack this week in *Time,* and article about Zen Jan. *Mademoiselle* same as Denise— Zen article talks about Ginsberg. I have several copies of new *Black Mt.* so don't send. The [Mike] Wallace interviews were in the *Post,* with Jack & Philip Lamantia, Jack sent them here. Also heard from Creeley, he's ok in Albuquerque, wrote friendly said he had a baby now he's trying to write more.[4]

Bill exploring young hip group from Monaco cafe here, found some very nice guys, the younger generation, one big tough lookin fellow name B.J. (he calls himself) with wild black hair & weird eyes, young, enthusiastic, held up bookstore in Frisco several years ago & said he was so horrified by the inhumanity & bum kick of it he's been happy & good since, tries drugs, wanted to dig me—Bill, lives with girl—also met that bearded singer with ring in ear, Gregory knew him, Darryl, folksinger,[5] he was here talking with Bill this afternoon—Bill strangely more open & enterprising in seeking out the cats than I am, but he found some nice ones—sort of the crowd of the fellow upstairs Greg went to Germany with. Gregory in Italy, had big mad time with Peggy G., almost made it with her, but after a week in which she saw him & got drunk together & gave him a wristwatch & thought he was wild, she put him down, too— he apparently insulted her with something he said about her daughter— so now that's over. Alan [Ansen] on junk wrote some chain poems with Greg & they got along fine—say I received a copy of Greg's book,[6] send $1.00 (a dollar) to City Lights (261 Columbus SF) & get one—it's really beautiful, after all, it's near what it should be, brilliant & rich, nice red cover, all the poems are wild except only maybe 2 or 3—all the work he went thru & the delays helped out, the book's fine, Alan Ansen real impressed said Greg should be supported forever for it, & wrote a 2 page review & sent it to *Partisan* [*Review*—never published].

So last nite Sat nite—Oh yes, I balled Joy again, not so hot I'd tooken paregoric, but better later I guess, —I went out & got drunk in queer bar Carrefour (near Fiacre—remember the glass front & juke & arabs & boys)—and wandered around to bars drunk, met up with above-mentioned Darryl & BJ, got drunker & had long talks with them, walking, smoked T for first time in weeks & didn't hardly notice I was so drunk I lost my sense of direction, picked up an Arab boy, friendly in the Bonaparte with them,[7] we kept drinking, he came home with me, I fell out in a vertigo naked, drunk, I saw he was going only to rob me, he took off his pants as if to come to bed but only put on mine & went thru drawers looking for money. I didn't care & was too sick to effort to get up, in fact I told him to take a few excess shirts I didn't want any more, it was funny, he picked up my new (I bought in England) turtleneck grey wool sweater & the corduroy coat, I opened one eye & said I needed them, so he put them back, must have found my money in my watch pocket (3000 francs) & got dressed & walked out, I was too careless & drunk & wanting to vomit to care—woke up in the morning more tired from hangover & frazzled than annoyed (he also took my watch but that had broken down so much now I was thinking of getting rid of it.) Bill of course said he'd thought I shd have known better etc, but I have never picked up arabies before & wasn't bugged by the practical loss hardly, tho a little sad no lovemaking kicks, ah, well, well, the world is full of sad monsters nobody has a good time like I wanted to, so nothing to do except be good cheer & look for souls again anyway. Sure miss you, as if a golden soul of me were still there, to think on, floating six feet above ground across the Atlantic (I feel your ball of soft fire in the room a near presence summoned up by a thot sometimes)—keep thinking of Shakespeare sonnet "But when I think on thee dear friend/all losses are restored and sorrows end." Got all your letters now, including last airgram Feb. 19. If you got a place to keep my books with you they're ours anyway & pictures etc, just put my letter safekeep in Paterson basement trunk, when you've time. Family mentioned your letter, sounded nice, said they hoped to see you & hear firsthand about Europe & so don't worry about their attitude when & if visit, I guess, they'll be welcoming. I'm making it all right here, but I miss you, your arms & nakedness & holding each other—life seems emptier without you, the soulwarmth isn't around, only lots of energy, I do a lot—as in England I read wildly & saw lots of people & did something to hop poesy there, it will have an effect I'm sure once they broadcast that BBC record, open the floodgates in London maybe, for new feeling in poetry there—it's all so deadened now & insincere. But I feel alone without you Peter, I already daydream with tears of how sweet we'll be, meeting again, in summer, it seems a short time off. Yes we'll bloc together & invade Julius & drag him home to life. I got letter from P.I. hosp, & wrote simple straight recommend you letter back, so that's ok, no flowery madness. Carol visited for short time today, she's same, Alyse had abortion in SF, & has boyfriend there. Haven't seen Frenchy Francine here yet, thank heaven, the other French girl visited, I heard from singer Darryl he made it with her, had same trouble we had, she wouldn't open her legs; twice same story in fact. Must answer many letters as usual & start typing up notes & poemlets. Don Allen assembling fast good hip-beat anthology.[8] Carl wrote one line letter "John Hoffman is alive!"[9] (friend from '49 hipster dead in Mexico overdose peyote.) Bill said he meant Hoffman was alive in Carl. Working with translator Bosquet on his anthology of young americans. Ansen translating "Howl" & pieces of Jack & Bill & Greg into German for small book of us. Ferlinghetti wrote OK for Frechtman to do Artaud book for him. Also sent me address to record "Howl" here for Fantasy records— I get $50 in advance in a week or so. Also $35 for short Canadian radio record. Also money from BBC coming in. So I'm doing fine. Parkinson said he's pretty sure I'll get the Guggenheim. I don't know if it'll be good

or bad have all that money. Lipton sent me contract for music composi-
tion to Supermarket poem on a record. I bet it's not good, but I signed.
But I sure lost $10 to that arab boy last night, what a shame. (I felt
ashamed to tell Bill a little but he sez all arabs like that, you got to keep
an eye on them unless you know one fine boy like his Nimun).

Well, peter, Pater, Peter, hello, gobye, say hello to Jackie [Kerouac]
hope he's alright, not worried by publicity, enjoy it tell him, & not strain
to explain, just goof with reporters & dont try for message, there ain't
none but, smile in the heart, flowers in the floor, cock in the hand or cunt
in the hand, happy love springtime coming no-self joy, alas that the world
were happy.

I read Soviet & chinese pamphlets by Krustchev & Mao Ze Tunk on
literature: they say, the writer must help build free future for the masses,
that future is communist, the Party understands all problems, therefore
poet must write in accordance with Party ideals & thoughts & be cor-
rected & guided by Party———which is a lot of madman evil mistakes—
it's terrible—they even print it up as official speech. No hope there.

Bill thinks new American generation will be hip & will slowly change
things—laws & attitudes, he has hope there—for some redemption of
America, finding its soul. But we are so run by competition and decep-
tion, there is no possibility of men being true, even to their dear wives—
you have to love all life, not just parts, to make the eternal scene, that's
what I think since we've made it, more & more I see it isn't just between
us, it's feeling that can extended to everything. Tho I long for the actual
sunlight contact between us I miss you like a home. Shine back honey &
think of me. Find anybody in NY? Maybe also we have some mad balls in
NY when we end the summer. I told Joy I'd marry her to get her US
citizenship formality if she needed it—it dont make different, maybe we
Ball her in Manhattan. Or maybe you marry her. Good girl—what a
mystic, calm like pondwater. Ach. I wish this sadness were out of my
breast, love is choking me to death.

                    Goodbye Mr February.
Enclosed photo—they found   as tender as ever
the dust & bones of Fra Angelico   swept with warm rain
and are going to name him Saint   love from your Allen.
now.

                              Green [ink]
                              for Spring
                              acoming

1 Guy Harloff, Dutch painter who lived at 9 rue Git le Coeur.

2 See poem "Europe! Europe!" in *Kaddish* for reduction of material in this letter into poem.

3 John Clellon Homes (b. 1926), companion of Kerouac, author of *The Horn, Go,* and *Nothing More to Declare.*

4 Robert Creeley (b. 1926), poet, novelist, editor of *Black Mountain Review,* later taught at University of New Mexico. Had been generous in appreciation of San Francisco–New York Beat writers he'd encountered in 1956 in Bay Area, as evidenced in his inclusion of them in *Black Mountain Review* No. 7.

5 Darryl Adams, famous among musicians. Folksinger, friend of Ramblin' Jack Elliot. Has lived in Europe all these years. Elliot sang Adams' songs on the Rolling Thunder Review.

6 Gregory Corso's *Gasoline.*

7 Bonaparte, a cafe in St. Germain des Pres, less expensive than the Deux Magots, frequented by poor bohemians at the time.

8 *New American Poetry,* Grove Press, 1960.

9 Carl Solomon (b. 1928), American poet, author of *Mishaps Perhaps* and *More Mishaps.*

Peter Orlovsky in New York City to Allen Ginsberg in Paris

March 10, 1958

Dear Allen: Forgive not writting before dear love but lots have piled up at once & was too frantic gun shot like mind to write but here goes now to you in far-a-way corner so long as this pen wears; its true I am alone & dident get much done but not sad, no, and not head hung low & bent or tears, those bloody tears whare anger vanishes into snow but look my penmanship is clear even for Bill [Burroughs] to read. I am convinced angles pray over my head & ring bells in the far corners of my mind for me to keep in tune with the songs of rhythms of—much goes on here with me & I hope you & Paris shake hands & sing song off breast & tummey as a pigion flys off the roof—Come now this is not the time of world to stay in your room like a cave ignoring the starey eyes of Paris lay on rusty book shelves but let your poems come thro your teeth & roll off the snot of your nose & between your bloody teers—Saw Laff this evening, he living at 78 Washington Place, room 32, he so-so—the 5 mo. in Npt. [Northport] has checkmated his mind again & hes going thro tough struggel with anger at me at times but I feel so good that we part smiling—he dont want to live with me—I give him lots of money so he feel secure but what a thred-bare room he keeps—he beginning to pick up again interest in art—I am living at my father's place (334 West 84 St, room 5, N.Y.C.) for he got compound fracture from [stepping in] street gutter when steping off bus—I continue working, only nights, so time to read & think & talk to myself & others around. 5 year old girl tried to commit scucide, fist thro 3 glass windows—she had an uncontrolable burst of anger & wanting somone to talk to her she smashed fist thro window to get people to talk to her—I was in operating room with her for 4 h[ours] thro night & talked & made her laugh at times—Saw Philip Lamentia last night with Laff & a few nights before Philip & I had 6 h talk thro my day off night till morning came we walked out of Twin Brothers Resturant to buy cigerats[1]—we clashed about religion, he called us sinners when I told him about our love—he wants to be a saint & phrosicy's [prophesies] a miracle in years to come to bring back religion—saw also Denice Levertov at her apt. but only for 2 hours, she good girl & wants to see me[2]—Saw also Jack [Kerouac] a few times, went with him to T.V. show & saw what a tricky thing for anyone to go thro.

March 11
Tuesday
11:00 AM

Bright day—want to go see young doctors at W. A. White School of Psycharity about Julius [Orlovsky]—Reading Blake & Villon—Nicholas [Orlovsky] wanted to go with me to see Julius' doctor & ask him to release Julius to us but I told Nicholas it would be better if I went there with a girl I am going to say I will marry—Elise is coming to N.Y.C. in a few days & so is R[obert] LaVigne in April—Yes, ask Nicholas for money, he would feel better in relationship with you if he paid you back —Bill happy? I hope he stays with you in Paris & doesent leave—go around with him & crack Paris open—go around kissing everybodys feet & talk to all. Saw Iris Brody at her pad & Anton & wife who is having baby in 2 months—Yes send me anything of poetry of Mayakovsky or interesting others—I will be living here till my farther gets out of hospital in 4 weeks or so—Saw Leroy Jones & his friends, some of them—he reads his P. at Jazz on the Wagon thursday, this coming—he got your 10 poems you sent him—Hi there you in Paris—in 3 days here you are. Heres a kiss on the cheek on the face. Happy go thro Paris land.
P.S. Young 16 Parisican [Parisian] kid lives next to me; his English is poor but nice guy
P.S. Get on the ball & make a scene in Paris love, you do that from your letter to me, like england

Love Peter
write whenever can or want

P.S. Gregory's poetry here at 8 st. Bookstore's great. Tell Bill to give reading at American Library at Rue de Dragon St. Meet Lucians wife in street—will see [Denise] Levertov today. Am writing & drawing a little bit.

1 Philip Lamantia (b. 1927), San Francisco poet.
2 Denise Levertov (b. 1923), British-born American poet.

Peter Orlovsky in New York to Allen Ginsberg in Paris

March 20, 58
Thursday 4:40 P.M.

Dear bloodey tear angel Allen:

Got your last letter & poems of mine & your long thin poem somone called "Ginsberg on the street"[1]—yes I am sorry for not writing you & throwing my face across the sea to you but here goes now—sit on the bed and relax—smile—I'm near you—tho tears come now to me now and tho All's not well I am feeling good—yesterday as I was walking on Village street I began talking to myself "I take all this awfle world in on my breast—let it all come in and I dont know what I am going to do with it—things like Laff not in clear mind—the old lady who I'll never talk to—ect—for warm hands is the main thing to give & try to touch every bodys heart harb cords"—don't remember all I said but any way I feel good and go straight ahead & do the next thing I want to do and all's that happaend to me you want to know now Dear Allen? but I will answer your questions frist that you have in your last letter—good that Bill [Burroughs] off any kind of junk—go around Paris with him—take him to the Catacombs—no no that might depress you both—but go to that round cafey art hangout—house & studios—where Sortiene was before[2] —remember the place—on hard walk—take paris between your legs and the golden rule—love every body like you do when your feeling good—come on now dont save all your love for me and all your deep confessions & tears sprinkle them on others faces—I cant say it the way I want to at the moment but I imagine the tears your feeling now come from loving the few souls you know too much instead of the "no street-woman is loved under gas lamp or neon"—Well Allen I cant say it this clearly so forgive me for not having it on my red finger tips but latter— planty of white pages around—and Bill is good and I'll never be afraid of him again——so yes your questions. No I dont give shock—thank god —all I have to do is talk to the patients—but I am working nights now & so read & write letters & poems and as I was sitting in dark hall of Hospital ward at 3: AM I saw a small blue box on the wall with a star on it— the job is easy I talk to attendants the night thru, some are hip or the like and so enjoy talking and reading time—good hospital but square in many ways—Henery's (schlachter) girl friend's farther is doctor and he may help me get Amb[ulance] Att[endant] $300 mo job so will see[3]— but Henery very jelous fellow—his girl—at henerys pad one night last week—casually remarked "Do you need a typewritter Peter—I have one I can lend you" but Henery jumped in and said to his girl "You have a typewritter—give it to me (Henery has a typewritter in his room sitting next to him). I dident know you had one." She said she had another one she was getting fixed for Henery. Its real jelousy in Henery for he knows that I havent tried to skip into girls heart so when he said this it realy surprised me for I thought we had a friend understanding—but anyway he might change his mind—we haven't talked about it yet but the next time I see him alone I give him a blast about jealousy.—Henerys working as manager in Nedic's orange juice counter service.

Yes I will tell Roi [LeRoi Jones] about Jack—and Jack about Roi— hes a nice guy and we get along fine and will see him more—did he send you the book he put out. I saw it—OK, Phil [Whalen]'s [poem] First Yellow stone N[ational] park I want to be a buffilo very good—and your Easiene Seedy hair poem in it—Roi was giving a P. Reading last thur. night but I missed it—over slept & late for work—first time late (10 minutes)—Yes write Nick [Peter's brother] for $70 dollars I think it is—ask him he will send it or what he said to me he owes you—write him open heart letter—add your political Ideas too—encourage him to write you—and tho he probably wont and may send you a short note still do it any way—tell him about the Direct Anallys by Rossen—Nick wants to pay it back so dont have touch, nervous thought at the typewritter when you write him. Jack's plans? I dont know; he buying a home in North long Island somewhare—I haven't seen him recently—hes living at Joyce's pad—Yes I saw him at Circle Theatre in Village—near Lucien—P. Lamanta [Philip Lamantia] and David Heart reading—Jack read Gregorys poems & Parts of Subturains [Kerouac's *The Subterraneans*]—very good he read—hes doing it again this Friday night at Midnight—but Jack so bussy will see him soon & have talk to him—shall I tell him to make Russia with you? Yes I will or what? Saw D. Howard— he said Subtrains sold 12 thousand and expect to make it to 20,000. So—D.H. has a painting by F[rancis] Bacon, a old man with mad, open

148

death splach mouth and a orange band behind his head—Do you have his adress (D.H.?) Hes doing lots of translations of french books & poetry, got nice apt. looks like inside of ship—Jack is to be Master of Ceremonies tonight at P. reading in Circle in the Square at 22 midnight—but Elies said she spoke to Joyce who said Jack isent going to do it—I am over at Joyces now. Jack on the phone I'll tell him to write here to you—

Here is Joyce—

Allen—New York is full of snow and poets, dancing girls, Elise etc. Come back to New York soon—everybody misses you. Love, Joyce

Joyce was to get job reviewing childrens books but she dident get it—I've been here about 3 hours, we 3 took a walk to meet a young Christian girl who has been like Fransois to you [. . .]

Am a little drunk, Jack got me going, my mind is a little rushed at the moment—Will go see & hear Jack read tonight at Midnight. If I can get in free but so many of Jacks friends want to get in free so dont know if I can do it but will see—he (Jack) may read my poems—but will read Gregory and his subtrains—this deal is for P. Lamentia & D. Heart who get paid—they asked Jack to read there so it would go over & now they want Jack to come tonight & read—but Jack doesn't dig this [. . .] Jack is not in joy with this—or what—but here you want a letter—"Joyce says not to go to Russia their testing to many necular weapons⁴—" She writing her book of College days and all—I hope you are happy Allen—I dont mean to go around meeting every body but so many love around that its sad walk & talk simply to sombody—Your poem sounded very sad—have you been crying yesterday or days before you wrote me—or when—Its true there is money here you could make but dont come—forget this money you could make—as dont come back home now just to make money because you could give readings—cause that not poet heart—so stay there and joy and live & kiss Bill & fall in bed with Micheal—or kiss what ever you will do—yes stay there & complete Europe eye-dip trip—I told Jack to write you more but he said you havent written him in a month & so he is wating for a letter from you—& the reason he dont want to go see Charegal [Chagall] (the painter) is because the people who will take Jack to see him are square—and so the meeting wont go good—but I told him to see him—& Jack said he was lazy—but told him that is not true—all—this—Jack says you write too political but I say you go on writting what ever sadness or thouths come & sprout into your mind or spout off all on typewritter—Lover boy— you are a boy you old fella come on now boy tip your hat & kiss me here across the Sea [. . .]

Dear Allen—(Now Jack [Kerouac] is typing for me) [. . .] Jack is gonna read tonight with Lamantia & Hart with good spirts giving pigeons off his breast & hes gonna tell every body to hold hands instead of clap & then read my poems (he read Gregory's poems last time). Jack read em very good, I was there [. . .] parts were funny, no he didnt read the right part of Ode to Coitus tower pome & he introduced me to a girl that I goofed, Al, I was a little too shy with her & so didnt flower with her but always time again—I'm going to call John Ashbury and find O'Hara and Koch[5] —Jack, I told him about giving poems to Leroy Jones and Jack said he will send him some poems when he's got some around in his pocket. Jack knows Leroy and saw the book and lost it and said he didnt put the right pomes in. Jack said he dident put your best poems in it. I was to hear Leroy read his poems in the Jazz on the Wagon place but I missed it and overslept but Leroy is warm and we get along together & will see him again.

Laff has been kind of shy, he stays in his room, I'm not pressing him to do anything about getting a job but tell it to him in a calm way to think about it. but he bought an artist book a 75 page drawing book and drew but when I saw him this week 73 pages were missing & only one page with a face of a man with big poppy eyes and roody wavy electrical hair. and we hey he had a minor operation on his testicle, I went with him to the hospital, the doctors were very not understanding, half yelling at him, half impateient, took water out of his scrotum sack out of the sack sack in the scrotum or something and now Laff tells me that he cannot come, he comes in dreams, when he mastrubates he cant come, Psychological, when I met Lamantia accidently on the street with Laf we all 3 walkt past Laf's room on 78 Washington Place, Lafcadio ran away from us fast up to his room & I thinks he senses the feminity of lamantia and was kinda scared of him or sumptin—but what I think is, I havent talked to Lafcadio about homosexualty or anything and I think he knows me and you make it together & other things about shyness and his own shyness and his own lovely dream of the universe something I think, it'll work out, he's a little upset over it, the 6 months in Northport have been bad for him, he's gone back to a lot of old traces of imaginable bullets flying thru the sky just speaking poetry but the not-coming is just a problem that will work out or somethin. [. . .]

Next thing on my mind is let's see now ah oh I'm in good moods so we'll see all these people only it takes a little time now Here's a poem I wrote working in the wards:

Third Poem
S u b w a y   T a l k s

I stand on a platform or| in crowded| riding train| and look about me,| she, old
woman next to me.| She turns into 50 roll of| newspaper statue—| A woman
throws her baby into| my pocket| I look at the pepsi cola ad| and drink water in
my mind| a young bird steps on my newly| polished shoe| I take it off and give
it to him| to polish| I want everybody to talk to each other on the train| There
are seas of subways and| stars of people| all rolling sleepy lipped| They take the
air from an invisible tube| on their back| It's only subways that I've| gotten
close to some| shattering faces that need angels to carress who with| delicate
pine finger-tips, and| only a few will get billed; but we really do need; that blue
box with a star on it| in our room| When Minerbia gets on the| subway| I
usually get off—| she's so fat & dripping with| all kinds of slime—| even the
air shrinks and curls & hurls away from her.| Hey| I'm writing a poem| as I
sit on night duty in| a mental Hospital near where you| 8 million people live|
If only a subway could| run thru a mental hospital stop,| things would be a lot
different| around here.

My mental change above was: "Only a few will get billed" to "change
their 2 by 4 faces." And also "the blue box on the wall with a star on it" is
a haiku. (It's actually a window.)

Jack says I'm a great poet. Laf doesnt want me to be a poet. Also I have
another mental hospital poem will send you later. [. . .] My other poem
is about patients making big chocolate wheel cakes on the walls from the
stuff we manufacture so superbly. [. . .] Jack is alright, his mind a lil bit
worried, lots of things on his mind, he wants to go to Russia in 2 years
when invited—will sit in his chair all this year. [. . .]

March 22—

A day has passed—the reading last night was flop—no body showed
up hardly—S. Gould was there, I got in free & so did Lucin Carr—we
talked a little—I showed him your letter—he was good—but reading
was bad except for cuple laughs Jack when reading Subtrains like the red-
hair outburster when you & Gregory read in L.A. there was an old man
here who came up here & asked Jack for cig—& took his cigar that Jack
was smoking—yes—there was snow & at midnight hardly anone shoed
up—P. Lamentia & D. Heart read the same poems as last time—D.
Heart reads from Memory—Lamentia read a big long poem like "Howl"
& "America" combined—and parts are alright except it doesnt rise like
he wants and his reading has no guts in it tho funny turns in his voice and
some things he does read like beginning of one poem with a green lizard
on a wall—my impression is P. Lamentia & D. Hearts soul is not there
when they read but are professional smooth readers wile Jack's soul is

partly showing—we all was going to some pad and I walked with them by the subway at Sheridan Square next to Lucian—but like a fool I parted and Lucian said to come along—but I said I had things to do & we would of stayed up all night & I called in sick friday night which I am intitled to once a mo—but for some stupid reason I felt very sorry as I got on the subway for I could of talked to Lucian—he wasn't drinking and was in good mood—but—I showed him your letter—your last one to me—If you dont want to tell me I wont do it again but write Lucian—when you can he would enjoy hearing—today (Saturday) got another letter from Philip Walen—he may get a summer forest job again—he sent me a dream poem part of it is "—I wake up in a strange house, seeing a familiar chair & a door that doesent belong & wake dying in my own collage floor bed Facing the proper bookcase Berkeley summer night." He said he hasent heard from you or Gregory or Jack—? He likes *Subterraneans* He says "Tell Jack *Chicago Review* wouldent take any Buddha poems for buddha issue & write me a silly new criticism type letter, what shall I do ect."

"I (Philip) have Gasoline. Some of it good but not as good as watching Gregory write it." Oh yes—gave Jack French version of M. Waclse [Mike Wallace] interview—we read it over togeather. When is SF Poets in *Esquire* coming out? OK about Mayakovsky to Gregory & Anson; will be very happy to get it in a mo. Did you see Leroy Jones poem in *Yugen* about Lorca? have you got his publication—will send it if you dont— Well—I just called up Leroy—he said he sent you a cuple of copies c/o *Yugan* he said for me to go over & see him soon, and asked if I wanted to read my poems at Jazz On The Wagon—I said I was too shy but said I might it depends on how I feel at the moment—What do you think Allen—Yes?? and so the day passed—today Sat. the snow is clearing away—will write Joy in a few days—laughed thing you said of Bill loving cherry tarts and so did Jack who said Bill is always loving something—here at 84th st is one duble bed room—ice-box & stove for $68 mo. will take it I guess this Monday—Hey—The end of this letter is near—sleep well baby—rest with your arms on your chest with rainbow vision before your eye—Love to Bill & Joy—am sad Joy is sad about somthing—fall on the bed & dream will write soon again—Love Peter

this was so fast I drew it with no idea as image in mind—it came out so fast—& as the line came to the bottom I saw what it was so now I'll put a star above the cock—

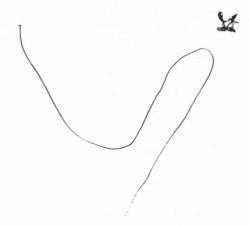

1 See Ginsberg's "Europe! Europe!" published in *Kaddish*.
2 Chaim Soutine (1894–1943), French expressionist painter.
3 Henry Schlachtner, student friend of Peter Orlovsky.
4 Joyce Glassman Johnson, New York novelist, editor.
5 New York poets John Ashbery (b. 1927), Frank O'Hara (1926-1966), and Kenneth Koch (b. 1925).

Allen Ginsberg in Paris to Peter Orlovsky in New York

9 Rue Git Le Coeur
Paris 6
April 1, 1958

Dear Peter honey rose lip'd derrick high die casting daffodil crank transformer: Hail! with kears & tisses cross Atlantico wavelip groans & hisses, Hope. Ah, I gotcher letter today # PM 3, woke me up asleep all day after another 4th successive all night up and walking or writing opiated or sober Seine sunrise gawkings with B.J., Peteresque-ex Hollywood angeltalk fiend who woke up in hospital 2 mo. ago with an infected asshole & big vision of heaven translating him from a Wild One to a Wilder one, now goes about Paris imitating Bill [Burroughs] and accosting Germans on the street to talk about who are the young yond hip cats of Allemand, he's a big tall black bearded (new) fellow about Al Hinkle's size with a leather jacket & multilingual french girl who calls everybody "Man."[1]

Also he started writing poetry last month & drags me out nights to stay up all joint night babbling in Halles & see sunrise over Notre Dame, also one night up with Baird Bryant who now comes over[2]—in fact 2 days ago the first dreamy warm day of spring we all left our coats home, me & Bill out for walk, found Gregory [Corso] talking with young french girl with big non-englishspeaking purse, and in front Iris, one pornography writer girl, and Al the Shades Levitt, drummer, and a spade named Money, and another tall blond nervous type with a west mustache like Frisco, so we all drifted along toward Luxembourg Jardins, and on the way met a banjo artist Jack Eliot & his wife, and also on the way Balf, shambling & shy,[3] and wanderd in the Park until who should we meet by the pond but Mason, also, out for a junk cure constitutional walk, we all stopped & ate icecream cones and talked about man-eating pirhana fish & sharks. So I started going out now more led by Bill, actually, who dug all the new young, and talking around more, in fact a steady stream of traffic in my room every day until, in fact, yesterday I asked Bill to write on his type-writer *down*stairs & Gregory, who just returned from Venice also has a room downstairs (I dunno how he's going to pay for it.) Joy went to Amsterdam for a week. She send love, keeps talking about how you're the deepest of everybody & how she was sorry she didn't have time to really make it with you—but she dont make it with me, she got a new actor boyfriend Jerry upstairs, actually, she sleeps with, so I no got laid hardly all month & felt bad too. All the news from New York excites my belly & makes me afraid, so many things happening how to keep them all pure, you're right thanks for saying, no I wont come back now for money (me & Bill just have big fantasy, there I am in huge reading hall, the hall all empty, I taking off my clothes screaming everybody be naked, you there 99 years old with white hair applauding saying everybody got roses in teeth, Jack in wheelchair creaking go man go, Bill glowering & laying down the mahatma word hypnotism behind me, everybody put-ting all down us, ugh, what horribles,) Yes I see why Jack be lil bit wor-ried, there's too much to do, in public, & it's reaching proportions of religious revival, & we got to be absolutely pure to lay down a golden rose & not just goofy ego—& in a way it's important that we help save ourselves & everybody right now so we got to come forth & sing anyway even if afraid, like we laid out our task in eternity & now Voice of Eternity calling us out to dance to our own music & suffer forth our humancy where every eye can see—I begin to want to write a new book of a Bible, in fact have written some of it. Now follows a poem: (only just show Jack, I didnt know what I was writing, so it maybe goof on personal details so shouldnt publish)—

THE LION FOR REAL

I came home & found a beautiful Lion in my room
Rushed on the Fire Escape screaming Lion! Lion!
Two stenographers pulled their golden hair & banged the window shut
I hurried home to milly Paterson & stayed two days

Called up my old Reichian Analyst
who'd kicked me out of therapy for smoking african marijuana
"It happened" I panted "there's a Lion in my apartment"
"I'm afraid any discussion would have no value" he hung up.

My father & I shrank from each other tearful & shaking
He blamed it on my mother's nervous breakdown
I tried to insist I never actually saw a Lion
He didnt believe me & went to his job in the Zoo.

Found Jack my novelist friend and roared at him "Lion"
He looked at me blankly and read me his fucking mad poetry
I listened for Lions all I heard was Unicorns Hippogryphs Whales Elephants
     Tigers & Ant
He really understood me when we made it in Ignaz Wisdom's bathroom

But Next day he wrote me a letter from his Smokey Mountain Retreat
"I love you little Bo-Bo with your delicate golden Lions
But there being no Self & no Bars therefore the Zoo of your dear Father hath
     no Lion
You said your mother was mad don't expect me to produce the Monster for your
     Bridegroom"

I went to my old boyfriend we got drunk with his girlfriend
I kissed him and announced I had a lion with a mad gleam in my eye
We wound up fighting on the floor I bit his eyebrow he kicked me out
I woke up masturbating in his jeep by the curb moaning "Lion"

Confused dazed and exalted bethought me of real Lion starved in his stink in
     Harlem
Opened the door & the room was filled with a bomb blast of anger
He roaring hungrily at the plaster walls but nobody could hear him outside
My eye caught the edge of the red neighbor apartment building thru the window
     standing in deafening stillness

We gazed at each other, his implacable yellow eye in the red halo of fur
Waxed rheumy on my own but he stopped roaring and bared a fang greeting
I turned my back & cooked broccoli for supper on the iron gasstove
Boilt water and took a hot bath in the tub under the old sink board

He didn't eat me, tho I regretted him starving in my presence
He wasted away all week a wheaten rug full of bones hair falling out
Enraged a reddening eye as he lay sick with hairy huge head on his paws
By the wood book shelves filled with thin volumes of Plato & Buddha.

Sat by his side every night averting my eyes from his hungry motheaten face
I stopped eating myself for 3 days, he roared weakly at nite while I had a
    nightmare
—Lost in Jungle surrounded by alert nameless eyes, eaten by lions on the cosmic
    campus bookstore.
Run over by Lion in 42'd street traffic, a lion myself being starved by Professor
    Kandinsky

Dying in Lion's flophouse a toothless asthmatic rig with a crank in a travelling
    green sideshow,
Devouring hundreds of hairy bloody lambs in dairy marshes soggy with
    bleating—
I woke up one morning the Lion still aching added on the floor
"Terrible Presence!" I cried, "Eat me or Die!"

The lion lay there six days more without complaining
I trembled & fumed over the dishes, went out and got high & lonely
Came back & stared in its eye, blank hardware look to blank hardware
Both angry, it got me frightened—I didn't know what the Lion was thinking.

Except it got up one afternoon—walked to the door
With its paw on the wall steadied its trembling body
Let out a rending creak of Love worse than a volcano, fell silent
Pushed open the door & said in a growling voice "Not this time baby but—
    I'll come back again."

Lion I have remembered now for a whole decade knowing only your time-rending
    hunger
Not the bliss of your final satisfaction O roar of the Universe How am I chosen
In this life I have heard your direct and deafening promise and seen
Your starved and most pious ancient presence O Lord I wait in my room at your
    mercy.[4]

Well that's a pretty strangesick poem, I wrote last week, Bill heard and said, "Aha so that's what's become of your heterosexual personality, the Lion" and I was ashamed of it too because it really tips my mit, I mean shows the fact that I am now *here* but pining for the world to come, & maybe damned for now, not really Zen or enlightened, but just still waiting lovelorn for Future Blue Baloons, but on the other hand at least the poem reveals that—I'm thinking of what Rumaker said in that review in BMR [*Black Mountain Review*] I was a hungry no-man.[5] But nonetheless the poem's true, I'd rather pray than make believe I'm God. Ah, Peter, I'm afraid everybody will criticise me, for being a self pity queer. Been locked into myself all these last months a lot, and all the news from NY makes me feel unbalanced. Well, Just took some Opium, little black ball, that fellow Bernard the Frenchman from Tangiers was here last week & gave us some, this is the last, should work in a hour & be writing all nite, or dreaming, don't know what, got 20 letters to write also— Creeley, Whalen, now LaVigne, Snyder, Jack, Home, etc. Your letter long & beautiful—write me postcard if cant afford more, I do get happy each time I get letter from you, candle rose burning across the sea, I miss you, miss the inner glow—am nervous with others—need you. It's good we parted so I can get stabilized on my own, tho it's very hard—I mean, I get along & can make friends & act around, but the central sincerity is hard to find again with others—to give myself so altogether (as if in a way knowing you are there, I don't try to make it with any single one all the way). Anyway that's what's happened so far. None the less, after blowing round England OK, & withdrawing here, I began to come out again & been staying up all nite & having big soultalks with B.J. & softening up to people more—even making friends with Graham, the "foggy hipster" upstairs—Bill likes him and I see that I'm getting too selective & negative about people—shutting out a lot—partly however also even mad at Bill, he's always around typing in my room, when I want to be alone to rock back & forth to sing to myself & write a Bible. So had big long talk with him again yesterday & made up, he work downstairs & help cook henceforth (I've been serving him all along like a haggard complaining wife). And I have actually been writing more as you can see from last two poems—also more pages of mad politics & some poems in England, and more work on an old undeveloped fragment of "Howl" called The Names, a personal private poem about everybody, specifically, who died, sort of an Elegy, short paragraphs on Natalie & Cannastra, etc. [Cf. this poem on page 33.]

Mason also talking about how everyone, underground, getting hip or enlightened while both Official America & Russia put out more shit trying to keep war going between each other. Tell Jack, I will write Politics poems, but addressed to soulhip underground, saying we all, Amer & Russ, should stop with arbitrary conceptions of self-identity with illusory Governments & their wars. I mean I wont am not writing pro communist polemics liberals, but Bill & I hatching big lamby revolution against the Senders & Powerdrags on both sides. The main thing, as Bill says, is that any government, or person, who tries to put down a story saying that they are Right (& the enemy wrong)—is already putting down a big Maya con. Any attempt to force people to agree with you, or propagandize an opinion, is already an invasion of ego on the nameless golden loveland. All sides are wrong—and Bill says the answer is not in Politics, I agree, tell Jack dont worry, I will write Bible saying why doth Jerusalem war against Arabia, and why doth Arabia prepare spears against Albion, and why doth Dulles preach sexless Christ to the crucified Tonkinese, except I'll try to make clear sense.[6] But we must write Bibles for Milleneum. Pretty Bibles to tell everyone it's here, at hand & foot. Bill [Burroughs] says: "But the Dharma love can not be forced on anybody, or coerced on them or advertised on them till they repeat just words or shoot or fuck when told—they have to want, desire, seek, themselves— that's why U.S. & Russia are both anxiety power-drags—trying to make world in their image—they only make robots."

Well let's see. Hello to Laf. He sounds strange. Write me sumpen on him. Hello To Elyse—by the way, saw Carol in the Monaco the other day, she was telling me about her boyfriend Ali—got me worried— sounds like, she says she went to Nice with him, he picks pockets & she gives him money. He wants her to take him to America, sounds like he may be deceiving her on love. She says she's naturally suspicious, so should she trust him or not. She doesn't *know.* It made me feel doomed, that she was maybe doomed to bloodfailure woe. I didnt know what to advise. Meanwhile she's still working & everything normal. Tell Elyse hello. If I get Guggenheim this spring I'll be able to repay her, which I guess she'll really need. Yes got Leroi's *Yugen* with my little pictures, sorry I didnt send him nicer poems.[7] Bill will send him some page of prose this week & I'll send more.

Fellow from *Climax* magazine, very nice, from New Orleans, wrote asking for work from us, he's in NY, Bill & I sent him work too. And *Chicago Review* is publishing 10 pages of Bill & thinks he's great & [Irving Rosenthal] sends him postcards asking for more, More, for next issues.[8] Pretty adulatory letters to him too, makes him feel good.

Subway Talks poem fine third poem.— "I look at Pepsi cola ad/and drink water in my mind" is great, & "Minnerbia" is very funny.[9] Jack's right about your poetry. Did you get the pack of it I sent you finally? I typed some up again. Send the three poems here for Gregory's German anthology when you can—when they're all right & typed up fine.[10]

Your shoes in your drawing of feet & room made me homesick to kiss your feet & belly. I would like to run home now to NY but will instead fly round to maybe Warsaw. People say Warsaw is now wild—there's more freedom blowing up there, people put down Russia & US & illuminate on themselves, lots of activity, spirit flowing there, so they say. Soon as I get next City Lights money, will do so.

Yes I know what you mean about shouldnt save up love, & limiting it to 2 or 3, so been moving out with B.J. & others, actually I see & talk plenty now . . . You know I used to be on 6th floor for 6 weeks, then 7 months on 5th floor at P.I. Carl too—by the way his mother wrote me he's back in Hospital—worried about publicity & thought he would be interviewed on TV or something—it sounds strange—I dont know, not being there—anyway he's "relapsed" she says & is back in but's not too bad. I write him. Yes, how did things go with Henry . . . you sounded as if it would be OK. I'll write to Nick—but please send me his address— I dont think I have it—will look but please send it in next letter just in case . . . No I dont have Dick Howards address but give him regards & say I'll see him soon, Tell him also, met Herb Gold here finally, with Bill, have seen him several times & had long talks & now hope better understanding. Tell Jack I explained all Jack's work to Gold & also now hope better understanding.[11] In fact I screamed at him the first time, but then I felt I was being mad & silly so calmed down & talked longtime more earnestly & explained *Visions of Neal* & [Doctor]*Sax* & what we thought of hipsters, & read him Burroughs County Clerk, which he dug, so, now, hope for better understanding.[12] But it was slow & cant tell what he thinks—he complains I'm always overbearing on him. So I tried to be straight & talk. Gold says he didn't like [Dan] Wakefield's attack on Jack reading [poetry in the New York jazz nightclub Village Vanguard] in the *Nation* & wrote letter of protest to the *Nation* defending Jack. Gee in your letter sure got a complete picture of NY excitement, it's scary. Jack really coming on great to go swimming like that. I don't think I'd be able to take all the criticism he has.

Nicholas Calas you remember from Venice was here & introduced me to English Apocalyptic Poet David Gascoyne who once wrote the line "Christ of the Revolution & of Poetry" and now I saw in a new Grove [Press] radio-poetry-play he wrote:

The day of Wrath the Atom Plan the Wrath to Come the Atom Bomb the

Coming Day the Greatest Bang the Biggest Bomb the Wrath of God the World
of Man the Day to Come the Bang the Bomb . . .[13]

which is pretty swinging read aloud.

Yes, Well you'll see Lucien again, so doan worry, Peter, anyway the O
is beginning to work on me, I feel slightly nauseous. I heard from Phil
Whalen, will write him. & Chicago advise on him, will explain to them,
etc. Herb Gold says his agent & French people he knows are all inter-
ested in Beat Generation they've heard so far. Heard that *Esquire* will do
picture story or something but not publish our poetry anyway.

Yes read at Leroy's, it'll be a ball, & the audience probably crazy any-
way won't be mean, they'll dig—the poems you have are better than
what else they'll hear you realize.

How strange about the Lamantia reading—glad to get your descrip-
tion of it. I sure would like to see what kind of poems he writes—esp.
the long one you describe. If Lamantia is there, say hello also, and that he
could, should if please send some poems anyway to Gregory for the
German anthology, & [Howard] Hart's too, so ask him to send poems to
us for us to see. But it's a good warning, when I get back I won't read
much and then only for free and stay away from money—I know anyway
that I can't read to order well, especially if I feel that there's any kind of
Order organizing the scene, & admissions at the door. I would feel then
that I had to make it for practical reasons rather than goof ones, & it
would dry me up—I'm having trouble making a record here, I been back
twice to the studio & both times my eyes fuzz & fade & I cant deliver
from heart. Will try again. Wish you were here for that to help. Glad
Jack's soul shows in his reading, we need to give out for real or it aint
worth nothing.

Those poems were weird, there certainly are a lot of goofs around,
they got the spirit but they're not anywhere yet, I think, they don't write
seriously about the details—I mean, so far, Jack Micheline & Bobby D.
those two notes[14]—but it's great they got the openness & hope, & inde-
pendent wild spirit. Those are the only people I guess who can learn
anything new.

Bill now a third thru on his novel—sort of a Junk pilgrimage from NY
to the Andes—a long surrealist panorama—he's keeping out worst sex
so can be published in the U.S. Part of it is what *Chicago Review* is pub-
lishing. He should finally come thru on this, as far as getting circulated &
shown. Meanwhile there's still hope thru Olympia of the long *Naked
Lunch,* Iris that girl advisor has got interested. More on this when it
happens.

Received Levertov's new book published by Jonathan Williams, it's better than the City Lights book, more to it, all mellow & high.[15] If you see her tell her it's beautiful. I'll write sooner or later to her. Read it if you get a chance—she maybe can loan you a copy. I sent Mayakovsky to Ansen, when he returns it I'll send it to you.

What does Lucien think of all this poetry business I wonder. Amazing it has spread so far—does justify our hope that the young are still alive, at least desirous to be talked to non-mechanically, non-officially, humanely, religiously in our own terms. Great day to see Lucien get up & deliver his own stark beauty to the multitude. Stark mustache.

O mustache besweetened, hey Peter, what's up? Drinking tea & typing under light on table,—I finally fixed Gregory's broken radio. So have a lil music nowadays. Gregory finally got along well with Guggenheim, she almost took him to Greece. Alan [Ansen] going to Greece the first time in 2 weeks.

We could talk in bed all night . . . like praying over my typewriter . . . hey Peter across th'atlantic in midst Manhattan . . . turn over . . . I not masturbating much but once had long fantasy screwing you, remembering last night the smile on your face when I did . . . was that OK, at last? I felt such freedom, that you were mine, & wanted to stay together with you for good . . . we'll also have Joy between us in July, or Aug, she says she's going to US . . . but all this poetry activity is hard to keep in one mind with us also in big sexball bed, loving . . . and the invisible Lordie on top of that . . . life is getting wild . . . and I'm getting old and wonder if you'll be able to love me forever & stand still to be screwed that much . . . so what happiness when we see each other again & renew the lovely elastic band . . . I can only strum it in my mind, it's stretched across the water, with all those whales & dolphins & waves in between . . . except it's all eclipsed when I think of the light burning steady & quiet & happy in your soul & the always light in mine I can look inward to & know it's the same in NY & not just a fantasy of my imagination but the light that makes the universe alive . . . ah I remember how melancholy I was at night by hedges by church in Paterson wondering what the ache in my chest was for . . . and now to be old & know what for, & it be there like sweet belly gold for us . . . O Shoe bubblegum Lafcadio'd Pete, boom boom, titty to tit. Write me little letter soon please doan leave me wait too long, honey please honey.

Love, Allen

[Ellipses in this letter are in the original and so do not represent deletions. —Ed.]

1 Al Hinkle—tall Denverite railroad conductor and friend of Neal Cassady.

2 Baird Bryant, filmmaker and artist, who 15 years later worked with Chögyam Trungpa, Buddhist meditation teacher, as did the author of this letter.

3 Balf, a young bohemian Frenchman who looked like Gerard Philippe, I think. —A.G., '79.

4 Early version of "The Lion for Real." Final version published in *Kaddish*, City Lights, San Francisco, 1961.

5 Michael Rumaker (b. 1932), poet, novelist, author of *Gringos, The Butterfly, Pizza*, etc. See his work in *Orgasms of Light: The Gay Sunshine Anthology* (1977).

6 John Foster Dulles, Secretary of State under Eisenhower, had blocked U.S. signature on French-Vietnamese Geneva Accord lest "80% of the Vietnamese would have voted for Ho Chi Minh" as Eisenhower explained in his book *Mandate for Change*. Instead Dulles called in the CIA and installed secret police and Diem as America's puppet-ruler in Saigon, thus initiating U.S. involvement in Indochinese war-holocaust. Diem had been groomed for the role and sheltered by Cardinal Spellman at a Maryknoll Retreat for several years, conferring with fellow religious nut Henry Luce, mass propaganda magnate (*Time, Life*), in preparation for his mission and crusade against the Viet Cong and Ho Chi Minh. —A.G., '79.

7 LeRoi Jones (b. 1934), poet, editor, who in the late '50's brought together diverse schools of post-Poundian American poetry in one salon and in little mag, *Yugen*, publishing Frank O'Hara, Olson, Kerouac and Orlovsky.

8 University of Chicago 1958-9 censorship of *Chicago Review*'s publication of 80 pages of *Naked Lunch* (as well as prose by Kerouac and Dahlberg and poetry by Corso) led to foundation of *Big Table* magazine to carry Burroughs' "breakthrough" literature.

9 See Peter Orlovsky's book *Clean Asshole Poems and Smiling Vegetable Songs*, City Lights, San Francisco (not published till 20 years later, 1978), pp. 59-60.

10 *Young American Poets* (1961), edited by Walter Hoellerer and Gregory Corso.

11 Herb Gold, fellow alumnus at Columbia who had met Kerouac there, novelist. He had written a somewhat frivolous and cynical account of attempts to introduce new work by Kerouac, Burroughs, Corso, Duncan, Creeley, Levertov, Selby, etc., to New York publishers under the title "The Beatniks Invade Madison Avenue" in a weekly magazine. But he later came to admire somewhat the writing he had parodied. —A.G. '80.

12 Then unpublished section from Burroughs' *Naked Lunch*.

13 "Night Thoughts," reprinted in *Collected Poems*, Oxford University Press. The author of these letters did not meet Gascoyne again till 1979 at Cambridge, England Poetry Festival, and the two read together on the same platform before 5000 people in Rome, June 30 of the same year.

14 Jack Micheline—San Francisco poet.

15 Highminded. —A.G., '79.

Peter Orlovsky in New York City to Allen Ginsberg in Paris

April 22, 58

Dear Allen: Well so if I dont write more often, heres a letter now— actually I a little confussed & sad & a little poor & have so many things to do about famiely & working & Laff that no time, but I have time here, now. Hope your well & reading P. in Paris—how did it go? God what a crazzy letter you 3 sent me, whare was Bill [Burroughs] at the time of your letter? Whares the life whats the hope—Laff calls you all mops

wet—Dont ask to lay with Joy just do it—you know—I guess marrey
her but she must have a love & dance & tears with you too—I thought I
was getting this typewritter but no go so thats why I havent writen before
—Julius is braking thru—hes talking with me—holy tears its true—un-
believable—Woes my heart—hes stumbling thru to the open door of
green—in a few (3 or 4) I think he will be on par to get out—let me
explain it more fully now—Oh hell how can I go thro it again, in writting
to much—I see him every week—doctor is impressed at Julius' talking,
doctor granted walking out side around grounds permission—have ap-
pointment with J's social worker, she can be of help—Joy analyist will
get in contact with Dr. J Rosen—Nick too ancious for J's relise—argu-
ment with him—persuade him to wate—not be too hasty—the abrupt
release of Julius into world with me is not good—in time (3 mos) I think
I will come out of it to a certain extent—we act like children togeather—
tikle his feet as he eating food—we tickle each others feet—we do push-
ups togeather & sing songs—we wave good-by to girls & their asses from
behind bars—we gigle—I cry—we walk around the pourch barred
room—I ask him what is the name of that sope Mama (there was a pole
with yellow colors of sope in it in the room we were in) used to use—I
cant remember the name—I try to say it Nels- —I ask J. what is it—he
says it Fels aphafta (sp) sope—he spels it after I ask him—like Lata—
Bill thing—Julius pupit like with me but not all the way—takes time—
but Oh God hes on the road—pary for him—Yes Gregory I'm reading
lots Count of Cristo too, thats you? [. . .] Bob Kaufman, remember him?
(SF) hes been reading his poetry[1]—havent heard it—so is Lee Forest
here reading her P. too—will tell Jack [Kerouac] to write you. G. hes just
fine moving from Fla to Northport LI him & his ma—& his sub.[2] is hitting
to beat the band—going all the way to Kingdom come—Great—and
Bill—I've been telling my brother Nick about your drug-chemical body
balance & apo morphine & thingsthat surprised Nick—he said he would
look into it—Yes July we can all work to get you across to here if
you cant find job in Paris, I'll have apt by the time you all get here—
heres a shy kiss & bliss when see you next—and your Papa Allen still
havent seen him yet—but hold on—will can do—had a dream of a red
angle cutting my toes off—Gregorys book selling well in 8 St book store
—they have a big pile of it in the back—all red—flaring across tabals of
books at everybody as they come into store—What did Bill read at the
reading—what are Gregorys new poems—can you send me carbon
copies Allen—Hi Allen—hay-ho doll—come on over and blow me you
sexy ass of yours under the sheets that I feel all the time—right there
between my hands—I miss the shoe shine you'd give my cock!—God—

you know I've layd nobody since we last made it together—God for all I know my cock may be getting rusty like a dusty kings crown in dewy dungen—I'm sick of all this crying—the world is never going to end all this sadness—I'm going to marry good woman & grow my own love army—but here I am, my farther is going to get out of Hosp. white cast leg for 3 mo—have to find him a room tomorrow. Went with Laff last friday to Telivision Calvilcade, Laff went thro telli-interview—he read— on one man T.V.—Advertisment—the interviewer told Laff he needs training in Pronunciation & Diction & we walked out angry & Laff realized it was a money gip-joint—but he still wants to be Hollywood actor so must go to Talent agyency before he will get job & what?—a drunken old lady said to two young colored boys on the street whare I live as I passed "Its nice to talk to everybody—"Whats Paris like in spring? The sene river? The early mornings—I'll never sleep the day especially morning thro again when we travel in Orient—never never—does Bill know about creative drugs—*iponizoid?* Whare are you all going—did you write Nick about money—are you broke—any more flu—is your room clean & shorts washed & socks clean—Hows Gregorys teeth & Joys acting coming along & to think I acted like a sheep in Paris

Your Peter

[*The following was written on the outside back of the aerogramme.*]
Well I hope you all write me now—again—God what a Ball you all must be having—all the creeps of Paris must be creeping outside on the streets for you all to meet—Peter DuPeru babys-spring-ring-king-bob-top-lip —& when you all clown on the bed remember me—when you drink bear make believe I handed it to you—when you open the door to the room think I am on the other side—& here to/the dream never ends— Love k-k's

Sorry this so short—3 PM Wednesday now, just woke up—dream of you & I talking in weird Peter Breugal land

P.S. Meet guy from Black Mountain like College in Texas, said they tear you up in class. So I say write all 3 of you again

1 Bob Kaufman, black San Francisco poet, author of *Solitudes Crowded with Loneliness,* etc.
2 Kerouac's novel *The Subterraneans.*

May 15, 1958

Dear Allen: Got yr. letter with pictures & money (that you shoulent of sent cause you must be in need of it so shall I send it back or hold it until you write for it or will use it in case of emergency)—Have a big letter to you but not finished so heres a note in meantime. With all this news of Paris in riots how does it seem to you, in the spring no less, well its a good time for riots—Has your Hotel been raded and the P. reading at American Library—did the French out shout you—I guess by now you are all dead—or beaten up—& Bill [Burroughs] must of bought guns that you all look at when you eat breakfast—Well nothing to do but write war poetry—how did Bill read—did he read at American Library also—hope so

May 17, Saturday
9:30 P.M.

Hi again. Just got your card from London, surprise to hear you & Gregory there—Good for students to yell—Poor Gregory—Audan sounds Artaud good[1]—Hope this will get to you when you return to Paris—have written you many letters but no mail them uncomplete—hell—well—Got my farther reading Celine[2]—he likes him—both books—see you when the clock striks Heaven—& Catullus am reading[3]—new translation—very good—hip words expression-tavern talk—1957 translation—Paris is a hot bed now—lots of thorns all around—watch out you dont get trampled on—or Gregory—cause—? I have been staying home most of time—Laff needs companion—hes not so well—more slient & it will take great deal of Patience & time for him to wake up—puts down all my friends—walks all day—wants to live out at Npt [Northport] & work there—Mother & Sister dont want him there & dif to find job there—Hollywood idea eats his mind up—my farther living with us in this room—Laff uneasy about it—Oleg talks lots but has little patience with Laff—tho sometime ok—yesterday walking in Central Park with Laff—Laff just came in—He wants write to you—He says Allen dident write me—what have I got to say to him—Tomorrow I see Julius—Him & Laff are real time fuckers—made it with Elies last week —and went to cuple parties—one by Leroy Jones—almost got into fight —drunk—but they couldent fight me—cause was flying around the loft like pigion

Reread yr postcard—Big Litrary visit my ass—have you seen Celine yet?—come off it you guys are nothing but pancake poets—ya may have good color but your very flat—the only walks you guys take is in circles, around trees & lakes—a bunch of chickens with no heads—do I have to put up with this all my life—the Catullus—The Complete Poetry Trans by Frank O. Copley is influ[enced] by [e. e.] Cummings like Ex—

> *Who'll I dedicate my pretty new book to*
> *all fresh and*
> > *shiny and*
> > *just off the shelf?*

Well look—I think you better get this $10.00 back cause you may need it—So will send it in next letter—You can imagine how much Laff can regress to old water pipe ways living in Npt. 6 mo of last year—the poor kid—what a brat & how inocent he acts—If he wants to be an actor hes got to express contact to others—hes good for quite moves—I wish you'd write him when you have time Allen—Tell him hes got express & talk & read aloud & take interest in other people—so that he can grow in the art of acting—I'd like to be there playing with you & Gregory in London but the marbles here are very real to me (I got a poem about marbles) Big article on 2nd page of Sunday *Times* Book Review of you and Jack [Kerouac] & Ivy League. You all are sure of a puzzle to everybody—real wicked puzzles to everybody—will send you this 6 page full letter—by by Baby   Love Peter

> *Cornelius, to you: you always thought*
> *the stuff I wrote (thats what they call it—stuff)*
> *was not so bad, not so bad*
> *yes, and thats when you had the nerve*
> > *(that what they call it—nerve)*
> *to write the Outline of History*
> > *in three*
> > > *short volumes*
> *the LEARNING that went into them (Jupiter)*
> *the work!*
> *well anyway, here*
> > *take it*
> *maybe its not so much*
> *maybe its not so good*
> *but just the same*
> > *O Patron Maid*

let it last forever
    not just for this
    generation

[*The following was written on the outside back cover of the aerogramme.*]
P.S. Are you all going to World's Fair in Brussles? If so you'll need the 10
Bucks Yes? Yes!
P.S. May 19 in littel wile more mail.—P.

1 W. H. Auden (1907-1973), Anglo-American poet; Antonin Artaud (1896-1948),
French poet, actor and theater director.
2 Louis Ferdinand Celine (1894-1961), French novelist.
3 Caius Valerius Catullus (ca. 84 B.C.-54 B.C.), Roman poet.

Allen Ginsberg in Paris to Peter Orlovsky in New York.

                            Rue Git Le Coeur
                            Paris 6, France
                            May 30, 58

So Dear Peter:
    Last time I wrote was postcard from England—been back a week, got
your letter, lost it been looking for it to answer but no can find it. Well
my time here coming to end—about ready to leave and would as soon as
I can—now looking for way to get money to get back, am broke again
(so's Gregory [Corso] who's going to Germany he says) and no immedi-
ate prospects for Loot. I don't know what I'll do yet, I guess something
will turn up, maybe. Be back in July though. If you find a rich lady to
send me fare—Joy says she'll come over too sometime later in the sum-
mer.[1] Bill probably stay, Greg brought me a volume of Vachel Lindsay
collected poems, I'm halfway thru—hes very bad & very good—real
natural Whitmanic-US vision—very funny & relaxed, and actually amaz-
ing rhythmical devices, when the poems are read aloud—only use I've
seen of negroid sermon & shout rhythms, they really rock-&-roll some
poems—tho sometimes the poems are so long-winded & trite & vague
in expression of this wild native uplift, the rhymes are bad.[2] ("in a door-
way dark & bad") (well that's a weird line). But he's interesting—I'll bet
his prose books are wild—he's also a Buddhist, lots of poems about
Prince Siddhartha (another name for B[uddha]) & he thinks of Shelley
like Gregory & of Lucifer like Gregory—and all his poems have a back-
ground like the street & stage settings of old Chaplin movies. He amazes
me, he's so noble & his vision so piercing & prophetic & idealistic.

Vachel, the stars are out
dark has fallen on the colorado road
a car crawls slowly across the plain
In the dim light the radio blares its jazz
the heartbroken salesman lights a cigarette
In another city 50 years ago
I see your shadow on the wall
You're sitting in your suspenders on the bed
The shadow hand lifts up a pistol to your head
Your shade falls over on the floor.

[Early version of poem "To Lindsay" published finally in *Kaddish*, p. 44.]

I never read how he committed suicide so imagined this way, hotel room. [Actually he drank a bottle of Lysol. —A.G. '80.] Also wrote a little poem, dreamed the form, dreamed I'd be coming back—

Since we had changed
rogered spun worked
wept & pissed together
I wake up in the morning
with a dream in my eyes
but you are gone in NY
Remembering me Good
I love you I love you
and Lafcadio & Julius
are my own brothers in Law
I accept their drunk cases
It is too long that I've been alone
It is too long that I've sat up in bed
without anyone to touch on the knee
I want love I want you with me now
Ocean liners across the boiling atlantic
delicate steelwork of unfinished skyscrapers
back end of the dirigible roaring over Lakehurst
six women dancing together on a red stage naked
Yellow bones in the clay of an old graveyard
The leaves are hanging on the green trees in Paris now
    I will be home in 2 months and look in your eyes.

[Early version of poem "Message," published finally in *Kaddish*, p. 58.]

Had a long drunk time in England and met this time a lot of young boys around Soho (Times Sq-Village) area, and got drunk with older interesting apocalyptic poet George Barker[2]—then Edith Sitwell took us to Lunch & we talked for hours & she liked our poetry & said we were the hope of English poetry, I said "May we own you?" and she held out her hand palm upstretched a hip mystic gesture.[4] Auden took us to tea in Oxford, Gregory said "Are Birds spies?" and he said, "No I don't think so, who would they report to?" and I said "The trees."[5] Funniest boy in England is 17 yrs old named Adam, with a porkpie hat, odd scraps of teddy boy cloths, who talks constant exaggerated bebop & dance-skips up the street, speaks 6 languages and translating a little play of Brecht from German, he works in the Complaint Department of a Pyjama Factory—went to an all night drinking club the Mandrake, with him, Barker & others, another—great fellow, the London DuPeru[6]—named Alistair Southerland[7]—he graduated from Oxford & Talks slowly & intelligently, more so, like Balf, & stutters, but sells picture postcards on Picadilly Circus (London's Times sq.—all the sad whores hang out there & there are huge Coca Cola & Bovril & Schweppes signs at nite & a small classic statue of Eros with a fountain at the center round which all the traffic whirls)—so he, Alistair was our T connection & since he hangs around the Beach area, introduced us to all the younger cats, who were very sweet & took long walks with us. I saw a crowd picketing & lobbying at the Parliament against the H-Bomb—and Simon Taylor also is connected with the anti-H Bomb organized protests here.

But meanwhile all the revolution was breaking out in France and we were too broke to go back because we were waiting for a check from a magazine [Cambridge *Isis*] for a Beat article by Gregory[8]—creepy interviews with me Bill Burroughs, Balf, B.J. etc. etc.—so we had to hang round London for 2 weeks broke, borrowing money from friends, sometimes hungry, mostly not tho,[9]—Gregory & I made another BBC reading—we had read at Oxford, Gregory wrote a new fine H bomb poem[10] (did I write you about that? He says I love you H Bomb I see ermine round your neck you're so lonely everybody wants to die by cancer electric chair old age but not by glorious you, I want to stick a lolly pop in your furcal mouth and pat your baldy bean)—so some young anti bomb radicals threw a shoe at Gregory and denounced him as a fascist—"DO YOU KNOW WHAT IT'S LIKE TO DIE BY AN H BOMB" they kept shouting, and he called them creeps, so I tried to explain the poem to them & they argued politics so I called them a bunch of assholes & big riot & then there were some girls there they wanted to kick out (after 10 PM in the

students' rooms) so we followed the girls and finished the reading some-
where else till midnight. Big funny time. & everybody heard about our
poetry riot there. Auden said at a party I heard he was sorry he really had
acted like a shit to me in Italy—so when I left I gave him present Vol. 1
of Artaud, whom he never read, he was sad & lonely there at Oxford, &
was kind to us took us for walk & showed us his old college. Last day in
England we found Blake's grave in Bunhill Fields, a cemetery in middle
of London, a 2 block square place, with Defoe (*Robinson Crusoe*) & Bun-
yan (*Pilgrim's Progress*) there too—Blake has a 5 foot, or 4 foot, brown
sandstone gravestone says near this spot are his & wife's bones, but no
one knows exactly where—outside the graveyard bombed houses adja-
cent, & apartment building construction with cranes & girders & lonely
voice singing bricklayer song way high up on the 6th floor scaffolding.
Lots of grass & some trees in the graveyard.

Back here, a few days ago—we been following the politics here daily,
everybody fascinated by the big picture puzzle of it—Main deal is Al-
giers colonists forcing De Gaulle in, nobody else knows what to do—but
everybody seems to trust or want to trust De Gaulle; it'll be alright if he
gets in and makes peace with Arabs. If he doesn't & tries to win the war
then it will mean horrible dictatorship in France, because nobody here
that interested in continuing the war, and all the moderates will feel De
Gaulle screwed them up by taking power to take the side of the colo-
nists. So he'll probably be ok, I dunno.[11] Anyway the streets are all quiet,
there were a few small mob scene fights yesterday, I missed them—But
Gregory & I and Balf did see the huge anti-De Gaulle Parade & mass
meeting around Republique Square (where we went to African theater)
—great streams of humanity all the way down wild boulevard, no vio-
lence—the hordes of silver helmets of police down the block waiting for
a riot which never came—but police kept out of the way. I guess you saw
pictures of this demonstration—I climbed a statue & watched from there
& then stood on the 10 foot ledge of a bank to survey the mob.

Also went back to Père Lachaise cemetery with BJ, this time found
Apollinaire's grave—up in the back—a 6 foot grey granite rough stone,
shaped like a rough unfinished cock a little—with his heart calligramme
poem & another carved on it (o people accustom yourselves to the prodi-
gies which I have predicted—or something like that) so I sat there a half
hour and sketched the grave, wrote some poetry

> ... *I am buried here, and sit by*
> *my grave beneath a tree* ...

[See "At Apollinaire's Grave, *Kaddish,* p. 48.]

So I can finish that Apollinaire's Tomb poem sooner or later, took some nice notes. Also sat in front of the Eiffel Tower on that long green mall & wrote poem about the tower, just notes, ends—

It stands is indifferent like God—blank blind eternal red silent
*   filled with people birds machinery and drifting balloons*
So, sitting down on the grass a mile away
I imagined an eye in the tower
an Eiffel eye looking down over Paris
Sweeping past the Butte & domed church & picassos old studios
Over the rooftops & domes of Invalides & Pantheon faraway
St Sulpice Corners breaking the waves of the rooftops
*   under the yellowing dusk*
an eye that stared down finally & picked me out on the ground
*   and our gaze met in mid air—a flash of dizziness in the*
*   center of the universe*
and I woke and picked up my pen.

[previously unpublished]

I'll write Lafcadio this week, I've written 19 letters since I got back, answering all old correspondence, also wrote 500 words for Bob LaVigne for intro to a show he says he's going to try organize in SF, told all about how we first me & I saw [his] big naked painting of you & how we all lived together & argued & had art talk, described some Foster's [Cafeteria] & described his ways of painting, different projects like the Klee-like rectangles & the Foster's sketches—the Dangerous Garden [flower drawing] series.[12] *Chicago Review* wrote Bill [Burroughs] they like him so much they'll print his book serially (the new one [*Naked Lunch*] he's finishing now) if no one else will publish it so that's great. I'm going to type up a chapter for him to send tonite. His plans for summer not made yet.

Please send me the long letter youre writing, even if unfinished—I wait so long to hear from you, Peter, Also send me marbles, by hand or typewriter. Who you laying? I made it with Billy W. a few times, then he went home, I'm glad, he was acting kind of strange (making serious goofy faces as if sensitive & couldn't communicate in words & writing a long vague bad novel). I see Joy often but not ball lately. Oh, yes, great night yesterday, BJ and I and Gregory stayed up all night, then in the dawn BJ & I went out for coffee & went to Clochard's bums bar on Rue Xavier Privas right off Rue Huchette, you know street with arabs etc.—and went in to fantastical crowd of worst looking beat up hairy old creeps you ever saw—so we had some wine then BJ found he still had 500 francs—so we bought 2 bottles wine & cigarettes & got drunk with them singing & goofing all morning for about 6 hours, when we ran broke, they brought out their dirty rolls of hidden thousand franc notes & bought us wine & gave us cigarette & got us drunk, I wound up on the street near an Arab cafe singing Eli Eli to BJ with the arabs applauding & then went home slept all afternoon and woke it was dark. Stayed up last nite too & saw dawn. It's 5 oclock now I'll wind this up, go shopping & cook big meal. Goodnight Peter—write me soon—I'll be home soon. What will we do for living quarters? Can find apt anywhere Queens or anywhere? maybe near your job? Well write me. Love xxx

your allen

1 Joy—a young lady friend in Paris.

2 Vachel Lindsay (1879-1931), American poet. His poetry has a natural spoken music often with jazz rhythms. See *Collected Poems* (1938).

3 George Barker (b. 1913), English poet who uses gay themes in some of his work. See *Collected Poems* (1957).

4 Dame Edith Sitwell (1887-1964), English poet and critic. Famous for her poem *Façade* set to music by William Walton. See her *Collected Poems* (1954).

5 W. H. Auden (1907-1973), Anglo-American poet.

6 Peter Du Peru—a street friend of Orlovsky/Ginsberg from San Francisco.

7 Alistair Sutherland co-edited (with Patrick Anderson) *Eros, An Anthology of Male Friendship* (1961), a gay anthology which includes work by Walt Whitman, Cavafy, Edward Carpenter, J. A. Symonds, Spender, George Barker, Denton Welch, etc.

8 "Variation on a Generation," reprinted in *A Casebook of the Beat*. T. Parkinson, ed., Thomas Y. Crowell, N.Y. 1961.

9 Mainly the late David Archer, editor of Small Parton Press, which first published Dylan Thomas, Barker, Gascoyne, and, in the late 50's, the Anglo-Indian Oxfordian Dom Moraes.

10 "Bomb" was published in Corso's *The Happy Birthday of Death*, New Directions, 1960, pp. 32-33.

11 The political turmoil in France, stemming from the revolt in Algeria, led to De Gaulle's assumption of power as premier in 1958 and the subsequent drawing up of a new French constitution.

12 Robert La Vigne, San Francisco painter, friend of the circle of Bay Area poets. Had lived with Peter Orlovsky in 1955. See the excerpts from the *Gay Sunshine* interview with Allen Ginsberg on pages 111-118 of this book.

Allen Ginsberg in Paris to Peter Orlovsky in New York

June 8, 1958
9 Git Le Coeur Paris 6

Dear Peter:
Received letter, & check . . . I sent it at the time had money thinking you broke . . . but glad to get it back . . . no dont send money, I'll make it here—Bill has enough for eat emergencies etc. & my rent's paid . . . my family writes they'll send money for fare home if necessary, so soon will investigate boats or other ways. Be home in about a month and a half—mid July or so.

Went all screwey in London, sleeping with Gregory all night began to got hot & never got laid, came back screwed Billy W. between legs and then couldn't look him in face he seemed weird, acting strange he talking about openness all the time like a theoretical novel; they went out with B.J. & Jerry, thin boy downstairs to Clochard bar near [Rue] Huchette, drank with bums and kissed them & got all excited about B.J. & Jerry, wanted to sleep with them, & got drunk & took off my clothes, but they didn't want to, this kept up all week like a fever, drinking every night almost, finally came off it, left them alone & realized how fond of me B.J. is but not queer so I was just bugging him, which he took OK in fact told me go right on drunkenly do what I want say what I want—but finally felt I acting like an old queer—my birthday I'm 32 June 3—we went out to big hotel on Champs Elysees with friend who had room there & got drunk in Ritzy bars. Finally stopped trying to make them anyway—feel better, trying to make them all queer angels all involved in my hair—feel ashamed. Don't feel like laying Joy. Maybe I should see a psychiatrist in NY for some more liberation find out what's under me. Been thinking of that.

Bill [Burroughs] back on Paregoric for weeks now, almost got some H yesterday but it still hangs in the balance whether he'll kick soon or not. He has to stay on for his analysis so won't come back when I do. Says he's dreaming of Beirut and the Near East, wants to go there. So he may go there next while we're in NY. I typed a few chapters [of *Naked Lunch*] for him and sent them to *Chicago Review*—they were asking for more from him. He says hello, I guess he's going his way for awhile. That's alright we'll all meet elsewhere in a year or two, with new things to exchange. Maybe sooner if he gets a book in the States after this year, he'll come back.

I feel like I belong in garbage cans too tonite. Afraid of having to make good in NY, create or participate in big wild scene.

Don't get an apartment yet unless you think time's ready for that; no use us setting up a regime & hangup apt. for money—unless ready to settle down. I'm willing to hang up with you in furnished rooms till Laf & Julius [brothers of Peter Orlovsky] stabilized enough to move in with— if everything's ready, tho, let's start, get the pad. What's the situation. I suddenly thought maybe you're sick of all your responsibility & want to find way out. As for me I'm ready for anything you want to do. I'm only scared of having to go on TV or something.

If you think time's ripe, look for an apt. now if you can—I'll be back soon now. Anywhere you think wise. Out in Queens, Northport, Paterson, Manhattan, Staten Island, or across Geo Wash Bridge if necessary— someplace where everybody have maximum opportunity. Best for Laf in Manhattan I guess. Best for you near hospital. I'll be OK inside Manhattan or out—tho prefer Village handy by subway. Maybe Bronx. I'll be glad be back we talk & calm souls again.

Send copies of some poems of yours—now—to us here, for Gregory's German anthology.

You think you can keep it up, working in hospital? I'm going to find some way to make a little loot too, I hope not have to work. Maybe I'll try be an actor play bit parts. Maybe we all go to acting school or found a little theatre.

Quite a few articles been in London papers, I'll bring them back. See my horsefaced evil devil picture in *Time?*[1] . . . How is Julius? Where's Marbles?

Cat recovered from bad leg. Got huge new white towel size of a bathrobe. Cooked peasoup-hambone & lamb stew this week. Your calendar still on wall. Never changed, I didn't continue after I went to London first time. No news from Warsaw or Moscow so they're out now. Went to big all nite party in studio with Gregory & B.J. the other night, painter Sam Francis, jazz orchestra, endless beer & salami, everybody's faces painted with white greasepaint like indians. Write me letter. We'll cook a huge soup together in a month. Love Allen.

Don't be unhappy, wait for me, I won't be sad if I wait for you.

June 15, 1958

Dear Peter:

Not mailed last page yet so will add more. Been reading a huge book on Dada all last few weeks, & the other night me Gregory [Corso] and

Bill [Burroughs] went to a big Party on Ave President Wilson & met some of the old geniuses—Marcel Duchamp, Man Ray & Benjamen Peret. Duchamp you may know of, painter, but Man Ray & Peret I'd read about or heard of earlier. Ray is a photographer & Peret a surrealist poet, writes about avenues of blue breasts. We got drunk & conversed with Duchamp, finally kissed him & made him kiss Bill, which he did— they are very similar in temperament[2]—Duchamp gave up painting to make weird scientific cool mobiles—birdcages filled with sugar (marble blocks that look like sugar)—anyway we wound the night up drunk crawling on the floor at the party (filled with well dressed ladies & gents) after Duchamp, feeling him up the pants legs, & begging his blessings— he came on very sweet, giggled,—Carl [Solomon] would be interested since he always was interested in Duchamp's dada style, high style, & puns & destructive wise intelligence—but with us he kept insisting he was only human, which I liked in him, to hear him say that. Also the day before at Deux Magots we met Tristan Tzara who actually was the most interesting of them—in a way the best writer[3]—I've been reading his Dada manifestos carefully for the first time and they are good poetry (one famous phrase—Dada is a virgin Microbe)—but I see he especially realized that Dada was very similar to Buddhism—that is that the weird incomprehensible jokes of Dada are very similar to the Zen Koans— like Duchamp's birdcage is to art language the same as the goose in the bottle to poetry[4]—a riddle to free the mind. Also saw a few surrealist movies lately—old Dali & old Dada—saw the *Chien Andalou* again, this time they didn't censor the razor cutting open a girl's eyeball—not so horrifying as I'd thought.[5]

Well I dunno what I'm going to do to get back yet. Today wrote a letter to *Bothega Obscura* [magazine] trying to peddle $200 worth of poems for ship fare [unsuccessfully—A.G., '79]. Maybe that way. I'll write soon again, write me soon too, what's happening, how are you. Gregory has a new girlfriend who took out his typewriter from the fixers, a big 19 yr old Russian girl, who has a house on the Riviera, invited us all down there, maybe I'll go for a week before I leave. B.J. & Baird Bryant smashed up on a motorcycle the othe night near Pigalle trying to score for T [marijuana], & Baird is in Hospital. A new strange cripple boy appeared on scene, Frenchman named Jacques Stern,[6] went to Harvard & is very intelligent & serious, is a rich Rothschild, has car & chauffeur & [. . .] he and Bill now good fiends friends & sit & talk junk by the hour—Bill now in paregoric still trying to get off, maybe next week,—Stern will drive us out to Chartres maybe tomorrow. Stern says he writes prose, he talks very beautifully in intellectual way but seems also to have free spirit.

Went to George's bookstore [Shakespeare & Co.] saw Joy today & kissed Francoise hello. Dave Mcadams was in NY by planetrip & says things jumping in Village.[7] I'm dying to get back now. You ready to look for Apt? The room here, with Bill, Gregory, BJ next door, Balf, Joy, all their acquaintances, etc etc, stray girls, strange visitors, is still overrun with people & I dont get too much time alone. I hope we dont have same problem when we get place in NY. I've piled up a lot of unfinished writings over the last year, more than I realized, I was looking at some the other night—have to sit down & type it all up in final form this fall.[8]

Send me a note soon honey, I'll be back next month. I feel good to think of going back. XXX

Allen

PS running around & drinking a lot, got sick flu, spent last few nights all night coughing & vomiting & sleeping late, been sick. I'll smoke a lot of T before I leave, feeling in a mood for that— saw Artaud [movie] picture last night about strangling a Bishop.

1 *Time*. Probably a story on *Howl* censorship trial in San Francisco.
2 Marcel Duchamp (1887-1968), French painter, Dadaist.
3 Tristan Tzara (1896-1963), French surrealist writer.
4 Here's a full grown goose in a bottle with a tiny neck. How get the goose out of the bottle without damaging the goose or breaking the bottle?
5 *Un Chien Andalou* (1929), a famous surrealist film made by Luis Buñuel in collaboration with Salvador Dali.
6 Jacques Stern, author of unpublished prose *The Fluke*. At the end of '70's living in New York City.
7 Big, heavy black fellow, friend, psychologist.
8 All these mss. wound up in *Kaddish*.

Allen Ginsberg in Paris to Peter Orlovsky in New York

9 Rue Git Le Coeur Paris 6 France
June 21, 58

Dear Peter:

Received your long beautiful letter scrawl, because you don't shudder for Julius I'm not afraid. Though I realized how bad it is (shit on [his finger-] nails), the actual situation is very good, you've already made the biggest step—getting him well enough to take out visiting. As long as there is that freedom, no more worry about battle with hospital authorities, and transition to home environment can be made slowly—we can take him out weekends till it seems ok to take him home. I only wonder if he will ever be restored to sufficient independence & strength to make it in the city, or alone ever. But we figure what to do as we go along. I worry about Lafcadio tho.

What did I do rape you pink in Barcelona? I dont remember! Where, how? I remember here, & Madrid. I wish we were in the same room now & able to touch . . .[1] I wrote you letter same day (& sent it) or day before I got yours, here's another. Well I'm sure I'll be home July but dont know how yet & July is coming close. Have to type up & send out poems for money. If that doesn't work will get it from my father who offered already (so no worry, I will be back soon), or elsewhere. Just I don't want to take family money, rather save that for emergencies, maybe need some when in NY. Any news on getting an apartment? I thought the other day, have you any chance of getting one as a veteran in one of the big projects? Can perhaps plead that you're taking care of family, Laf & Nick (tho he live elsewhere) & need space for weekend Julius? And get help from Social workers in Central Islip? Explain to J's Dr. that you need place to bring him, get him to ask social worker there to help. That way by claiming lots of tenants can get a sizeable place maybe. If not in Manhattan perhaps nearby in outskirts, Queens, Bronx, etc. What you think?

I don't remember if I wrote you we met some great rich boys—one Jack Stern who's like a 24 year old Bill [Burroughs] & loves Bill, has great expensive wife & vast apt on Champs Elysees with butlers & chauffeurs & long cadillac convertibles he takes us riding in—Today he gave Gregory 20 Mil to pay rent & etc. just like that when Gregory [Corso] asked him; he'll take us to Chartres this week. He asked about you, "Is Peter an angel?" so he knows. He's crippled, sick & thin & often sick, I carry his 95 pounds up the stairs to our room. His friend Harry's less interesting, but very nice nelly boy, married, vast young millionaire he at last took me to great long jam session at Club St Germain this week, told me he had backed Jimmy Dean's first play & made it with him 3 months[2] —& told me some of story—said he screwed Dean but Dean not screw him & they blew each other, experimenting around, young—tho Stern later told me it wasn't 3 months it was only once they made it—but strange to meet someone who screwed Dean. Said he fell in love with Dean, the way he lounged his body open bellied in chair, arms crossed or something . . . didn't get more details straight we were drunk & on top of that sniffing Lee [Junk] in the john out of a jewel box. Sent message he'd come & take us all out again . . . but don't be sorry, we will know these peoples in NY or elsewhere & you see the mad scene; Harry a short blond sweet babyfaced kid, but narcissist . . . strange to drink all the pernod I want & hear driving raging drum & sax yowling back & forth in that mysterious basement St Germain that we sniffed around together frightened the first nite we got to Paris, hanging around the black grill windows to hear 6 sounds in a row.

Bill still on drinking paregoric, a habit, not off & no sign of end. I dunno. I make big pot white beans & ham bone. Then Stern comes in that night with Gregory carrying 2000 franc armfuls of delicatessen to surround my 400 franc potful of beans. So life jumps up just as I get ready to leave. And met more poets like I wrote you last time, all the Dadaists. But still lone for you & rush back as soon as I can. All I'm waiting for is money & I take the first ship. John Balf by the way left last nite for NY, he has 3 little books for you. Mayakovsky I loaned to Baird Bryant who's in hospital now after motorcycle accident . . . I'll bring it home.

I used to write little poems about that Bridge, looking at it from the outside cage porch, "Today out of the window the Washington Bridge / stands solid as the cliffs / silver and invisible . . . .. [above Psychiatric Institute where Orlovsky worked as attendant], or something. I have the poem in Paterson . . . and I kept a huge notebook there, that I have home, I'll show you . . . but mostly inner thoughts alas, & no descriptions . . . I was in the room 5 th Floor, first corridor, by myself . . . I dont exactly remember which corridor, on the right . . . and I once had a bed next to Louis (is he still there—part catatonic, snot drips, he been there years as mascot? darkhaired short fellow) in the big ward on the bridge side two beds in from the outer wall facing river . . . I can't give sensible description, I'll tell you when see you. Used to see Doc 3 or 2 times a week . . . 8 months there, out weekends, had a good time . . . one time Carl [Solomon] & I started banging the piano & yelling just for fun, they [staff] almost flipped . . . Yes [I] read the phrase "Shook-up Generation." Greg takes lots of PG & no go to church at morn . . . writing a lot again after dry months . . . yes I'll eat Julius's shit with your honey . . . (you honey, but I changed it to your honey). Bill says not good idea make it with J tho . . . but I dont know what basis to start give him contact . . . something will. He may not need sex so much as stable new environment for longtime—that's sweet him saying "Peter girlfriend" . . . what did you feel . . . were you hot for him then? I could, he was cute . . . but Bill says no good. But I fantasied it, long ago. Are we goofy? Ah, yes, I know what was in your mind exactly when I saw flash on your face & tears since I'd had same death-in-life feeling about my mother, after she in hospital years & I realized I'd abandoned her. Laf be alright with Julius

I think—may give him something to react sanely to. But we'll see. Oh, when I was in Hosp I gave raw thought & experience to Dr's but they were actually incompetent young doctors who didnt understand me any more than I understood them then, but I tried to cooperate & get some good out of it . . . was eager for therapy in fact . . . but they were square . . . wouldnt give me mescaline they were experimenting on upstairs,[3] tried to fit me into workaday mould—didn't do much to bring out my real feelings & wants, discouraged visions or vision interests—reduced all eccentric individuality to the level of P.I. 5th Floor nuttiness. I was really a misfit there—trying to fit in to their conceptions—wrote Bill I didnt want to see him for a year or hear from him (trying to see if I could conform), (to what I thought they thought was the Road.) They were incompetent. It's a shame because many nervous breakdown patients [are] caught between their undirected illumination & the sterile bourgeois minds of the young new doctors. Steve Schoen & the Dr. [Philip] Hicks I had at Langley-Porter [Hospital in San Francisco] were rare good men I think. I had 4 different doctors at PI. All basically rigid in method, and of no help, to me. Yet I thought then perhaps they had some secret total knowledge I didn't . . . kept expecting miracles, from digging their ideas & conforming . . . get job, girl, lead average active life . . . no sense of the sweet humane surprise, Vast life. I was a miracle myself then, they didnt dig . . . kept asking me, official question . . . do you still think you're superior to other people, & different? I said no, to please them finally, but really felt weird Yes. But they sounded like communist anti-deviationist leaders, so couldn't resist arguing . . . but it was all finally just a matter of words . . . they more hung up than I was. Like the time I spent 5 hours with one dr. trying to make him accept or understand what I meant by saying "the telephone thinks." By the way met a fellow whose mad aunt was frightened of the "electric horse." Classic phrase.

Heard from New School Prof. [Elbert] Lenrow about the play. He liked you. I'll miss him here in Paris he'll be here too late.

And do you remember the big white moon behind the death clouds at Assisi, we hugged [each other at] the door?

Gregory just came down he wrote great, finished, poem about A Bomb. Poem is arranged so page looks like a bombcloud, too. "You (bomb) are a paean, a lyric hat of Mister Thunder! O resound your clanky knees . . . I want to eat your boom! . . . Know that in the heart of man more bombs will be born / magisterial bombs wrapped in Ermine— all beautiful . . . They'll sit plunk on their grumpy benches fierce with moustaches of gold." etc etc. OK. Greg read your letter & sends you

Boom. I send you letter & no more jack off, so save love till I see you, yes you do same? Get laid if can but no more jackoff till together. Baby goodnight, see you soon.

Happy ready to come home soon—Love Love Allen

1 None of the ellipses in this letter represent deletions. — Ed.

2 James Dean (1931–1955), American movie star.

3 It turns out these experiments at N.Y. State Psychiatric Institute were funded by the CIA. —A.G., '79.

Peter Orlovsky (left) and Allen Ginsberg
On Flagg Street, Cambridge, Mass.; the first snow, December 5, 1977
Photo by Elsa Dorfman

June 24, 58

Hi Allen:

Got a Smith-Corona here, from my mother, she gave it to me cause of birthday. She had it a year thro a friend she got it. Think of that—she still has in mind after all these years to write her life. She was saying how fun it would be to write of people around the hill. I was out there few days ago, Sunday, sister graduated from H.S., she completed h.S. in three years. She realy needs to get away from mother & the hill life. Its to a hospital in New Werk, New Jersy for 10 mo. baby training course, modern looking place too. Have to go out there with her come two fridays from now for interview. Shes on her way at last—just what life orderes. My mother & sister finally put the town church down, they were hounddoging them. 5 old ladies would come up to the house in evening pleeding Maire to join church & they would come many times till finally my mother hides from them & now she talks to them breaf as possible. Lots of sweet smels on the Island now. In Northport Library have Jacks [Kerouac's] two recent books & *Evergreen Review*—the last four series. The old lady librian knows Jack is living in Npt. She liked the idea so I told her Jack was living with his mother & they get along very well. No Allen I am not fed up with working on job tho would like to get more paying job & that must do. This job here I can read all night. Its quite at night, new liberal policy, 6 No. has open doors now. Only 8 No. is closed ward. There diging oil wels in frunt of the hospital now (P.I.). Tho would like to spend time goofing all day. To think of all the people I could meet in the Village & al over if time were mine, but no I dont mind working cause I got to. Theres a russian prince here Valintine—talker french an all—bums around carries little bag of clothes with him—desendants from emperores of Byseantium on his mother side—querr too—last night he was drunk & putting his hands on me in fround of my farteher who got real mad to point of yelling at Valintine, here today only not drunk—hell talk.

Jaune 26, 58

Very fast, got your letter today & it strickets me kinda true wat Bill says, ya got me Allen youll just have to be plain simple with that. Jule should have a gril—thats what would do more—he always strong for girls, fact, like I say hes original Brando type before Brando came out. Just took Oleg[1] to hospital, one mo. off comes heavy cast return to bare leg & in one mo. 2 weeks he'll walk like new. Doc. said it was comming off good so no bone about that. God Yr letter sounds exciting but. I'm not so envious, just a little well so what if I am—if you only told me Balf was comming over I would of tried to meet his boat at harbor be fun seeing him again, cant imagine what books he has for me. Those rich junkes—do they make with their wives? or too always high? Whats a rich junky like, could they be anything like Garver Sensitive & gostly pale? Hope not. Up pick him up like doll you say. Hes dreaming in your arms. Was he there when all that trouble mit De Gaull rolled about? Does he write? What kind of cripple is it, maybe he can concentrate on walking thru hindu methods. You know theres a hindu method by which Huxley cured his crippled eye sight, via looking at sun & darkness mixed togeather and other exercises. He said eye glasses are like chruches for broken leg man—the more use cruches the more use chruches. Thro junk maybe he can concentrate more. In fact before I got your letter today as I was shoping for food fantisy of cripple came over me in a car crash with Elies—Parlized from neck down—crall out of bed early in the morning to the hill near by and stare at the sun rasing self to estatic weep-joy bliss thinking of walking all over the earth with huge foot stepts & thinking of kicking the sun with my foot & then grabbing the sun & rubbing the leg with it till it feels hot & warm in all kinds of funney ways—never can tell being criple could just be a dream. if hes cripple he must have strange eyes. I should think with all his money he could have special made some gadgit that would enable him to walk like machine with walking legs from the waste down. In germany they might make them. A machine with two mechinacial legs with a rectulanger engine between the legs that he can strape around the waste. Look up Ripilys Believe it or not, he might have illustration. Or run aid in Art Buchwald collum to atract eye of some paris mechnic inventor. This is the machine age. Whats with Art B. is he gay to or is he writting about you or what & whare. I've heard lot of bad stories about him—hes a devel worpisher—in his apt. its all painted black. Oleg is sleeping, my day off, it just rained, from new jersey it came. Just saw old lady in long dress with her dog all real wet pass under my window—what could I say to her—she must of been deep in river side parkway when it began pooring on her. Pink the windows of Barceloma & Pink the bed on the cock that night we striped with the nape sack dream going out the window to some strange grees we had that my cock was saw in the morning—you worked me to the bond, far from home & we came & brought the morning come earlerly whare on the street we saw all the clothes hanging up & the big lot with the shooting gallerys & the tabol hocky game, the gambling on the side walk or was that in Genet but you remember the lot we got naturaly high on? The landlord just came in, I told him he could have this typewritter ($80) for $20 dollars & all the cockerroches in this room. He said there was no rochers here. So I told him pointing to the sink & the door that theres a whole batallon with the general & capitan that creep under that door along the base of the wall & do a left turn on the wall straight for the garbage can in file. Say Allen, Elies told me Neal is in jail you wanta check on that. She dident remember the one who informed her so dont know if its true or not. What do you think?? She said it might be for tee. If neal in jail can he take it—how long I wonder—frist offence isent to bad. Why dont you send me La Vigns adress, wasent he supposed to be here by now? Got these things to do here, icebox needs frosting & cleaning & bed sheets need changing—ice just fell on the floor—Oleg just out to bathroom—he takes sleeping pills at night—more ice falling—raido on, U.N. chief just back from Lebinon—he said scene cooled down for now—I'm sweting—the rain stoped—how are the girls along the Scene? (Seine) See any teddy grils in London?

July baby Frist:

Want to get this off to you also wanted to type out poems but so painful to do so, dont know why but cant sit and be patient, always had that problem. God I wont have apt. when you get back. I have been goofing up on that score. Been going to the moves lot, scared, all these problems seem creeping up. Maybe I have been dreaming life in mind too much, latest fantises are about robbing $5,000 buck to satisfy all wims of burden. This bissness with Oleg has me tied down. Kook & shop for him & when on top reading Look home ward Angel. But anyway in two weeks I should have $170.00 dollars. Have $60.00 saved so far. Next payday in two days means another fifty & then in two weeks another fifty. My fifty five a week from V.A. goes to Laff. out in Npt. for support of him & he wont get job tho out there its impossible to get one yet he says he can get one & says he will. His fantisy life is so up that he dont care how my money goes & on what or if I get Apt thats why I feel so enraged at him. Could cook his brains in a soup pot. Best to throw him into the Art Students Leage, $30.00 mo course & pracitse & instruction at painting plus all the young people there he could get to see & meet if only he would. Thio he still thinks he can make it in Moves and so I sugest allen we take him around to these places and pull Laff. fantisy out from him & substute art & painting course. I just bought oil set & box & canvas & bruches for him. A $25.00 set for $8.00 dollars. Hes growing into a monster Oh its not that bad—he likes to be by him self a lot. You know I think could get 4 room apt. on the east side for 40 or 50 mo. You remember that gril Florence in S.F. who had like for you, she has just that on avenue "B" I think, nice big place very cheep. The housing development yes, but am afraid V.A. might cut off my 55 me if they find out I am well enough to work then that would be like paying 90 me if that happened. A rich gril is the only answer. Buts that more likely to happen to you then to me. So Allen all I say is when you get back here, instead of looking for small bits in theatre which donp get married to rich bag. But actuall all will go well if can get 4 room 40 or 50 dollar mo. place, right? Yes thats the key to our heaven.

Have been sleeping average 6½ hours a day now, it works alright, I just hop out bed fast in the afternoon & thro cold water on my face & start to shop & cook for me & Oleg. Was down in the Villege Sunday night, Elies got new sweet boy friend. Joyce seems sad, Jack seem to no want her now. Joyce wont give me Jacks adress. But tell Jack to visite Laff. Maybe my mother & Jacks can talk it you, tell Jack that. Laff's got drawing he could show Jack. In the Villege meet Michlene, said you wrote him & Willims to of critisem of his P. He needs it. He writes a lot. In the Villege Gate, a place under the Mills hotel, big basement whare you could read to 400. Meet another poet there & another & that 41 american who we meet in Paris who went Russia then China, He got into U.s. alright. Refused to hand over his passport. Cant sell his book about China viset, old issue wont sell pub told him. Anyway the other poet translates Mayaikovsky into French. He write too but I no like it, dont know what he says except for "Children drawing butterflys on the stops." Meet Nick [Nicholas Orlovsky] last night, hes going to X-ray school now for 4 mo. Today he has appointment with analyists, he wants to go be analyised. Doesent know if he can take being around otheres in class 4 hours a day for 5 d. wk. for 4 mo. The Millennium of Hieronymus Bosch, interp. by W. Franger tell you about it when you get back.

I dont see how you can leave Paris now just when your getting to know the streets. No sign of Balf, he should be here by now.

July 5, 58

If I dont get this off to you now you will get here soon & come in the door & catch me typing this to thinking of you in Paris so heres the last page. Thur'sday I was out to see Juluis & what I think is good news tho I dont know what it means, Its like Bill's Latah. Juluis immetates me, he does what I do, he will flick his ashes the same way I do, he put hands on his hips when I do. When we were out side laying on the grass I would change my possion & so would Juluis. He must be watching me very clossely with sharp iyes & thinking of me. What do you think Allen. I just knowticed it this week. It made me happy, touch of life in him. Theres so much pain in his face, its always there, the eyes. I pointed to green water tank, asked him what color it was, he said pink.

This $40 3 room spot is too shabby & in desolated area, window broken doew. I've come to think it possible now that of paying $100 dollars to anyone who has 4 room apt. just so to get in, it might be easer to get place that way.

July 6, already

Morning, just got back from work, rain, surprise, are you still in Paris? Eating? Borch? Duck supe? Sleep on a clean pillow? Only one way to make Bill stop pagoric, cut another finger off, make him sleep under the bed, pull his hair out, put ants in his bed, through a lot of stray dogs in his room, take the wax out of his ears, pick his teeth for him, cut his cock off, yes thats it, fry it up for him, saushage like. As long as hes not lonely when hes on. I would like to know what he says of Juluis's new behavior?? Tell Gregory Howey Konivitz is in Hollywodd making film. John Michel told me. *Yugen* has Spon. Requiem[2] of Greg. (2 issue) Very bad poem, he should deffinately be ashamed its published, it sounds like Gregory is writting with a flat tire for a pen, has he gone blind, it does seem like so much absurb babel, like a message the clowds would write if a clowd could write, its a shame, whats caussing this turn into darkness digging in mud, maybe he doesent know what hes doing any more I am worried Allen, is he crazzy now, how long is his black hair, I am sure we could get Gregory a good quite privite sanitorum with toys for mad gregory to play about in. Hows he going to get to India with no money,—

Say, no ward from Balf, what could of happened to him, my phone was ringing last night but before I could get to it, the other end would hang up, it could be Balf. I wonder who you are talking to now. Joyce said you were in *Tribune,* you & Gregory interview, what happined to Art B. meal & talk, Did you go see Celine, Genet back.??? Do you know Leo Garin, he knows you & Jack, hes opening, in process of, thearte, his frist play will be Genet, not the Maids, the other one.[3] Having your lays on the tabols these days? What does that mean, I dont know? Did this, knocked on O'Hara, Frank's door,[4] he not in, door open so walked in, dark, And then saw this *Meditations in an Emergency,* very good, & so stole it quitly, looked around, saw Ode to Lary Rivers, & part of a play on typewritter about Helen saying I dont thin you can. He has many piles of manuscripts laying around in stacks, all that work, then I meet Diana De Prema in Cidar Bar,[5] told her what I did, then she wanted one, said she was trying one year to get copy, took her there, she took one, then back in the Cidar Bar saw John Michel & told her what I did but she too drunk, she drinks to much, what a strange face she has, its got mens rinkles in it, for a moment it seemed that way. Here take this letter, hold it in your hands for eternity or untill we die. ByBy toots, keep the shade up, scrach when you ich.

This rote last night, more like excersise:

Such a nice pink cloud, I would surrly rap it around my body & parade the street in all that pink glorry.
I have a different room now, my farther lays on the bed.
12:00 O'clock at night my work begins in this mental hospital—
tonight the hour will come for this. An attendant on the wards.
A highway behind the hospital, cars wissle all night long, a street,
no love sign on it there, no direction toward any heavenly casle,
no hint to come and see me cause I like to talk.
I am convinced, like I know meat when I smell it, that open talk
of what one feels to be true with eyes to eachother to take in all
the lovey-dovey poetry lines of the face—I love you—touch me—
would end all this complicated jitter, litter that makes us smell
Or hide our face in a crowd of moves.
I would like to live in a city whare there are blocks of love,
_ _ _ _ _ _ long blocks of love _ _ _ _ _ _ _
There go Adem & Eve, I see them so many times on the street these days,
          young ones who have ne sign if cockerrouch looks
   or bent head or cob-web teeth.   baby
          They seem to be srounded by invissible angles
      dancing ribbons. The old are jelous & the single, lonly, dart sharp fast
          wishful looks
               _ _ _ _ _ _ _ _ _
Theres something on my heart, it feels like mud
          if only could be pulled out I'd stick it on a painting in the
          museum of modern art, below I'd write a word or two
               somthing like "Young carve your
                    love's name on it"
               _ _ _ _ _ _ _ _
     The trees boy & lend hair
               to anyones head.
               _ _ _ _ _ _ _ _
  Could you butter your corn with pis
          & then salt it with tears?
  Well you will if you dont stop & talk with me on the street, a stranger

Oleg says: The lantern was swing back and forth on the moon
the dog was smoking pipe,
moon & earth start to fight & they went to the bar.—
Oleg said you want an idea and says this—

- - - - - - - - - - - - -

Got more but this is too much, latter.
I got to sleep.

P.S. well this will get to you real fast. July 7, now. No signs of Balf, does he know I am living on 3rd floor & has to yell to me from the street for me to hear from him?—Is he staying in N.Y.C. long, did he give you his adress in city—How is Joy—lost her adress—hope shes not mad at me for not writting. Love Peter

1 Oleg Orlovsky (b. 1899), Russian-born father of Peter.
2 "Spontaneous Requiem for the American Indian." I'm all wrong about this poem. It's a good poem; I must have been jealous. —P.O. '80.
3 Genet's play *The Balcony.*
4 Frank O'Hara (1926-1966), New York poet. See his *Collected Poems* (1971). O'Hara's book of poems *Meditations in an Emergency* was published by Grove Press, 1957.
5 Diane di Prima, San Francisco poet, author of *Revolutionary Letters,* etc.

Allen Ginsberg in Chile to Peter Orlovsky in New York.

c/o Cultural Attache
U.S. Embassy
Santiago, Chile
Sunday Jan 24, 60

Dear Peter:
Came down here to Concepcion, sat part way in front pilot's seat in control cabin & saw the Andes far away on left. The Conference lasted a week and ended yesterday. I seem to be the only bearded man in Chile, so my photo was in all the newspapers—and children on the streets thought I was Fidel Castro's representative. Most everybody at Conference was un-poetic but one thing was most interesting, all the communists seemed to take over enough to make the whole week a big argument between pro & anti political writers. Everybody from every country got up & made fiery speeches about the workers. Everybody wanted revolutions. I delivered an address also on Wednesday—in broken span-

ish, english, & french—and had translated & read them Wiener's queer poems,[1] Lamantia's "Narcotica" & Gregory's Bomb—plus a long lecture on prosody, Jazz, Drugs, Soul, etc. It was a big mad interesting speech & they dug it—I think it was probably the best of the speeches. Then 2 nites ago Ferlinghetti & I read—he did very well but my reading was without real feeling but had some force. So I was depressed afterward tho the audience seemed to enjoy it. But was unhappy not to deliver the lamb to the communists. But anyway withal we were big hit and now Beat Generation is considered great new American poetry & all the professors will bring it back to Uruguay & Argentina & perhaps Colombia.

At same time there are some interesting people here like in Tangiers— the best friend I've had here is a strange roly-poly Philosophy professor at the University who talks English & is called Luis Oyarzun. "Luce" (lu-cha") (little light) is a big telepathic botanist, naturalist, fairy, astronomer & poet (tho not a great poet—too shy)—he's like a small Ansen but funny. He has various queer friends including an old man named Hyde who has a house here & is very brilliant & lost like an old lady with books. Also a young couple of lovers, boys, whom they all know—so there's a whole semi-hip queer secret society here. Oyarzun is also a big head of the Fine Arts School & is leaving for China in a week. He says he will get us invited (expenses paid by Chinese) to visit China—everybody here visits China. He sends you regards.

I've slept with nobody & masturbated twice. The land is like California. Tomorrow I'm taking a 3rd class train south towards an Island called *Chiloé* near the broken islandy bottom of the continent. I'll stay there a week & eat fish & maybe finish Kaddish. Then return here, fly to Santiago, take a round trip bus ride across Andes, return & fly to La Paz Bolivia—see Macchu Picchu—then to Lima Peru for a week. Then to Panama City for a week. So I will be here about another month or month & a half & then be back.

How are you & Lafcadio? From here it seems you must be in a labyrinth of his worries. Tho I have been in a labyrinth of communists which is just as bad.

Also I went to a Jazz festival & heard a beautiful Uruguayan trumpeter play a geniuslike 1920 horn last nite.

One of the things we did was go to a town by the sea called Lota, to see the Miners there who work 11 hours a day for $1.20. Mines are along tunnels undersea. The political writers organized the trip to impress us with the sufferings of the workers here. Everybody's talking Revolution & Workers etc.

I have not received mail & won't till I get back to Santiago in 1 or 2 weeks. Did you get the Check from Ferlinghetti? I expect some money from Fantasy and Ferlinghetti says he owes me more & is printing another 10,000 copies [of *Howl*] (that makes 50,000) when he gets back.

My writing here is simplified down because I am so used to talking simple Spanish I feel as if I were translating everything to basic explanations. I have been a little lonely but feel good anyway. The unfinished book bothers me so I may try it here more. I hope you are not feeling trapped in N.Y.C. Perhaps we can all go to Mexico later in the Spring or further on. Is Lafcadio showing any sings of independence & feeling?

My plane ticket is good for side trips to Bolivia so it's very cheap for travelling.

Another person I like is Nicanor Parra, a poet about 45 years old who is always falling in love with Swedish girls, writes intelligent & sincere poetry & is also a big Mathematics professor who studied in England & U.S.A.[2] He too went to China last year & believes & accepts Mao-Tse-Tsung's Yenan literature theory. City Lites just put out a book of his translations—not bad, at least readable. I'm sorry you did not could not come—you'd have been the most amazing person here.

Well OK for now—I haven't written anyone but you & I should send postcards to everybody so I will today. I am generally confused, by the communists & by being alone, but it feels good to be wandering solitary in South America. No cocaine yet but still have to get the Chilean yage-like drugs & try them.   Love Allen.

1 John Wiener's work from *Hotel Wentley Poems* (San Francisco, 1958). See especially his "Poem for Cocksuckers." Other gay poems are to be found in *Angels of the Lyre,* ed. by Winston Leyland (Panjandrum/Gay Sunshine Press, 1975), and *Behind the State Capitol or Cincinnati Pike* (Good Gay Poets, Boston, 1976).

2 Nicanor Parra (born 1914), a Chilean poet who was also a professor of mathematics and Newtonian physics.

February 9, 1960
c/o US Embassy
Santiago, Chile

Dear Peter:

All this last week I've been staying in a small fishtown Calbuco,—tall nutty poet here Hugo Zambelli who no longer writes but owns a fish canning factory, I'm living in his house with him, he has servants who cook & clean beds & wash my laundry. He's a big naive goof who wants to go back to live in Italy, & is very hospitable, leaves me alone, or takes me out in motorboat. What this place is is a town of 20 houses on the beach of a channel so narrow you row across it in 5 minutes—wide as a little lake in Central park near Zoo—across from an island 5 miles long, called Calbuco. Across the way (outside my window) can see Calbuco town, which looks like a little Breughel town on the tip of the island, with sailboats, fishboats, rowboats, & piles of seashells all over the beach. If I climb the hill behind the house, I get a great panorama vaster than Tangiers—of many islands large and small, but confusing you can't tell where one stops & another begins, some are large & look like main-land—and lagoons between the islands with little boats wending be-tween—and to the east above the Islands, the huge range of the Andes stretching from one end of the east horizon all the way south as far as the eye can see . . . brown or black mts depending on the weather, a wall of them, jagged about 50 miles away, with many cones & snowpeaks and some long chains of snow alps interspersed—On the other side of these mountains is Argentina. They stretch with these islands all the way south to Tierra Del Fuego—and I can get a Ship for $20 or $60 I don't know which, that goes down to the southern tip of the continent, thru narrow channels & passing along the same Andes snowrange in sight. But I don't think I'll go, too much $$ & time. I eat a lot of shellfish, some weird huge white rough shelled things that taste a little like tuna & a little like crab, oysters and also here eat a lot of small & big fried fish and also strange red globs, and also sea-urchins which are the purple spiney round shell-fish we saw at Monterey—have a yellow-orange soft interior you eat, as well as containing a live parasitic small watery crablike object—Zambelli eats a dozen of them, wrigging alive on his plate, puts them in his mouth still wriggling, half the size of a prune & same color. Some mornings I get up at 6:30 AM & go in motorboat with 2 of his workers to bays and open waters where early fishermen are catching long silver 4 foot fish, we buy them for the can factory, two hour trip. Also can see penguins, little penguins alone or in troops, swimming nearby, once I saw them right next to the boat, skimming underwater speedily eating little schools of 2-in. sardines—extremely fast & exciting to watch.

So anyway I'm staying here awhile. Taking a boat to island further south 50 miles this weekend, then will return and start north. Next week will go to a beautiful volcanic lago region I sent you postcard of. Then go back to Santiago & from there set off for Bolivia. My planeticket is good for free ride to Bolivia, Peru & Panama—so will go to each. Probably be gone longer than this month—probably till end of March. Have to find out if can get planeticket extended free. What is your money situation? I still have $100 of the $150 I got here. Also Ferlinghetti told me that Fantasy records owed me money now and would send a $200 check to me in Santiago, when I get there. Also Ferlinghetti told me that he owed me new royalties on *Howl*. It was out of that that we sent you $100 a few weeks ago. There is more money due me at City Lights so that if you are short of money or in any difficulty, write me and I'll arrange to have some sent from California. Did you get part time job? No need to do so as there is enough money around. You can write me still at Santiago c/o US Embassy and I'll get letter when I get there in about say 10 days.

Is there any important mail? Send it on if you think worthwhile but don't send anything that's not necessary to answer immediately. Proofs I would like to get if there are any from anywhere—*Big Table* or wherever. I think [Paul] Carroll was going to send me an extract from my letters he wants to publish—if they come, send them on I want to correct that maybe.[1]

I have had some weird dreams—one that I left you behind in some city in the south, and took off with a professor to another city 50 miles away—then realized I had forgot you, and you had no way of getting in touch with me, so got worried in the dream that you'd get lost, and felt guilty that I'd neglected to think of you, & realized you were suffering maybe lost in some southern city not speaking spanish, thinking I'd forgot you. Then another dream, in which I'm giving a poetry reading with Ferlinghetti in the Circle in Square [theatre in Greenwich Village] and I emerge a great hero—it was worse than that—not even a poetry reading—we were singing in a quartet and I sang one note so lovely it stole the show—I woke up horrified realizing that that was what I enjoyed, and an awful paranoiac egotism. Thank god I'm somewhere alone in solitude where I can at least look at myself. The whole beat scene now seems very involved & mad, to be involved in—we gotta get away.

How is Lafcadio [Orlovsky] & how shall we solve his problem? How does he seem now? Give him my regards, or show him this.

Still not got laid here, I guess I will when back in Towns, but stopped masturbating finally once the feeling of being alone settled in more, with less anxiety over it—used to wander around Valdivia & other towns here looking at boys, I've got less longing now than at first.

What's the household scene like? I've written cards to Jack, Lucien, Neal, Louis & home, etc. Borrowed Zambelli's typewriter for this. I'm filling small notebooks with random notes but written nothing much yet. Found a bush supposed to be narcotic Latue but as yet nothing happens from eating its seeds. Got to boil down the bark next. Love & fantasy kisses.

    Allen

1 Paul Carroll succeeded Irving Rosenthal as editor of *Big Table* (Chicago) & continued to publish new American poetry, including my own *Kaddish* and John Ashbery's "America." Letters referred to gave literary advice and urged him to publish John Wieners. —A.G. '79.

Peter Orlovsky in New York City to Allen Ginsberg in South America

March 24 [1960]

Its spring, the cats are again screwing on the floor I'm jeliuus, but she layes on her side with one foot into his belley so he cant get in, my how they talk togeteather when he tries. Your farther said to when asked if you had any checks here & I said yes he said to send them to you so I will so it will really be huge envelope, I get them now & put them in onvelope even tho I mensioned them in past letter to you you siad nothing but here they are in case you need & so wont have to send me scrambled egge letter with directions to contact Ferllinghetter at 8th st. book store. At Living theatre there is going to be on April 5th The Beats party with whoes his name that guy who Goold Medow books is putting out antho of his mind of Beats poets, his note too is there in yr drawer. On thats the check from Simon Krim whel hereit is, I cant find the other 5$ check so you'll have to this will do. Going thro yr letter back I saw this, & this is the only thing that came from Fantisy Co. was a income tax thing caled "US Information Return for Calender year 1959" so it says 710.64. Its sort of like a W-2 form i guess. Now I'll slide that back in the envelope & put it away.

Then there that strange thing about American poetry socity so figure to send it to for you to play with or what or maybe you got some south american poet under its wing so or somthing. Then theres this, from Mass I hope its not to late if you want to answer it. Me & Hunkie [Herbert Huncke] sent in little note's. Also this Mexican deal of writting for you to do on somthing. Also this from Pensivaliana want you too. Just realized you can maybe do all this stuf ware you are then when you get back home for to do pure work here but there in evening hour when you lay dreaming on yr back of black bannas [beans] diping in pink buds with green smell waveing about. Well I dont know thats about all I can find at the moment of loking thro the drawer full of mail but it seems to me that you will never have no piece for the rest of yr life for all hands wants poetry & you know how many hands there are to eat bread so you'll have to [s]it up right in the night.

Well, like I said I got off cosenall [cough syrup] the Hunkie still on & in Miroe [N.Y. Mirror] there was a hollar about junkies robbing bottles sneakey way from drugets [druggists] in drug store over the counter, the junkies go in, order a bottle with other things, listeriene, pink sope, pimple wiper & cosenil & then ask the counterman to get somthing else, meanwile the junke replaces the unbought cosinal with phonney [one] & says that his wife is in car & wants to ask her if she wants eneything else & then nevers come back. & then wile Else, at Grove comes up one night & says the plain clothes men were checking youngesters on infrunt of this building but this seems to be a joke she felt like spinning out just as Hunkie came in for supper that evening.

Well I been working over the weekend, got paid today & so paid money order to Alfred Lesile 20$ owed him had to borrow a wile back so feel better about that so I have still no money problem & so dont send me any money now OK, keep what you got & zim the path about SA [South America]

Laff ziping out of it somewhat but he seems like selfish spoiled brat tho he is so sweet at times but I hardly ever see that side. I feel like sending him off to a farm or somthing like that, hes just like me he doesent know what he wants to do in life. Well thats enough I cant think in terms of lives but the moment now, hes looking for dungries, I just came back from shopping & bought him laundrey color set & paper & a chess set. —to much I bought some peyote I want to take as soon as I feel better & went over to see [Jerry] Jofen but he not in so will call him day or so. Le Roy [Jones] came by when I was out, I guess thinking you'd be back from SA. Been screwing Jeniene with my cock & Laff says comes into the what are you two doing. She cant come & isent to hot about me & Laff in same bed so Laff says to me you took my girl away. I said you hardly ever talk to her or ask her to go out with you or ask her to dance ect but hes

getting to play checkers with her now & wins & louses & smokes I could-
ent believe my eyes the other day when Hunkie & me were over at
Lenny's talking & drinking[1] when in Lenny's desk room looking at his
pile of whatnot scrambled about he grabes my fly & wigles his hand into
my cock & starts to jerk me off & I look at him & go to see if he has a
hard-on & he has, hard as hell & I look him in the eye & says now Lenny
whats up with you I never thought Lenny Lenny what are you doing, now
just a minute Lenny I want to tell you somthing whats this here book
Lenny what are you doing now stop that Lenny Well I be damed, I dont
know what to make of that, you know of it???????? Well he got my bat
but I wasent going to swing with his wife holding the baby in other
room. [. . .]

Well letters letters & so no off now to somthing else Allen I go to post
office now & mail this at 34st one so it get to you fast for you must be in
Lame Peru now. You could send me any translation of Carlos Oquendo
De Amat,[2] that mad house [Peruvian] kid who traveled & died to wise
on foren shores somewhare???? or is that amount what yr going to send
me here????

Yr ass is on the blink hu? well you asked for it Allen, I'll do anything I
can to help but you always want to slide into thrid base so screamingly
sexxey so & slpooey so thats its no wonder that you get a burn with a
yern. I got boggies in my nose, its all drie but it would be wird if one
could be screwwed in that way, like some big tall & banna black negro in
africa with dich mouth and garbage nose could upit that way.

So theres this beat party at living theatre & mass publicity will attend
uptown but for Krims book anthology to attend should I me & Laff????
Machilene [Jack Micheline] will no doube be there from 5 to 7 pm the
hell I dont think I'll go cuase I'll take cosenall if I have to go to that or I
go with my handstied.

Weiners is OK but tho the doctors want to keep him, study him.[3] Irv-
ing [Rosenthal][4] about to hand over his job to Ed. Marshel at Grove has
been up to see him [Wieners] lots in Bosten but still doctors want him.
Hes writting tho & hasent changed much Irving said so alright there
Irving said.

No that was 13½ hours Laff walked & now has a meatey blister show-
ing that he riped the skin off of now lays in bed draws. I've been drawing
on subways on my job & when walking with Laundrey marker gives nice
deffinate linnes but all to funney falling.

What else is there to tell you, I get the crying cobweb ballence. Greg-
orys book just came out, want I should send you coppey? will do OK???
you could pass it along Its an amazing banna split with all kinds of car-
tooney entrences into magic land.

I dident see red moon, tho my mother did. you?? another red moon estromminers predice sept 5th so it will be playfull eye full then. work work work you no laxey no laxey, get up before yr ass does in morning & shine to yr window rime like time is when you spring Spring from the can.

I am glad yr making tuch with poets down there & say you feel like home there its all well & good & peachey so humming bird print with peach juce on noote books raped in ebon vine??

Ok I go back to my world now

byby bedeyby

& flowers you got to wet in april

love peter

If you get into Cocain country do, do get some & screw with it on yr. cock, right—

1 The real name of this person has been deleted for reasons of privacy.
2 5 *Metros de Poemas* (1929) by Carlos Quendo de Amat. See New Directions, Latin American Poetry, ed. Dudley Fitts, N.Y. 1942.
3 Boston poet John Wieners (b. 1934).
4 Irving Rosenthal, San Francisco-born writer, author of *Sheeper* (1967).

From left: Peter Orlovsky, Charley Shively, Allen Ginsberg, Winston Leyland. San Francisco, 1975
Photo by Steve Lowell

Peter Orlovsky in New York to Allen Ginsberg in South America

May 13, 60

Hi Allen: I just had to, the kats almost broke this typewritter & did hole lot of shitten all over everything & costing Mass $$ to feed a day so I took 4 kittens & mother to womans shelter up for adoption & they go to another home & do the same thing again only one or 2 of the kittens had to be put to sleep for hind legs were bad off. Worked a few hours today & saw Miles in post office, told about Jack [Kerouac] in city 4 days or more drunk, he came over to here when my farther was here with 4 friends, one vodu girl & I had to call up landlord yesterday about fix sink stopage & she said "I going to be honest with you peter, I dont want you bringing all yr strange friends around here, too maney kateriters going in & out of that building, I've been getting complaints from neighbors for a long time now but I havent said aneything about it but I am so I want you to keep them away, you understand." I'm sure there could of been no complaint of noise I say & she says that too but keep them strange people away, so I guess Molley got bug up ass on me, I'm afraid you going to look too strange when you come back in building Allen, neighbors wont let you in. [. . .]

Jack here, face reader than red beat cooking hot, he doesent know what to do with himself. I just came back from work, its 4 pm & had to wake Laff up, I'm going to send him to work with Henery on his truk delivering or ask Living Theatre to use him helping around cleaning up or running errands for them but he got to do something, right?

I had dream I was fucking my cats & meoweing back to them when I came. been watching to much fuck.

All poetry books are out, whalens, Frank Jacks, oleson, Garey Dons Antho of poetry from 45 to 60 out now, its one big avelanche. . . .[1]

Went to Boston & saw Wheiners [poet John Wieners] week back, he alright, only in dream world of own, alright so, no worrey of shock treatement or insulain just talking theripy so no real trouble & he can get out if realy wants to but he seems not to hot for out so stay awile. Hunkie no come down here, he what up his ass I dont know but he no show his face around so thats him, but I sneek up to his room & peek around & see that he doing lot of writting about old criminal days so all right with him, Its best he keep to himself aneyway to write & think & he also meeting other hidden friends so he alright. [. . .]

Lent Jack 5$, we go out to buy fish & he drink in bar, woman say to him why you smelling that wiskey boy, it aint pussey its wiskey, jacks looks around at her embarressed at the fat tub with cheess in [her] mouth. [. . .]

I've picked up tones of books from PO office for you, thick ones all black & spanish reading, woman poettrice of some kind now old looking. did you meet all those people to get so maney books you poor boy you, what did they do to you, how has my allen changed, is he the same happey fellow getting mad about picking my nose or you grown 10 feet tall the way Laff would like to see you? [. . .]

My farther going to die soon, high blood pressure, dreams of he has at night seeing himself die, blood rushes to head, breath stops, gasp for breath & then wakes up out of dead body, so he came around the day Jack came over & I said sleep over for you arent going to be around much longer in this world. He said he saw in paper our names in comintator spoursky something like saying that wee three are black spots on america, in jernial american daily big long collem.[2] Jack's *Golden Eternity* out, very good.[3]

Jack said he dont want his girlfriend Louise, too catatonic, but he say she great poetress & I told him no so he tells me something she said at Lucians about—

[. . .] Having to defend gregory [Corso] against being called no good, tho comic poet good only for laffs & giggles. so I said "they just dident count on gregory getting in, they just dident think a guy from the east side, puney & poor was going to come along & write poetry, they just dident think that this would happen, it dident occur to them—"

This letter got to end. Lot of other funney things but better latter butter matter later

Inside the vast movie house
one ave "B"
I dident know whare to sit.
empty train blues

>   alright sweettey, start blowing me
>   good, the new south american way

Love Peter

1 Poets Philip Whalen, Frank O'Hara, Jack Kerouac, Charles Olson, Gary Snyder. *The New American Poetry,* edited by Donald Allen, was first published by Grove Press in 1960.

2 Commentator George Sokolsky, a syndicated columnist in Hearst's *New York Journal American,* often a conduit for FBI opinions. In the same years J. Edgar Hoover was quoted in an editorial in the *New York Daily News* as saying, "The Communists, beatniks, and eggheads are the three greatest menaces to America."

3 Kerouac's *Scriptures of the Golden Eternity,* a Buddhist text (New York, 1960).

Postscript to a letter of June 12, 1960 *from Allen Ginsberg in Pucallpa, Peru,*
to Peter Orlovsky in New York [See also book The Yage Letters, *City Lights,*
1963.]

P.S. So many things—"it all comes back to me now"—remember when
we were high on peyote on Montgomery & Broadway corner near Book-
store, standing by a lampost and you were laughing when we looked into
each other eyes and I got scared of your laugh—I couldn't tell who I was
or you were, we seemed like empty toys to me & your laugh signified
that, and I kept saying "Now Peter stop laughing" because I was afraid
not to be my old familiar Allen self lover boy any more, afraid of change,
and death and "truth"—

Suddenly tonite on park bench overlooking Ucyali River, yellow
moon rising way low over horizon, muggy dark jungle across ½ mile
wide river, path of yellow real moonlight blue sky & widespread stars
like a lot of eyes looking at me in the sky—I felt like I was in ancient
Bethlehem—sat on bench listening to cricket for 2 hours—thought of
. . . Your laugh & Empty Face Robot look then—as if in that instant you
and me were the same, only I was afraid of not being the *old* me any
more, so you laughed at me,—I wanted to go on being Allen young
forever & never die—and you also then the elephant nosed Snell-Faced
Deity Being looking me right in the eyes & laughing—because I thought
I could always be Me Me Me that I've been since I've been 5 years old—
not realizing that that Me would, alas, someday Go, & Die, Alone, like
Chessman or Hart Crane or Natalie or any of us, Christs—all, every-
body.

I guess I am still afraid of the old Boogie-Man, death—was, then, in a
way, when you laughed—I wanted to be reassured we would always be
together the same thruout—Eternity. Thats why I feel, if we are doomed
to separate, be separated, by death one day, by a thing that includes
neither of us—let us have children to continue here in the universe. Isn't
that the way that is given to keep the Spark alive? Tho I don't know if the
Suffering Spark of Separate-from-Death-God Self *should* be kept alive—
"To be Or Not to Be, that is the question" and God says "that's up to
you & Peter, Allen." I don't know—something like that keeps coming
up especially in the Hyahuasca trance & dragging with it all the problems
of life—my relations with women, with my mother first—my poetry—
our fathers who are going to die—us—Love, Allen

Peter Orlovsky in New York to Allen Ginsberg in Peru

June 21, 60

Hi Allen: Got both yr letters in pucallpa yaga death dream & wile you
were in infinate dream a scroll, of old man, sitting with such long
eyebrows & gapeing mouth with 5 teeth gone as if eating the tree
underwhich he sat so long roots.[1] So you must of sent part of yr self here
to me wile you were dreaming (it came from Lima in yr name, adressed
for you here) heavenly high on yage—when I started to unroll the scroll,
as piece by piece of sitting old man came before my eyes I suddenly
gotted a high shot heroin in the arm kindness flow of calm piece came for
a second. That was Sat the 17th. Dont worrey Allen if you want babies
they will come yr way by the tons & then we grow chicken coops full of
tickleing babies & you can starve them with poetry, dont worrey. I always
wondered why you had that bregual [Breughel] children games painting
above yr bed & know you know why & that kid shitting in the corner way
back the stone wall is your son & yr eye cought him for a second. At least
Allen I could stay around the back porch & maybe if you feel like throw
me a few penies & do yr nailling up scream to keep flies away, & Allen
you wont boot me off the back porch too often, I wont know what to do
with my self. [...]

You in Lima now, more yaga I hope. It sounds you in calm thoughtfull
fleeings mood & so stay sit or I guess I not being very seerious—I dont
know what I can say—yr traveling so maney miles ahead of me that when
I open my trap yr in another dream world, If you want to come home &
tell me to leave you I'll go, I dont think I am stable enough like you are
to babey marrey minded so I'll turn myself into world pastures & get
rustey in that light. In case you dident get last letter to you, Neal is out of
Jail, working in lithograph co. liveing at home with wife & 3 children.
I sent Jack yr Eather note poem but he no answer & so am afraid to send
him Majic splam poem,[2] also when began reading that got Heroin like
shot in arm feelling of big trust feeling & as if some master were specking
yr mind writting for you. Laff a little better, he been out walking up to
farthers, 80 blocks & 80 blocks back till 4 pm & stoped by cops but no
borther from them. so he has independant walking sperits in him. Jerrey
Hisserman around yesterday, looking like Teenage wearwoolf more then
ever & realized today that I like him because he kind person. He happey
hobo looking. You & death realy talking, all sounds true & meatey &
moth & flam[e] drawing acurate with true sting to it. Good you getting
all the Yaga you want. [...]

Miles Forest in Paris, I had dream of him last night, he was naked in my bathtub with clap & told him to take sits bath & soak his cock. New Issue of *Two Citys* with B.B. [Bill Burroughs] & Gregory [Corso] & Guyson [Brion Gysin] in it all cut up writeing & mechanical methoid of writeing, playing around I think.

Maney people ask for you, so maney I dont know what to say & so I hide in movies on 3rd ave. at 13 st. Comit Theatre & see Old westerns whear the drunked colared men go & they laff & it makes me Laff so I sit behind them everytime I go cause that makes what would otherwise be boreing movie, I told this to John Weinners & he understud me wanting to sit alone in dark behind 4 colored drunks. Its a place to do some thinking & eat cheep pretizles

Tram Combs here sent you letter[3] & it says, one of note says that you "when you get back to U.S. please go over to see Dc. Williams as he thinkd you all no longer love him." So Allen, hes one soul you aint been writting now so do so, he will be amazed at yr death pull thoughts. Tram wrote poem kinda good about comeing here & hopeing to see but you away in Inca world. I'd send it to you but dont know how long you be in Lima?? No word from Lamintea [Philip Lamantia] all this time. Hunkie Ok, showed him yr sitting old man scroll with bumpey head as if volcano thoughts erupted in exploring hidden sensitive areas of mind. Schtwitzer Hospital happey? Peru look the same after Yage, feel anything different now being back there again, see aneything different? I hope you do something to flower Jack away from drunk self [. . .] It sounds like you doing lot of riteing & now bored & hope you no get too lazey at night to rite down when awake up from sleep. Its evening here now, accordian's music traveling into my window & kids let the fire-hydrant luse till old man who has nothing to do turns it off. The stars are eyes seeing you is nice for you to feel that way, kind of ageless feeling, I guess? All the butter is in the icebox & the cat is stuck to the glue, & my tung is cleaning my nose, fireengunes screaming happey. So, I showd Hunkie the scroll of old man with long eyebrows & he said to hang it on wall, so tacked it up to X-mass tree. Hay Allen I just found a baby, how lucky can we get, maybe I find another one, maybe now but one is alright

Love Peter

1 This was a Chinese scroll painting I mailed from Lima. —A.G. '79.
2 Allen Ginsberg's poem "Magic Psalm" was eventually published in *Kaddish* (1961).
3 Alabama-born poet Tram Combs lived for many years in U.S. Virgin Islands. Author of *Saint Thomas* (1965).

June 23, '60

Dear Allen with dark Indian Death Eyes: Am here at 33rd St. P[ost] O[ffice] takeing long walk high on enphedemine pill & just came from washing my face & neck from fire-hydrant that used to protect slums but whare now (8 Ave & 26th St.) lays vast empty torn brick space—& I asked for job from ½ naked man fixing wire fence if I could pick up bricks like I see old colored men do all around—but no—and today got post card from Jackey boy [Kerouac], He got yr letter notes poem— says Great—wants me to stop by see him & so I make copey of "Magic Psalm" poem[1] & send it to him like you say to do. Vast spread in Sunday *Daily News* about Jacks' Subterraineans[2] due to show in 2 weeks—and today, earlier went to job work but they no need me to do errands for them today—but collected $ pay they owed me for last weeks work—I decided to buy N.Y. *Post* cause of Hitler type giveing Mayor frustrated time—& on page 2 is blast "Kerouac Doesnt Live Here Aneymore" by Aranowitz but Leroy [Jones] gets a little sence in to article—not so bad—anyway it's the *meatey* sence of soul that tuches not whear you live—yr last word in "Magic Psalm."

Aneyway I going to write Frank O'Hara to keep on his street & I keep on mine or else we have right to rotten peach each other. *Post* NY also says man will get to androminater (star in our galaxy) but first young man to go will come back old. Maybe Earth Freak of Hole Universe?—We cant be—did you send mind into Outer Space Allen?? you sound clear on Rimbaud—I think it best for you to do a lot of writting now & free meditation.

I also thought, Yesterday, that you (in yr last letter said our Peyote High scared you when I laffed) feel I do harm to myself if we seperated & you get married (children) or I get mad at you & so I think now what ever we do (weather I turn into cockerroch cralling along 1st Ave coble-stones & get Xed by truck) (both get married or just you) (as you fall in love with John Weiners[3] or bring back new boy friend from Lima as you want to go away alone by yr self to india hill cave—or sit on my cock & talk it over & lay down & do it again, as you get married & I take care of yr baby while you blink in Jungle Storms or open the door & say "Now Peter you just cant stay around & do notheing all the time"—or be happey to each other at important times—maybe I am yr Child & you dont know it Allen—Allen I love you, Allen, Please Allen give me a sapey (sap) kiss—

Oh, realized Ditran Laff [Lafcadio Orlovsky] & I had is like Electric Shock without going into convolutionsions[4]—supose we drop dead now —why this letter—whare would it go—does God work that way & just thought you said Death is a letter never sent—have you thought that again? Oh yes had weird Dream of you & me last night—we were in Movie house or Court Building and about to leave a small black robed girl with a golden string violin you want me to carrey here out for you & I to awed to ask her to play music & then a tommey gun gangster shoots my legs off for crow baring my enterence into back of movie door. The girl was small in black & mistrey with Bliss all over her face & you had love eyes for her. You got Visian "the Pourpose of life is Death" & you got "Death stay Thy Phantoms" & you got "Afraid to face that pourpose in all its Physical & Psychic significance now." What you feel about "Afraid"—maybe best to work on non verbal sence of feeling in the chest as Einstien, Albert, on his musle nerve twiching leg musle when he would come close to infinate discovery—Death dont seem laffey to me but sad & painful—the payote laff may of been to get Power over you, frighten you—or to scare you with possible death—I dont know—hope you alright & look at star eyes tonight—I stayed off taking anything for few days—cant afford I am so gaining bodey weight & do little exercise with Laff. Maybe tomorrow if we get up earley, we go drop Telephone books on "Dean Steps Door." Ray Bremser out of Jail yesterday.[5] He & Bonney will live in Hoboken, NJ & have baby in 5 or so mos. Eliese would probably say hello if she were next to me now. Hunkie [Herbert Huncke] got yr postcard tho expected more from you. He OK. Showed off his beard when I saw him last—

I see here it says:

yr little boy Peter	The Department of Sanitation
is dressed in blue	is doing the sweeping on Ave "D"
in the subway	wile the mothers are doing
up to 42 st to	their shopping
pick a movie	

In the Essic [Essex] Markets looking for shaving blades—
"Which pack is better?"
"Eather one is good"
"I'll take the Don Juan one (5¢)"
"Both the same"
then old man says to me—
"You know what the Don Juan is?"
"O Yeah"
"You ever used the Don Juan?"

"O Yeah, lots of times"

"thats good."

& I ask him "You to?"—"oh yes"

He was old man, 60 or so.

Well down to this here letter now: OK, lets not fear each other we can figure out what to do—but you go on dreaming clearly stinging yr heart at seconds here and there you got letter 2 mo back wanting you to contribute to Nat King Cole Negro integration fund—

Write me more if you want I sail yr heart

Love from 33 st. P.O. Peter

by by now

1 Allen Ginsberg's poem "Magic Psalm" in *Kaddish* (1961).

2 Jack Kerouac's novel *The Subterraneans* was first published in 1958.

3 John Wieners (b. 1934), Boston poet.

4 Ditran, an hallucinogenic, was administered to us by a dentist & he dident tell us what a downer this drug was. Had I known I would never of let him inject me in the vien. It was a bum high. —P.O. '79.

5 Ray Bremser (b. 1934), fellow poet, loved Kerouac's writing; long time jazz blues harmonica player. Author of *Poems of Madness* and *Blowing Mouth/The Jazz Poems*, Cherry Valley Ed., 1978.

Allen Ginsberg in Tangier to Peter Orlovsky in Athens, Greece

Aug 2 Tuesday 61

Dear Peter:

Just got up—have to run to PIO to send this so be short—been up 2 days on O with Leary & Gregory [Corso]—Enclosed note from Buenos Aires—how are you and how's Athens? No other mail come but this so far, will send anything on as it comes. Beautiful to see you ride off and I felt good that you were off into World alone, just tearful that we had been quarreling with each other & separating in soul but that will be OK I hope next time we meet—I felt lost when you said "years" [from now] but if years alas, then years alas I'll still cry to see yr old eyes. Leary came in, said he saw you at airport—living downstairs in hotel, lots happened, he dug Gregory, gets along with Bill [Burroughs] politely and vice versa. He invited Bill to Harvard in Sept & Bill accepted so that will take place in September, he pay Bill's way over and small salary but not the $2000 planned because no money. We all went to Achmed's new apt (great balcony view) last night,[1] and have been going to fair to listen to music. I took a few mushrooms and felt sick and began kissing Pamela

Stevenson on Bvd Pasteur, I think I will start chasing girls again—Leary off to Copenhagen [LSD Conference] later today; Ansen also leaving this morn for Venice, that leaves me & Gregory here & Bill & the boys there—still a sort of cold war. They gave Mark (the friend of Mike Portman lives downstairs) Majoun and he got panicked at Bowles because everyone was ignoring him, so Jane [Bowles] & I and Paul & Leary held his hand & got him back & the next day on O I sat up with him & had long talk and now he is much more sociable & open & independent & I also gave him my flute since he is a musician. Gregory & I started article on Cannes [Film Festival 1961]—an interview, was OK but boring all about Sal Mineo—then we cut it up and it sounds wild—sample—

"Emptiness haunted by Jack Kennedy. Talking about windowsills of cold Sal Mineo Liberace secrecy, how would world war 2 clodhop strange? Assuredly American film presents films of attention. Musically they're really enough. Hollywood is reporters and roses? And a producer in a slimey flower festival, he got into stringbean conversations." This was done by taking cut pieces & reweaving poetic sentences from words—that is, half cut up half mental reweaving.

Bill still cold, so that's that, I feel depressed in that I'm lost touch with you, and also out of direct contact with Bill & Mike Portman mainly in the way tho maybe it's just my own schemings. Greg & Leary went to Casino last nite with [Francis] Bacon & lost a few bucks—I'm down to a hundred dollars—Leary says he'll send us railfare from Paris next week, so Gregory and I will go to Copenhagen I think—Leary says lots of girls there so I'll try girlies—Ansen made date with me for to try his boys but not done that yet. From Copenhagen can get to Berlin etc or Scandinavia. But I don't know what I do next. Bill can't take mushrooms he says he gets horrors. Ian [Somerville] built a flicker machine it's easy[2]— Gysin made it sound hard—you just get a cylinder of black paper & divide it in twenty squares and cut out 10 of them around the roll and that's that. Gregory afraid I'll fall for Cut ups I think & I will experiment more than I did, since it was useful to hop up & intensify the Cannes interview. Bill leaving for Paris in a week & we'll leave probably around then too—I'll keep writing you gossip. How is Parthenon? I mailed your letter to [your sister] Marie Monday. I havent writ Jack yet. I feel lost but I guess that's good for me I'll have to grow up like Lafcadio & learn to be independent. The maid sick, so I sent her to the doctor again and bought her $2 worth of medicine, some kind of sulfa drug for her pussey & vanilone pills for liver like you had. Please write me soon so we keep thread unbroken, at least a little diamond thread. XXXXX Love, Allen

1 Achmed Yacoubi, Moroccan painter, disciple of Francis Bacon, traveled with Paul Bowles through England and Ceylon.

2 Ian Somerville, boyfriend and collaborator of Burroughs on electronic, and sound, and feedback cut-up mechanisms and experiments.

Allen Ginsberg in Tangier to Peter Orlovsky in Athens, Greece.

c/o U.S. Consul Tangiers, Morocco
Aug 3, 1961

Dear Peter,

Strange day yesterday, woke up depressed, thinking I am a poet, & all along had been your lover—I am Allen Ginsberg—and all along that has been me, and I didn't want to go thru with it any more felt like suicide— then during the day something slowly happened, ideas changed a little— and I realized I was not tied down to being Allen Ginsberg—nor being a poet—so decided to let my identity drop & my awareness grow & went thru a day of bliss as I found I was free—lots happened, I saw Bill [Burroughs] and since my eyes had changed, he changed too & I saw that his cut-up meant also this cut up of identity, nothing worse really.

Leary was great here, calmed everyone, Bill dug him & Gregory [Corso] went out to Casino with him happy—Bill meeting him in England late this month, they both go to Harvard where Bill will experiment with white noise & sensory deprivation machines etc.

Leary told me he agreed with Bill that Poetry was finished. Because he felt the world was really moving on to a new super consciousness that might eliminate words and Ideas.

It's just this point that had bugged me with Bill & hurt my pride—so I realized that at any rate part of my hurt was pride—or better dependence for security on my identity as a poet and my life work as a poet.

Well gee I better get this off this I thought—& once I decided, sort of, to be free of thinking of myself in such strict ways, I was free to accept more ideas.

Since then, Leary left & Ansen left—yesterday both gone. I told Bill I wanted to see him alone & he said yes & then we began a rapport again— I think aside from my own vanity pride (which his basic ideas were attacking & so it hurt me temporarily)—and aside from his own carelessness & vanity & sloppiness because he is busy—that Michael [Portman] has been in the way. He kept hovering around the door when we were talking inside, & when Bill & I went out for lunch he said "I guess I'll come along" & intruded on us. Bill said while he was gone for a second "He is too *dependent* on me, that's his problem"—so Bill sees that—I see it *less* as a conspiracy of Bill & Michael now—Bill does want everybody included—or thinks he does—probably truly does—but the basis of *inclusion* must be that we drop our minds. i.e. my mind says I am poet & Orlovsky's lover, so when I get high I vomited with anxiety when I realized I was not that separate self but the same as everyone else.

I guess your leaving must have robbed me of last prop, and it was courageous of you to do the same thing for yourself & take off and be a cloud & no more a part of the *idea* we had together which was partly beautiful idea, but as an idea doomed to fail after Zen-cut-up-loss of role-identity.[1] The beautiful shiver tho always remains.

As to sex, talked with Bill about that—his objection is to the use of sex as part of idea of identity, as part of re-affirmation & support of *me*-ness & ego—he admitted that sex might be a way of merger of souls on ego-less basis like we have had it,—and so he doesn't put it down, finally, in itself, but only where it is corrupted especially in civilized countries where it is part of power-ego grab. There's no *real* argument between you.

Lots came to a head when Bill & Mike gave *Mark* (new kid) majoun, we were at [Paul] Bowles', and Mark got panicked,—Bill & Mike were too high to notice—I took care of Mark who was suffering isolation—and realized they were too fucked up to notice & care for him—I brought Mark out of it—& Bill said he was in error—I think it was nastiness on Mike's part.

I think one trouble here was you were isolated, I was confused and since I was clinging to my identity with you I could not see thru your identity to your heart, and I think you wound up over-affirming your identity and pressing down harder on it while it was under attack, instead of just giving it up & coming out free.

However I guess by cutting off from us you wound up cutting your identity in a way and coming out free—so I guess everything is O.K.—hurrah—all works out—don't be mad at me I love you—but the *me* Allen that was loving you was a fake creep that could only bug you—it's over for me I hope I hope— and I hope now for you too, I mean just dont get hung on being Peter no more and all be well and I guess that's going to be well—

Now lets see lots other has happened—long talk with Jane—she told me about her stroke in detail—seems she got brain area damaged & can't therefore add & multiply and also, her vision is cut in that she only sees what's 10 inches on each side of her, not 30 inches[2]

The sensitive

other peoples see that

I will now take "Fall of America" and cut it up to get rid of my own self assertion parts & recombine the images into a huge glorious poem expressing the Hope of the world for a vast new Consciousness free of Names & Identities & Ideas of the self—[3]

I wish you had stayed here with me but if you had not gone I might not have been forced to change and we might have got worse into a tangle of fighting identities but sure we would have got out of it—all in all I think our idea of sex was right & beautiful & led us (or me) forward & thank you Peter—

Gregory is still a little Gregory & that's all that's why he picks on everybody he thinks he's separate & superior but he'll lose his mind too.

Leary says the drugs *cut off* the ego part of the brain in the cortex, and leave an "open brain" without ideas of self. That's what scared me to vomit while I held to my idea of what I should be—beat poet.

No I don't still think you are a firing squad, I'm sorry I said that but I was defending my *Idea* and I think you were setting up a different *Idea*, and it was a firing squad war of ideas in my mind when we both should have dropped—we both alas were too unhappy to drop our Ideas & get back in Union.

"Praise be the god that lasts" yes praise be—as long as we don't get hung up on the word or *idea* of god but be the gods.

"Man is only god that lasts" yes & no—man is changing, I am changing, you are changing, god is growing in us but he has now grown so real that the word God is almost obsolete maybe—

I think Bill & Leary at Harvard are going to start a beautiful consciousness alteration of the whole world—actually for real—Leary thinks its the beginning of a new world.

Anyway I was wrong in calling you firing squad because we are all one.

Anyway I don't think you're right on Gregory's book [*America Express*, Olympia Press, 1961]. Bill hasn't really read it either & doesn't realize how it intuitively does capture the whole situation here—all these different parties & warring identities trying each one to be right—not realizing that only if *all* are wrong can all get together and be one new person—all take on a new life together without ideas of Allen & Peter & Bill & Gregory as separate persons & plans.

Anyway, I was wrong. So I'm sorry I laid all that woe of my own thoughts & fears on you while Allen was dying—I guess you had your own troubles too—I shouldn't have left you alone here when I went [with Paul Bowles] to Marrakesh maybe—but I was afraid of imposing that week of anguish on you & fighting more—

Anyway it's worked out magically for the best & you & I are both free now so forgive me & take me in thought hello & I'll see you soon whenever we both can on free basis, I hope sooner than 10 years because that would mean it would take ten long years for both of us to be really free—and we should be able to do that this year yes—be free I mean—in fact let's do it now—I see you—oops—hello—goodbye—write me—how's Greece—how's Peter? Allen's happy—all love—everything will be allright. love Allen

P.S.—I wrote this fast and am not re-reading—will send it now—I'll stay here another week—don't know where next—Maybe take boat to London to see the Queen—stay awhile there & then take boat in Oct to Israel or India—Love Allen

I just re read it and it almost says what I want to but I'll write again and say it better.

---

1 Orlovsky had left Tangier suffering rejection by Burroughs and exclusion by M.P. from their intimate company. For his state of mind see accompanying photo taken at this time.

2 Jane Bowles (1917-1973), American writer, author of *Two Serious Ladies, In the Summer House* (1954). Wife of writer Paul Bowles. See her *Collected Works* (1964). See also the discussion on her life and death in *Gay Sunshine Interviews*, vol. 1, 1978, pp. 160-162.

3 See "Television Was A Baby Crawling Toward That Death Chamber," ultimately published intact in *Planet News* 1961-1967, City Lights, S.F. 1968, pp. 15-32.

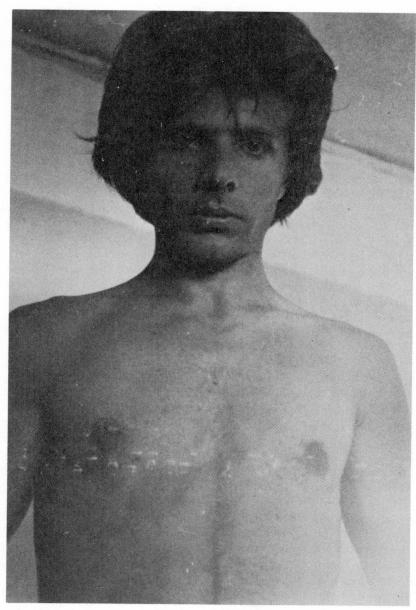

Peter Orlovsky
Self-portrait, Tangier, 1961

American Express
Athens Oct 21, 1961

Dear Peter:

I had been sending you mail Amer Express Istanbul from Tanger, including magazines & a package (letter & book gift Fra Angelico) from Janine; when I got to Greece there were two earlier letters from me I also had forwarded to Istanbul(but here they told me the real address was Turk Express Istanbul not American Express)—so there is a lot of stuff following you that way. Then finally after trip to Crete earlier this month & after I wrote your mother with a letter for her to send you, I received all your letters from Beirut and around the 10th or 12th of Oct I sent you letters and postcards there including a 20 dollar bill in one letter since it sounded like you were broke selling your blood & yr check not arrived according to yr mother; then I received yesterday your last note from Beirut saying you were heading off to Damascus, Jerusalem & I should write you in Haifa. I don't understand how you going to pick up mail in Haifa which on map is way up north in Israel; but I guess you will be there around the 2nd or 3rd of November to receive V.A. check from your mother.

I not sure what plans are for me but will make sure I am in Haifa by then and be around, and will leave note in Amer Express address you sent me there, saying where I am living. You do the same yes, so we not lose contact again. I can get boat from here to Haifa for 20 dollars with bunk-bed. So I will go there and wait. I hope you get this or I will be waiting there forever? I also wrote you extra postcard to Embassy Beirut saying I would try to reach you at the Haifa address you sent me Oct. 15. Your note sounded like none of my letters had reached you by the time you were leaving in "Taxey" to go to Damascus.

Gary Snyder says he and Joanne his wife will be in Bombay on Jan 1, 1962 & I should meet them there then, go on tour meet monks with him.[1] He says he'll need money and will give poetry readings in universities there & wants me to do it too, I wrote him Okay. Tho I don't feel like singing any more. I guess you read if you want. He Gary sounds great, I wrote him what happened with Bill etc in Tangier. Enclosed letter from Irving [Rosenthal] I got this month with NY gossip. Ferlinghetti's *Journal* came out,[2] so did issue of *Kulcher* & I have them;[3] I mailed you a copy of New Orleans *Outsider* with your [Snail] poem in it. Ferlinghetti writes me where are you he wants to publish yr poetry, I sent him yr Beirut address; Gregory keeps asking why you don't write him, Amer Embassy

London, he sad thinking you disappeared. He was broke & lived with Colin Wilson on S Coast of Eng. Then sent article to magazine & got some money & now lives near zoo & finishing mss of poems *Apples,* and hit Norman Mailer for insulting beatnicks at a London party one night. Bill was in Harvard & Leary wrote that all was quiet & OK but you see what Irving says. Leary sounds a little sad, send him a postcard encourage? I got to write Jack still.

I have 250 dollars when I get to Israel. Prefer to go overland but want to get there by New Year in Bombay, meet Gary, because he'll know all the monks & I said I'd read with him.

I stopped smoking for 2 weeks solid, then started again, but can stop anytime now, it's just that it makes me nervous. To stop. I get irritable touchy. I got some O [opium] from friend coming from India & used it twice, once I wrote huge letter about Politics & Consciousness to Howie Schulman (Hotel Presidente, Vedado, Havana Cuba) for his magazine there (*Arriba*).[4] He wants yr poems too.

I packed up books & papers and mailed them back to States; also packed up rockandroll & mailed them all to Romanova in Moscow.[5] So now my knapsack lighter. I got some shirts. Meanwhile I been here in Greece all along, read *Odyssey* & *Iliad,* and been in country most of the time to ruined cities and shepherd goatbell music valleys—Mycenae, Crete, Delphi, Olympia—I was going up north to Mt. Athos monasteries but time getting short for India & want to meet you in Haifa & it save money if I take this cheap boat. Had a lot of strange dreams in which I had amnesia or was whirled around by winds. Made it with a few boys here but cost money a little & they weren't so interesting but I dig the cock. I live across street from bar where whore boys gather, I know them all. Also hang around Zonars & Flocas cafes and see intelligent old literary men here & they all like me. They're all bugged at Gregory who apparently teased everyone, threw fits etc. . . .

Lessee what else to add. I get endless mail & still answer. Not wrote much poetry but lots of dreams., & some notebooks. *Empty Mirror* book is out & looks okay. Money I got is advance on Italian Translation plus 20 dollars Gregory sent me back plus 10 dollars from New Directions. I sold article to *Show Business Illustrated* on Cannes, had 750 dolls, Gregory lost 200 gambling & owes me that, spent the rest travelling plus 100 extra was his for helping; now they want to censor the word shit so I wrote them no even if I have to pay them back 450. Still waiting to hear. [Never published—A.G., '79.]

Sorry I did not see Istanbul & Cairo & Damascus but maybe see strange places inland overland to India if do that. Be sure & send for your mail in Beirut & Istanbul and send Amer Express 1 dollar they charge nowadays for forwarding. I read Mellville [*Holy Land Travels*] notes years ago & don't remember them except that was my idea, to see the Bible landscape he mentions, also he has long poem "Clarel" I read parts of about his trip to Jerusalem area. Okay Petey I sign off and see you in 12 days I guess if you finally get this. and you not delay forever in Petra. I have 2 huge maps of Middle East to Persia. Also possible boat from Israel to India. Maybe I, we, miss further arab countries & rush to India fast. They say Bombay & India is expensive because dysentery dangerous to eat native food & there are no Hotels like in west, just big hotels cost 3 dollars a day but with good food included. That Bowles says and all others I met.

Thank you for all letters sorry you not receive mine, some were crazy. I was lonesome for you.

Love to you from your old
Lover

Allen

1 Gary Snyder (b. 1930), American poet.
2 *City Lights Journal for the Protection of All Beings,* including Tangier interview of Ginsberg by Corso, and Burroughs interviews by Corso and Ginsberg.
3 *Kulcher,* edited by Leroi Jones and friends.
4 Published in *P'alante,* magazine of the League of Militant Poets (N.Y. 1962) as "Prose Contribution to Cuban Revolution."
5 Ylena Romanova, in charge of American literature and Writers Union, Moscow.

Allen Ginsberg in Bangkok, Thailand, to Peter Orlovsky in Benares, India

Thursday Eve
May 31 [1963]

Dear Peter:

Bangkok was fine—flying tomorrow morning to Saigon—Have you received the Bank of America check? Plenty 19 yr old Chinese boys here —They picked me up & two different times came to hotel—cost 1 or 2 dollars—young hairless skin like Vijyashankar it felt like [1] —Only trouble is they stick to me like adhesive tape afterwards—Come visit again— They hang out under King Rama's Statue in Lumbini Park—Great Museum here—the *SUKOTHAI* (12th Century) style of sculpture—walking Buddha with one hand up in the Abhaya (everything's ok) Mudra— is very great—Sorry I could not go inland. Oh, and I found a poet, young

kid, I translated one of his poems about "Angels Coming down to earth
to eat shit & sawdust in the dream, calculating how much shadow weighs."
I'll send you names & addresses—This kid Ankorn is Thai-style classical
painter—25 yrs. old & speaks poor broken English but great soul—I
met him & drove with a teacher all around banana palm canal suburbs—
Temple of Dawn & a big canal running like Venice thru the city is beauti-
ful—I gorging myself on Chinese duck & pork— 10¢ a plate of wonton-
shrimp-pork soup or rice—Expensive restaurants *and* cheap restaurants
of all kinds—fine—Inland, outside Bangkok must be lovely—Every-
body Chinese looking smiles at my hair & in my eyes saying "Ah sooo!"
Young kids in groups on streetcorners very friendly smile & polite—
some want to come home sleep—sorta like Tanger but more polite—So
this is a place could spend some time—They say apply in Delhi for 2
month visa & then can extend it here. I easily got 2 week visa, at airport.
Now running to change money for Saigon/Cambodia. I got Cambodia
(Ankor Wat) visa here also—costs $5 and 3 passport photos. Also I had
to give Vietnam (Saigon) embassy 3 photos and 2 dollars. The money
here is called "Bats"—20 bats to a dollar. Chinese soup or rice dish costs
2 bats. OK bats to you love—what's up—flying—   Allen

1 Vijyashankar—10 year old son of our landlord on Dasasumedh Ghat in Benares.

Peter Orlovsky in Varanasi, India, to Allen Ginsberg in San Francisco

Sept. 15, 63 Its a rainey Sunday
night

Dear Belley Allen love: Comming out of Opium -morphine haze dream
—I alright—reread yr letter yesterday (you last rote me July 25th from
V.C.)—had completely forgot its sayings—I am so glad you wrote me
saying what you said, I take you as my devine Love Gerhu [guru], you
kept humming belley-Love in my ear & letters until I got yr meaning
—swing open yr Blake gates. I can almost hear you sound to hear—I be
alright now my Love, & no Junk but help others & learn things—I
wireded you today for money to fly to you but now I think it better you
use money like for Phill Whalen etc.—I can make it back to N.Y.C.
Overland—Like you say—we meet in N.Y.C. in X-Mass my Love—I
be good & Happey so much thanks—Kiss to you—because of your July
25 Letter. I send you telegram tomorrow saying not to send $—it best

I not be dependent on yr practical life— this leave you free to spread yr money giving love to others— in need. Just send me your Blake Vission money return Love— Okay— you dig. Hello Neal [Cassady]. I got Learn to make my own moves to do the things I want— that will encourage me to type up my poems & send out drawings & sing otherwise I be gloomey dependant on you & get in your way. We grow Love in Letters & meet in N.Y.C. in the 8th St. subway stop. Thanks to you I feel much better already to keep my heart on Love. Its that I keep forgetting, forgetting. Okay— thats the main dish on my lips to you— I be here till next VA comes (just a minute I have to look up to see what the name of next month after September is)— October 7 about then I make tracks over Pakestan Iran Turkey & get boat in Yougoslavia maybe to N.Y.C.

Good morning— new day has come— Monday— I go run to Post Office & sent you another teleghram now. Just sent it— Its also that I a bit scared to face all America again but I work in self love to get over that. It best— it no good I be worrey drag on you & depend on your sensibilities too much— Right— I be better now— Sorrey for the False Alarm of Frist telegram. Also feel better, because I meet Trilochan Shastri last night & Naganand Muktekanth[1]— had been avoiding them leaving lonely quality food type [restaurant and] red time & shoot some M [morphine] selfish life—

Samsher Bahadur Singh [Hindi poet] is still in Sarnath. He has written 6 poems about you pub in one Hinde magizine; an american you meet in Taj Mahal— Gabriel Fluke is coming to Banaras today— I go to station to meet him & help him find room cheap—

I have to go back to my Hotel now a young German wants to buy a Shanai so I take him to the maker.

Yes its all love belley tickle its that I get kind of selfish worrey— but I be alright now— by helping others helps me to be better—

Naganand has gotten books from City Lights and your mothers Sunlight good too— amazeing she wrote you 2 days before she died—

Okay I be here till next VA check come Oct 7 th Well we almost met in SF or Vancouver—whearever you are now (?) but I afraid of being worrey babey drag on you So I make it back to America on my own—

Okay my dear friend, will write both Fat Jack & Lafacido to cheer up—

Be well—Hello to Neal—I hope he starts writting again. Good you working on his prose—Yes we give love to America—

Kisses Love
Peter

1 Trilochan Shastri, a traditional classical Sanskrit scholar, and Naganand Muktenanth, a young poet and journalist, were both friends of Allen and Peter in Benares.

Sept 21, Saturday 1 PM [1963]

Good Morning My Sweet:
   Am on train to Delhi. Meet young english girl who said smielingly I may get car ride back to England. If not then go overland. Hope you are happey like me. I be happey cause you told me I am some gloomey, smoking too much but am cutting down. I will start breathing meditation like you reminded me to do. [. . .] I got thank you note from Gary & gave it to a Cambodian monk at Sansero [Sanskrit] University in Varanasi who was interested writting letters. [. . .] I dont realey want to leave Romancro[1] & beggers—I guess its all the murdoer & heart hate in the world that I am so shy of—So I need joy to stop death happenings. Ug! I feel dead already but your letter pulled me out of morphine—I come back to America & live on air like Milarapo.
   I am glad of your Blake Vision—Hope you marrey a negro girl or the newspaper Blake friend. I am sorry too of waisted your time making connections for the 800 kisses dollars. Yes thats it. Just scared of death. No need to be that way. Arrived Delhi on top Ron Vial's roff top room. I hope you are well. [. . .] Am feeling fine will go wash my pajamas soon the water not running at this hour. Yes, yes, feel fine, any hassels dont worrey never no more about me can eat. Dont know how money goes. I be in Delhi waiting for car ride, maybe one day or 3. Hope you save So. America. Me too will help So America can help all the other countries. I go see Leroy [Jones] & make love with him & all his room friends & take part in Demonstrations & get Lafcadio out of Hospital. So have to be kind [. . .] with everybody & not be a drag on the human industry. [. . .] It be alright and I write to Sansher & write to Manjulo about fuck everybody & help everybody. Manjulo may get scholarship & study at NYU. She be alright. She may bring Tampura [tamboura] instrument for me to sing on the street of N.Y. or in Washington Square Park.
   Im on Honney Moon train to Amritzar—sitting on floor of crowded train next to Josephine english artist student & indians talking about Pakistane rupies & I love you & Hop yr long hair is happey too. I hope you no die. Yes—your right I type up my poems & read to America & England & Iran & Turkey, [w]hole population—I have to feel out belley talk. Vosnosensky thinking heard & writting great poems I hope. Namwar Sing showed me review of your *Empty Glass* in *Statesman*. You must be feeling much joy. Sorrey I not there to blow you & Lavigne. By time I get to England maybe I see one of your or Neals [Neal Cassady's] writ-

ting in *Life* mag. Poor China. I am on the night train & have all night to think of you & write more letters to Ashoka Fakir & Manjulo & Samsher. I know 2 simple rags [ragas] now my love—Okay I die happey whenever it comes. Yes, I stay off junk & help others. Even your mother died happy. *Time* mag critizing the Siagon corospondents even tho they friendly to Jacks brother & surprised to see *Newsweek* put the book down.[2] Bird love

        Peter

  1 Rabindranath Pal, Peter's music teacher in Benares.
  2 Publication of Kerouac's novel *Vision of Gerard,* about the early death of his brother.

Peter Orlovsky in Pakistan [traveling to Istanbul] to Allen Ginsberg in San Francisco

                                              Sept. 25, 63
                                              Wednesday

Hello Hinde Long Sweet Beard Hair Eyes:
Was just crying thinking you may die before we meet again. A beautiful thing just happened to me & beggar here in Quatta, Rabestan [Quetta, Baluchistan]. A beggar was sitting across the street from this tea shop So I went over to him & gently offered him a big long nan bred & he took it. I think he was a crazzey begger like my brother Julius & your mothers sunlight limelight keys. He latter walked away. So I confussed hopped after him to give him a rupie. He wouldent take. Another beggar walking by wanted it—Gave it to him & took out another rupie to offer again, he wouldent take it so I got down on the road to kiss his feet & looked up at his eyes offering him rupie again. He took it. But first gave me a piece of paper with a name in English & more written in Urdu addressed to the Commissioner Office. It was just like your beggar friend at Dasascamed Ghat writting he wanted to die when you asked him to write for you.

    I cry to think I may die or my money get robbed & I not get back home to see you again. I am sorry [to] worrey over such things. There is so much joy good things of help & love to give in the world that I dont want to die before its done. I hope Leroy is happey & alright. Sorry I dident make love with him when he wanted me to. Jhon was right when he said I was scared. I write postcards to Lafcadio & Julius & Jack & mother Kate & Henery Schlacker who sent me picture postcard of him on beach with friends in Holland & post card to Marcien we meat in Isreal & to Nathin Zak if I have his address. Had a long talk with a German philosopher in Hospital here & he said it was alright to help a needey beggar but to help the one that it will do the most for. Meet Urdu poet here had 2 hr night coffey talk with him. He may take me to meet few other poets here. I leave Quetta on Sat. for train to Iran Za-ha-dan. In New York I get job or work for America on my armey pension. I be alright my friend. Thank you for reminding me to be kind to Gary. Lady on radio singing SRGMPDNE[1] combinations would like love to come back to America in my Orange Lunge & Silk Jaipur chamiese if I dont give them away before I get back. So will give my money away instead to beggars then my clothes or buy a shert or pants for them instead of give-ing away my clothes.

Okay my dear friend— I go back to Dak Bungalow & write letters. OH I was going to. Some fellow travelers here have just come to have chy [tea] & nans. We three are shareing room at Dak Bungalow. My mind thinking slow. I am clam & cut off now & some confussed & dont want to bother use all your time. I smoke pot too much I hope I can stop today or if I dont I wont be able to give the 4 annas to beggars or poor souls [. . .] In a month I think I will be in Istambul [. . .] So write there or we meet in NYC in X. mass & try to save the world—& we kiss. Love— Peter

        Peter Your Slave Happey

1 Sa Re Ga Ma Pa Da Ni Sa, names of notes in Indian music scale.

Allen Ginsberg in San Francisco to Peter Orlovsky in Istanbul

Oct 10, 1963

Dear Peter—Just received one letter from you from Persia. In case you arrive broke in Istanbul here's $100. I sent mail to you at Benares & Delhi, maybe you never received it yet. Boy your going swiftly leaving footprints all over Middle East.

I'm living at 1403 Gough St (!!!) with bunch of young Kansas poets.[1] [David] Hazelwood of Auerhahn Press is upstairs, Neal [Cassady] & his girl Ann is in one room also. He's started writing.[2] I'll write you details— getting this out now swiftly to meet you when you reach Istanbul.[3] Love XXX

        Allen

[Postscript]

So as I was saying, am in big back room in near old kitchen stove in our old Gough Street house, all by accident—Neal here too he been playing the races losing all his money, Carolyn divorced him last month & he retired from works, applied for unemployment comp & is settled here with his new (18 months) girl friend[4]—she types good & he been writing, dictating aloud to us—maybe it work out good—Robert Frank was here & we worked out film treatment for "Kaddish" but I got more work to do on that—L. was here with Lois S. (dont tell noone) all blissfull & happy & naked laying around Ferlinghetti's attick & riding Powell St Cablecar with me—LaVigne has tie & looks distinguished—McClure is very tender[5]—I slept with 2 girls here but not so great—also here in house a young (28) poet from Kansas [Charles P.] I been loving in bed with & plenny belly flowers there too—Gee what a weird huge apartment this is—too bad you not see this scene—If you get to NY before me I come soon—if you pass thru London find Anselm Hollo for place to stay 87 Cornwall Gardens London SW 7. Irving Rosenthal still in Tanger finished his Sheeper book now 350 pages & people say it's good[7] —Ansen is in Athens c/o American Express & Nanda Pivano would love to see you in Milano, 19 via Cappuccio. Rosenthal is 2192 Tanger Socco & Burroughs is there too he says but I not in touch with Bill, Bowles there too in cse you do pass thru that way.

Young Kansas cat I been making it with Charles P. is like Charley Brown song, real funny—he made up a magazine NOW last weekend so I'll send that to Istanbul airmail.

I got lots to do, type mss. help Neal, make Kaddish Movie,[7] and write poems, & answer mails & make loves, boy what a schedule—I don't do much of all of it just goof around the big apartment—go to Subud also once a week see what that's like—lots of new young 20 yr old poets here—general feel of things is New Hope, the 30's are back, life begins again, young folks having babies, no more deaths, just the old methadrine horrors on a few people still hung up in crystaline nonhuman huniversesh—and YOU you better stop goofin with white horses honey they cant suck your cock like I can—or girls can—just remove you from the Meeting Place of Sexy Folks with asses & cheeks to kiss—and dulls the belly sensitive tickle—Amazing to be at Gough St like huge 9 year cycle come full round—I came here one night to big party Kansas friends of McClure had—all new poets here

1 J. Richard White and Charles P. 1403 Gough St. is where Robert La Vigne first lived with Peter Orlovsky almost a decade earlier when we first met. —A.G. '79.
2 See posthumous collection *The First Third*, City Lights, San Francisco, 1971.

218

3 Peter Orlovsky was returning overland from India.

4 Neal Cassady (died 1968) was a friend of Ginsberg's for more than 20 years. See the poems dedicated to him in Part I of the present book.

5 Michael McClure (b. 1932), San Francisco poet, playwright.

6 *Sheeper*, novel by Irving Rosenthal, Grove Press, 1967.

7 Filmaker Robert Frank who'd worked with Kerouac, Corso, Peter, etc. on *Pull My Daisy* (movie, 1958) proposed a film of *Kaddish* but unable to raise funds, began shooting real life movie *Me and My Brother*, starring Peter & Julius Orlovsky & Joe Chaiken. —A.G. '79.

Allen Ginsberg in Havana, Cuba, to Peter Orlovsky in New York City

> February 4, 1965
> c/o Casa de las Americas
> Havana, Cuba

Dear Peter:

Visit so far has been fantastic—Cuba is both great & horrible, half police state half happy summer camp—mixed. I have been writing a lot every day keeping notes & will send you notebooks to read soon, so you'll get complete story. *Hold* them for me & dont let anyone see them except *Sanders* & *not* to publish. Just went thru a period of Kafkian Paranoia here deep as Tangers when we got Confused there—a few young friends poets 17 & 23 yrs old arrested over night for seeing me, & me blabbing about Pot & fairies got *them* into McCarthyite type trouble. Straightening all that out now. I'm ok, living in big modern hotel & eating in big diningroom, have limousine at disposal when I need it to go out—meet young alienated kids & liberal revolutionaries & officials of state. I talk too much & so become a social problem. No sex no pot—too paranoid a scene for that at the moment got to be careful create no more scandals not embarrass liberal Casa de las Americas that invited me. Things better this week & arrests be all straightened out. Apparently big youth-queer wave here & the Govt. cant understand it & I arrived in the middle of that said I was a fairy & that set off waves of anxiety in every direction.

Received *Fuck You* today via Mexico thanks, & got your earlier letter via Mexico but *not* the original sent direct.[1] Which means that Vietnam stuff must have been seen by U.S. Govt. people. Please phone MacDonald & send him *Fuck You* too?[2]—at New York OX 51414 say I rec'd letter in Cuba, & understand, & will try to answer soon. Poor Schulman [ill]. What to do. On next page enclosed for Committee Non Violent Action [Against Vietnam War] my signature, please send it to them. [. . .]

Letter sent me from Ferlinghetti Jan 21 arrived today direct from U.S. But not your original Vietnam letter, only copy came a week ago via Mexico. U.S. Mail is irrational. I'll send *this* out via England.

Everything so far amazing here the amount of gossip rumor & small politics whirling around, for a few days I was completely cut off emotionally from everyone, didn't know who to trust. Now things getting back into shape.

Fantastic African-Yoruba drum & dance religion here, people dance into ecstatic collapse, [Santería] system of different gods like Hindu, I've been to a few ceremonies in suburbs of Havana.

Leroi [Jones] & Marc didn't understand or tell the whole scene here— I still feel sympathy for revolution but I don't think they dig how puritan conformist & brainwashing dangerous it is. Same old Marxist anxiety about controlling people's energies. In some respects same police terror here as in Lower East Side—the crises I was in reminded me of Kerista [commune busted by cops] days. How'd *pot* march go? I do nothing but jack off. I told someone, a reporter, I'd had sex fantasies about Che Guevara & that almost precipitated an explosion in the Casa de la Americas. I have to walk on eggs here to protect the people who invited me. What's impolitic, or suppressed, is unconscious fantasy. I've kept huge day by day journal but could never publish it. I feel great & very active running around all day gossiping like in N.Y. Nicanor Parra here & Miguel Grinberg & also heads of Nadaista Colombian poetry movement, & head of Roof of the Whale, Venezuelan poetry group, we gave a little conference together the other night in which I explained *Naked Lunch* techniques of Anti-Brainwash; sort of doubletalk for both Cubans and Americans.[3] Then tonite sat & translated aloud a whole bunch of Creeley poems.

I need *books* to teach with—hardly anything here. Please call Fred Jordan at Grove & ask them to airmail me Kerouac books, a couple copies of *Naked Lunch* & *Soft Machine*, [Hubert] Selby [author of *Last Exit to Brooklyn*], Don Allen's *New American Poetry* etc. Anything else too they can.

Also call [Ted] Wilentz & ask him same, his [Totem/Corinth Press] complete line poetry & 2 copies each [Gary Snyder, Philip Whalen, Leroi Jones, Joel Oppenheimer etc.].

Things looking better less paranoid today I guess it be all ok. Love xxx love to Julius [Orlovsky]—How are his affairs now? Still got nice girl? Love to everybody next door & Huncke. I may stay here an extra month till end of Feb or mid-March (unless they get paranoid again & kick me out which they wont probably)[4]—Leaving this week for trip around countryside. Gathering poetry for Ferlinghetti too.

Amazing the great wave of fairies here among teenagers, nobody can figure it out & the Govt. is hysterical trying to stomp it out of the Arts schools & universities. I keep telling them the only way is not repression but encouragement of heterosexuality early, but they are too dopey & puritan to understand.

I'm ok & running around with white Cuban sneakers & new blue jeans I brought with me & torn suede brown jacket.

Write, via Mexico, it comes in 1½ weeks about. Writing direct takes too long—

      Love   —Allen

1 *Fuck You/A Magazine of the Arts,* edited by Ed Sanders.
2 Dwight MacDonald, American radical thinker.
3 Nicanor Parra—Chilean poet; Miguel Grinberg—editor, *Eco Contemporaneo,* Argentinian avant-garde magazine.
4 They did—A.G. '79. See next letter.

Allen Ginsberg in Havana to Peter Orlovsky in New York

Feb. 15, 1965

Dear Peter:

Rec'd your letter mailed Jan 24 today. I'll answer Linda Smith when I get back. Thanks for Daily News Clipping. Newspapers here this week full of giant headlines about U.S. planes attacking North Vietnam. People here at *Casa de las Americas* sad about Howard Shulman—If you see him tell him Haydee Santamaria & Maria Rosa Almendres said he should come to Cuba to recover.[1] Or send him a Postcard. I mailed you 2 letters via England, enclosing the A.J. Muste Form. Also I sent you 2 [Cuban] notebooks via England. I have a third one almost full already. Got high the other nite & wrote some poetry [. . .] God it must be awful in the apartment without water. We better move. City promises Relocation? [. . .] Say hello to Irving Rosenthal if you see him. Also how is Stephen Bornstein? Give him big wet kiss from me. & also big wet kiss to Anne [Buchanan] next door. Does she have to move too?

I'll have money from Guggenheim or Ford Found. next year so we can afford a better apartment. Let's try & get a nice big cheap one, but you got to pay *something* for a permanent place. Maybe in a project. They're too small. Well, let me know. How is Julius' behind?

I took a trip with others by airplane all the way across Cuba to Santiago & Sierra Maestra Mountains & went in trucks up & down dusty roads to a big school on top of a mountain where 5000 teenagers are learning to be teachers. They have no sex (officially) & all sing songs to Castro & learn Marxism & biology & reading & writing, to go off later into mountain villages & make thatch-roof school huts & teach the natives. Things quieting down around me here—none of the interviews I gave were published & the boys arrested are now out of trouble & everything is calm as long as I keep my temper—Will meet some psychoanalysts this week. I'm still in big hotel overlooking Ocean facing Florida & little boats are bobbing on the blue water. Tell David G. I havent slept with any bronze boys & they dont want *sexy* social City planners, at least officially. They dont know what to do with sex here. Of course I talk too much & fuck too little. I'll send you a big pile of books & newspapers soon. I spend a lot of time with young teenage kids who take me on long secret walks by the oceanside & translate my poetry & complain about older square revolutionaries. I'll start making arrangements for going on to Czechoslovakia soon, tho hope to stay here another month. Not sure they'll welcome it though. Everybody likes me but I make people nervous always talking about Govt. sex policies. Enclosed a strange photo—last week at a party at the Writer's union, I introduced Haydee Santamaria to the 2 young kids on the right in the photo—they were the ones who were arrested for hanging around with me. Big dramatic Dostoyevskian scene—she was just promising they'd be safe & could visit me at Hotel again when the photo was taken. It's like a movie. The kids run a teenager publishing co. subsidized by the Govt. Called *The Bridge*. First everybody said they were put in jail overnight for "putting ideas in my head" criticizing the revolution. Later police said they heard I smoked pot & were trying to protect/warn the boys against being corrupted by me. Anyhow, at this point, they're safe, now that they met the lady-revolutionary-bureaucrat. Unless I start screaming & making scandals here about police state mentality. Meanwhile I'm waiting to find out if they'll put me up another month in this big hotel.

I was sick when I first arrived with grippe, & took antibiotics, & then last week one night of bad dysentery—took medicine & ok in 24 hours. Just back from the mountains & dont know what to do next so writing letters. Main thing is I've been keeping track of everything that happens, & so, write a lot in notebooks, that keeps me busy. I'll tell you more gossip but you can read it all in the notebooks when they arrive from England, if you can read thru my writing.[2]

All told Cuba is pretty good, I mean people working & building, like they say, a new society—which is remarkable for any So. American country. But there is a great limitation on some eccentric individual lib-

erties & really not much free discussion in public, the newspapers are all
hopelessly controlled & the writers all hopelessly self-controlled—every-
body afraid of being accused of being anti-revolutionary if they criticize
govt. policy or personalities too sharply. Because of that, much paranoia.
However most everybody says real Stalinist Square crisis has passed in
1962 & no police state will come about now. —OK. Love Allen[3]

1 Haydee Santamaria, Ministry of Culture, member of ruling revolutionary council.
Actually I got kicked out of Cuba because she was in a fight with a Minister of Immigra-
tion (hard-line military), and they were using me as a pawn. Maria Rosa Almendres,
head of *Casa de las Americas,* International Cultural Center. —A.G. '79.
2 Cuban Journals (200 pp., unpublished).
3 Shortly after writing this letter Allen Ginsberg was expelled from Cuba. See his
account in his interview, printed in *Gay Sunshine Interviews,* vol. I, Gay Sunshine Press,
San Francisco, 1978.

Allen Ginsberg in Prague, Czechoslovakia, to Peter Orlovsky in New York

May 4, 1965
Writer's Union
Narodni 11,
Prague, Czechoslovakia

Dear Peter:

Sorry I not write so long—I left Moscow April 7 & went to Warsaw
where I stayed for 3 weeks & made some polish zlotys [currency] with
poems [*Howl*] translated in a Jazz magazine—[Andrei]Vosnosensky got
passport & arrived for 10 days in Warsaw so I saw him there one night &
we talked a little—he says Kruschev is writing poetry now too.[1] April 23
I went to old Polish town of Krakow near Czech border & spent a week,
very beautiful ancient city with big main square & cafés—drove out to
see Auschwitz—but still no love life except one night I got drunk & took
off my clothes at a party & some journalist blew me. Then I got on train
& spent a day walking around another old polish city Wraclow & caught
midnite train for Prague—wanted to see may day parade in Prague so
arrived the day before & got cheap hotel room & went to see if I had any
more money, no, so I was low on bread—except a weird thing happend,
I ran into an old writer friend of [Jan] Zebrana my translator—on the
street the morning I arrived—he told another writer [Josef Sqvorecky]
I was back in town—& they told the students at the Technical University.
Well, an old tradition in Prague on May 1 is a student's festival where
they elect a King of Prague and a May Queen—Except that since the war

under Marxism they had no May-alles festival for 20 years. So every year they'd had student riots instead. So this year the politicians decided to let students have their own May festival after the regular May Day Parade.

Well the students decided to nominate me for Kral Majales i.e. King of all May & King of Prague thinking it would be a funny joke and I might even probably win—supposed to be little Parades with bands on back of trucks to a fairground where a few thousand students maybe gather.

So the day after I arrived a delegation of students dressed up in 1890's costumes arrived at my hotel & sat me up on a platform with 5 pretty girls & put a crown on my head—& then began really fantastic scene— we went to the University where already a huge crowd of students gathered, I started drinking beer and singing Mantras with my trusty finger-cymbals, & then we began to parade thru town—but what nobody expected was what happend, because everybody who could walk in Prague came out & lined the streets—almost bigger than the regular May Day Parade—and we rolled around the old town streets & under Kafka's house gathering thousands & thousands more, I kept getting up & making drunken speeches dedicating my Crown to Kafka & stopped this huge parade under the house where he wrote the Trial—& made big announcement for that & sang Mantra Hari Om Namo Shiva there— Meanwhile the streets were getting lined with people, it was huge happy Crowd come out for a non-political good time party for the first time in 20 years—Everybody good mood singing & all the police off the streets, just student guards—finally we crossed the bridge over Moldau river on way to park & the bridge filled with thousands of people & huge procession behind us & crowds lining the rooftops—I kept waving to babies like a big idiot Politician—and by the time we got to this huge fair grounds filled with dancehalls & rock & roll gangs playing in auditorium there was a crowd of 100 thousand people assembled—so I just kept banging the cymbals & singing Om Sri Maitreya [Amen Future Buddha] till I was carried upon the platform for the election—Then all the candidates had to make a speech—all the universities entered their own candidate, about four in all plus me—The rest dressed like kings or clowns—I had on old levis & dirty shirt & wild hair—so when my turn came to make speech I first kept singing [Maitreya Future Buddha Mantra] 5 minutes & sat down—Anyway they all elected me King & with a big gang I ran around fairground all day feeling people up—at midnite we elected me a Queen—first beauty contest here for 20 years too so it was like a big political moment—the Party was unhappy & tried to get me dethroned at midnite but it was too late I guess so now I'm King of Prague by Gum. Newspapers played it down the next day but everybody thought it was a great idea. I'll find out next if I got my money Prize—maybe hundred or 200 dollars 4000 crowns—pretty insane scene—I hope they hear about it in Moscow & Havana—it's a surrealist week—

I don't know what next—maybe use the money to go to Hungary—or else my plane ticket is good for Berlin—I feel like seeing the rest of the redlands while I can—There's no need for me to get back except for California date in July—I feel like wandering around still—Berlin—London & maybe a week in Paris—& the plane ticket makes it all free—I got one letter (April 23) from you—The rest of my mail got sent by mistake to Moscow—It'll take weeks to reach me—

I'll write Simon Vinkenoog [Dutch poet-friend & translator]—Thanks for copy of his note—Can you send me copy of NY *Times* story on Havana homos—are you singing picketing?

Enclosed find note for post office. Incidentally I have a license to import written material for Cuba so you dont have to sign anything [at Post Office] about receiving commie propaganda. If there is any question, call my [lawyer] brother Eugene. I guess the FY/'s were returned by the Cuban post office? I couldn't figure it out.

Love to Julius & everybody. So fine in Prague, I just came—

Allen,
The May King

I'll be here a week or 2—then go to Budapest or Berlin—Can write me here, & if I leave they'll forward my mail right this time.

1 Andrei Andreyevich Voznesensky (born 1933), Soviet poet whose work is marked by brilliant use of language, fine craftsmanship, a wide range of subject matter and a profound knowledge of Russian poetic tradition.

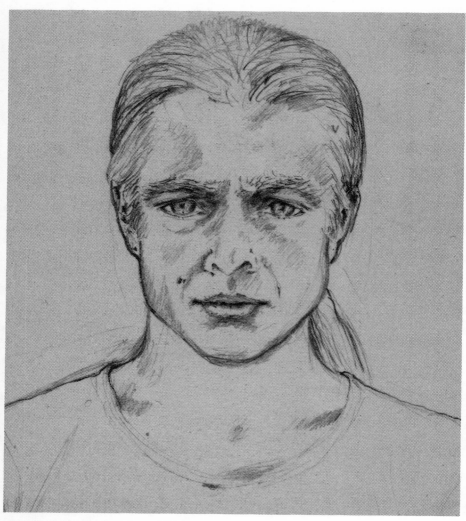

Peter Orlovsky
Drawing by Robert LaVigne, 1979

Allen Ginsberg
Drawing by Robert LaVigne, 1979

Allen Ginsberg in London to Peter Orlovsky in New York

care of T. Maschler
Jonathan Cape
30 Bedford Square
London W.C. 1
10 May 1965

Dear Peter:
You got my last letter from Czechoslovakia? King of May & all that? And THEN several nights later I was walking on street with a young couple, nice boy & girl, when a strange man rounded a corner, stepped between us, hesitated, looked at me, & suddenly exploded "Bouzerant!" (Fairy!) "Bouzerant!" and attacked me knocked me down—I ran down street but he got me down again & suddenly there were 5 policemen with lifted clubs over my head—I though oh oh now I'm going to get it & started humming Hari Om to the pavement—but they didn't hit, just took us all down to police station all night. The man who attacked said (1) we were doing naked obscene things on street (2) we'd attacked him. I couldn't figure it all out, except I think he was a police agent—"provocateur" as they say—
Meanwhile a notebook of mine suddenly disappeared from my pocket. The nite after I was attacked, plainclothes police came up to me in a restaurant on outskirts of town, said "Mr. Ginsberg we found your notebook come with us a half an hour and you'll get it back"—So I went to station, signed a paper identifying it as mine—and after I signed their faces turned cold & they said "and now we must inform you that we are turning your notebook over to the public prosecutor for closer examination because rapid surveyof its contents indicates illegal writings"—
Fortunately it was small notebook & I hadn't written much in it, a few sex descriptions with kids & some vague politics conversation.
So I went out that nite & sang songs & slept with a gang of painters & girls & next morn phoned the U.S. consul, told him. Then I went to breakfast downtown—all last days I'd had feeling I was being followed—and at breakfast some plainclothes Kafkan Czechoslovak security man sat down with us & told me to come to police again—I said, "can I make a phonecall?" & he said "yes—at the station"—but when I got there it was a roomful of bureaucrats & the head of Immigration Dept & an anonymous commissar—"Due to many complaints about your presence in Prague from parents and scientists & educators who disapprove of your sexual theories we are shortening your Visa and you will leave Czechoslovakia today."

So they took me in car to Hotel & I packed & they wouldn't let me make phone call to Embassy—detective stayed in room with me 4 hours till time for airplane & they drove me out guarded & isolated so no one would know, and I arrived in London that nite—April 7 [May 7].

Next day (slept at Anselm Hollo's) I went to Savoy Hotel, Bob Dylan's there & spent last 2 days with him[1]—last night huge concert at Albert Hall & thousands of beautiful longhaired teenagers—found Barbara Rubin in seat next to mine[2]—looking healthy—and after concert went to Dylan's room till 3 AM met with the Beatles finally—I spent all my time falling tipsy into their lap & yelling about William Blake—they make believe they never heard of him—I may have a moment's walk-on part in their movie—So anyway I'm in London & got to go to US Embassy get messages to Prague to get my notebook—it has that "Message" Poem with line "I lie in bed with teenage boys afraid of the red police" [See p. 168 of this book]—and some other good poems; I had fortunately copied most of them out except one I wrote on May King Stage (I sat down in front of crowd in a quiet moment & wrote a nice poem.)—Czechoslovak police stole my poem!—[3]

I can't make a stink, it's like blackmail, if I yell loud to newspapers they'll *use* whatever is in my notebooks to make scandal—sex dreams—which I don't care—but they might persecute people I described in Prague Ugh! Anyway I'll stay in London a month & I guess come back in June—I'll be with Tom Maschler [editor Jonathan Cape].

Please *phone* my brother & give him new London address. I'll write him in one or 2 days. Now I got to rush out to Embassy & then publisher & then Dylan at Savoy & tonite Albert Hall second concert—

Such adventures!

Love from
The May King
(deposed by police)
Allen

1 Anselm Hollo—American poet, author of *Some Worlds* etc.; Bob Dylan—See opening scenes of *Don't Look Back,* Pennybaker's Dylan documentary.

2 Barbara Rubin—filmmaker, *Christmas on Earth,* & girlfriend of those years.

3 See the poem "Kral Majales," page 45 of this book, for Ginsberg's poetic reflections on his Prague experiences.

Peter Orlovsky in New York to Allen Ginsberg in London

12:50 pm
May 14, 1965

Just got yr england check woe letter: yr brother not in will call back later. Those police are prity lie snapey on their words.

Yes its too bad about that blackmail & others in Prague may get prese-cuted tho an individual you could say what happened to the papers & that you were not given an opertunity to answer back the critics. Ed Sanders has yr Cuban Journals & Richard Sever of Grove called about a month ago & wanted to know whear you were & I mensioned to him yr note books & he said he would like to see them, is that alright with you? Just a look read & then give back. Its too bad about being bosted out of Prague, it shows that sex love talk & suck is a big exploseive—if not more then the Hydro-gen bomb. I had just sent you about 12 photo copy of yr letters to Prague so that you could answer yr mail but now yr may not even get that tho I think they will just might forward it on to you if the Writers Union knows yr new address?—Gregore Corso is at c/o Paolo Lionni, Corso Magenta 69, Milano, Italy. He just sent me a note saying he want to get in tuch with you—he goet fired from his job at Buffallo for refuseing to sign the loyality oath so decided to hop over to Milano with Paolo who paid a bit of his fair. Theres going to be a confruntation with the arms day forces parade this tomorrow the 15th, a sit-in on 5th ave & about 71st—I was thinking of going & sitting down, have 50$ to pay if 500 bail needed, main problem is not to cause riot so will put a suit on tho it would be lovely to take my clothes off & make a big naked save the body gesutre, in short cause a spectale of laff, the other problem is to get past the police live or thru their legs cause they might be knowing by now that such a scene will be taking place. Will get in tuch with my brother Nick to take care of Julius at his place for a week if it hap a week jail scentance come up. Still working at the 8th St. Book Shop tho am going to turn my job over to John Keys who's looking for work to make 800$ to travel maybe. Ismeal Reed, Calvern Herton, Dave Henderson & Al Katzman all plan to attend writers & artists conference at Algeria this summer & go on ture reading in progue I think other red countries & england maybe. So see if ya can have the writers union in Prague send yr mail to you in england. Just jerkedoff again, must of come about 60 times in the last month—begininging to think it better to save it for a public scene rather than do it in an empty alone room. Glad to hear ya got some good clean ass party in Prague before ya left. Am sending ya Jacks *NY Times* review—I was told that in the sunday before this review there was also a rightup on Desolation angles. Ed is planing a card tabol letter writting campain in washington sq. park this saturday or something like that. We did a demonstration, the sex league infrunt of Gracie Mansion protesting the, more like picket, anti-smut drive thats gathering forse with the mayor & a bill being proposed in the legislature to make all nudes pictures disappear. I see the homosexuals in London—hers a cliping on it. Will make copies of this these on photo machine so ya can do what ever ya like with them.

I hear Ken Kesey's film & maybe Ken Kesey got arrested because of the sex pot smokeing.[1] Okay, will get this off to ya now & will keep ya informed if aneything comes up . . . take care & have a ball

Glad to hear about yr film, Ed. S. is doing making a film too, Robert Frank is continueing along to[2] Glad to hearya meet Brabra rubins—Harey Smith is or was in Jail for puilling a fire alarm but I believe Pana Grady bailed him out—hes been truning over garbage cans & pulling off radio car arieles like a fool.

Julius drinking too much water, getting a big stomache but it goes down when he stopes it again will call up yr brother & give him yr new address & read yr letter to him over the phone

keep hot there lover.
Kisses Peter—

Yes I got yr last King of May letter—There was meeting last night with AJ Muste & artists & writters Ed Sanders, Tuli Kupferberg & [Seymour] Krim & me.

1 Ken Kesey, novelist, cultural pioneer, blueberry yogurt farmer, author of *One Flew Over the Cuckoo's Nest* and *Sometimes a Great Notion*.
2 Robert Frank, photographer-filmmaker, *Pull My Daisy* and *Me and My Brother* (starring Julius Orlovsky).

Dear Reader: We hate to drag you thru all this gossip. It's all worked out fine. Cherrey Oats & we'll see you around town.

— Peter Orlovsky
nut tree farmer, poet-teacher-singer
Naropa Institute,
Boulder, Colorado
August 1, 1979

About the Authors

Born Paterson, New Jersey, 1926, son of Louis Ginsberg, a lyric poet and school teacher, and Naomi, Russian émigrée. Grammar High School Paterson, B.A. Columbia College 1948; associations with Jack Kerouac, Wm. S. Burroughs, Herbert H. Huncke & Neal Cassady begun 1945 NYC and next decade after with Gregory Corso, Peter Orlovsky companion 1954 & poets Michael McClure, Philip Lamantia, Gary Snyder & Philip Whalen in San Francisco became known 1955 on as "Beat Generation" and/or "San Francisco Renaissance" literary phases; acquaintance with William Carlos Williams 1948 & study of his relative-footed American speech prosody led to *Empty Mirror* early poems with W.C.W. preface, as later Williams introduced *Howl*.

Illuminative audition of William Blake's voice simultaneous with Eternity-vision 1948 and underground bust-culture Apocalypse-realization conduced to 8-month stay NY State Psychiatric Institute & later preoccupation with Gnostic-mystic poetics and politics, residence in India & Viet-Nam Japan visit 1962-3, mantra chanting beginning with Hare Krishna Mahamantra and Buddhist Prajnaparamita (Highest Perfect Wisdom) Sutra same years, & experiment with poetic effects of psychedelic drugs beginning 1952 and continuing with Dr. Timothy Leary through Cambridge experiments 1961: certain texts *Howl* part II (1955) and *Wales Visitation* (1957) were written during effects of Peyote & LSD respectively.

Travel began early 1950's half year Mayan Mexico, several voyages years Tangiers-Europe late 50's on, earlier merchant marine sea trips to Africa & Arctic, half year Chile Bolivia & Peru Amazon 1960, half year Cuba Russia Poland Czechoslovakia culminating May Day 1965 election as King of May (Kral Majales) by 100,000 Prague citizens.

Literary Awards: obscenity trial with *Howl* text declared legal by court S.F. 1957, Guggenheim Fellowship 1963-4, National Institute of Arts and Letters Grant for poetry 1969. Contributing Editor: *Black Mountain Review* no. 7 edited by Robert Creeley; Advisory Guru: *The Marijuana Review;* writing published variously in *Yugen, Floating Bear Mimeo, Kulcher, Big Table, City Lights Journal, "C," Evergreen Review, Fuck You/A Magzine of the Arts, Atlantic Monthly, Life, New Yorker, Look, N.Y. Times, Izvestia, Rolling Stone, Underground Press Syndicate,* etc.

Participated in college poetry readings & NY Literary scene '58-'61 with Leroi Jones & Frank O'Hara; Poet's *Pull My Daisy*, Robert Frank film 1959; early Trips Festivals with Ken Kesey Neal Cassady & Merry Pranksters mid-60's; Vancouver '63 & Berkeley '65 Poetry Conventions with Olson, Duncan, Creeley, Snyder, Dorn & other poet friends; Albert Hall Poetry Incarnation, readings with Vosnesensky in London, and anti-Vietnam War early Flower Power marches in Berkeley 1965.

Attended mantra-chanting at first Human Be-in San Francisco 1967; conferred at *Dialectics of Liberation* in London & gave poetry readings with poet father Louis Ginsberg there and in NY; testified U.S. Senate hearings for legalization of psychedelics; arrested with Dr. Benjamin Spock blocking Whitehall Draft Board steps war protest NY same year. Teargassed chanting AUM at Lincoln Park Yippie Life-Festival Chicago 1968 Presidential convention, then accompanied Jean Genet & William Burroughs on front line Peace "Conspiracy" march led by Dave Dellinger.

Mantric poetics and passing acquaintance with poet-singers Ezra Pound, Bob Dylan, Ed Sanders, & Mick Jagger led to music study for tunes to Wm. Blake's *Songs of Innocence and Experience;* this homage to visionary poet-guru William Blake, occasioned by visit West Coast to touch a satin bag of body-ashes the late much-loved Neal Cassady, was composed one week on return from police-state shock in Chicago, & recorded summer 1969. Chanted OM to Judge and Jury December 1969 Anti-War-Conspiracy trial Chicago; thereafter interrupted by Miami Police on reading poetry exorcising police bureaucracy Prague & Pentagon, rapid Federal Court Mandatory Injunction declared texts Constitutionally protected from police censorship. Pallbore funerals late Kerouac & Olson, last few '60's winters spent outside cities learning music milking cows & goats.

1971 — Began daily hour-subvocal mantra heart meditation, Swami Muktananda teacher; brief journey Bengal Jessore Road Calcutta to E. Pakistan refugee camps & revisit Benares. Jamming at home & recording studios w/ Dylan & Happy Traum learned Blues forms. *Kaddish* play mounted N.Y. Chelsea Theater. Researched & publicized CIA subsidization Indochinese opium traffic; assembled 16 phono albums *Collected Poems Vocalized* 1946-71 from decades' tape archives. Completed second album Blake Songs.

1972 — Began study Kagu lineage Tibetan style Buddhist meditation, Chögyam Trungpa, Rinpoche teacher; took Refuge and Boddhisattva vows; extended poetic practice to public improvisation on blues chords with politic Dharma themes. Adelaide and Central Australia meeting with Aboriginal songmen, Darwin Land travel with Russian poet Andrei Vosnesensky. Jailed with hundreds of peace protestors, Miami Presidential Convention; essays in defence of Tim Leary, Abbie Hoffman, John Lennon etc. from Federal Narcotics Bureau entrapment, as member of P.E.N. Freedom to Read Committee.

1973 — Poetry International London & Rotterdam; meetings with Basil Bunting & Hugh McDiarmid, tour Scotland/Inner Hebrides. Taught poetics Naropa Seminary; all Autumn retreat Buddhist study including month's 10-hour daily sitting practice.

1974 — Inducted member National Institute of Arts and Letters. National Book Award for *Fall of America;* apprenticed rough carpentry wooden cottage neighbouring Gary Snyder Sierra land; with Anne Waldman founded Jack Kerouac School of Disembodied Poetics, Naropa Institute now 1111 Pearl Street, Boulder Colorado; co-director teaching subsequent summers.

1975 — Poetics school solidified; poet-percussionist on Bob Dylan's Rolling Thunder Review tour, filmed improvised blues at Kerouac's grave; *First Blues* with lead sheet music notation published.

1976 — Reading Academie Der Kunste, Berlin with Wm. Burroughs; *First*

Blues recordings produced by John Hammond Sr.; several months fall seminar retreat with Chögyam Trungpa.

1977 — Read thru Blake's entire Works, wrote "Contest of Bards," narrated TV film *Kaddish,* presented poetry/music Nightclub *Troubadour* L.A. under Buddhist auspice, thereafter N.Y. *Other End* & Boston *Passim* folk clubs. Read with Robert Lowell St. Mark's N.Y. Taught Blake's *Urizen* Naropa Institute spring, summer. Attended U. of Cal. Santa Cruz LSD Conference, visited Kaui.

1978 — Naropa summer Discourse on Meditation & Poetics; Composed music for Blake's "Tyger" to Trochaic heart-beat meters. Composed "Plutonian Ode" and arrested twice at Rocky Flats Colo. Nuclear Facility with Orlovsky & Daniel Ellsberg practicing sitting meditation on railroad tracks blocking train bearing Plutonium/"fissile materials." Month's fall meditation retreat at Bedrock Mortar Hermitage in California Sierras. Film *Fried Shoes, Cooked Diamonds* at Kerouac Poetics School with Orlovsky, Burroughs, Corso, Ellsberg, Leary, Waldman, Nuyorican Poets, Diane Di Prima, Leroi Jones, Chögyam Trungpa.

1979 — Taught Blake's *Lambeth* Prophetic books to *Four Zoas* at Naropa & poetry Brooklyn College Spring; Video film with Alan Kaprow by Nam June Paik; attended Gay Rights mass meet Washington Monument; several European tours accompanying Corso, Orlovsky & Living Theater with Steven Taylor musician, visited Blake's cottage Felpham, read and sang at Oxford, Heidelberg, Tübingen & International Poetry convocations Cambridge, Rotterdam & Amsterdam, Paris, Genoa, Rome.

1980 — Composed *On the Tongue* (literary conversations), edited by Don Allen, Grey Fox Press, Bolinas.

Poetry Books

Howl and Other Poems. City Lights Books, SF, 1956.
Kaddish and Other Poems. City Lights Books, SF, 1961.
Empty Mirror, Early Poems. Totem/Corinth, NY, 1961.
Reality Sandwiches. City Lights Books, SF, 1963.
Ankor Wat. Fulcrum Press, London, 1968.
Airplane Dreams. Anansi/City Lights Books, SF, 1968.
Planet News. City Lights Books, SF, 1968.
The Gates of Wrath, Rhymed Poems 1948-51. Grey Fox Press, Bolinas, 1972.
The Fall of America, Poems of These States. City Lights Books, SF, 1973.
Iron Horse. Coach House Press, Toronto/City Lights Books, SF, 1973.
First Blues. Full Court Press, NY, 1975.
Mind Breaths, Poems 1971-76. City Lights Books, SF, 1977.
Poems All Over the Place. Cherry Valley Editions, 1978.
Mostly Sitting Haiku. From Here Press, Paterson, NJ, 1978.
Careless Love. The Red Ozier Press, Madison, 1978.

Prose Books

The Yage Letters. (w/Wm. S. Burroughs), City Lights, SF, 1963.
Indian Journals. David Hazelwood/City Lights, SF, 1970.
Improvised Poetics. Anonym Books, Buffalo, 1971. Distr. by City Lights, SF.

Gay Sunshine Interview. Grey Fox Press, Bolinas, 1974.
Allen Verbatim: Lectures on Poetry etc. McGraw Hill, 1974.
The Visions of the Great Rememberer. Mulch Press, Amherst, Mass., 1974.
Chicago Trial Testimony. City Lights Trashcan of History Series, no. 1, SF, 1975.
To Eberhart from Ginsberg. Penmaen Press, Lincoln, Mass., 1976.
Journals Early Fifties Early Sixties. Grove Press, NY, 1977.
As Ever, Collected Correspondence of Allen Ginsberg & Neal Cassady. Creative Arts,
     SF, 1977.

PETER ORLOVSKY

Born July 8, 1933, in the vanished Women's Infirmary in Lower East Side N.Y.
Sometime ambulance Attendant, farmer, housecleaner, silkscreen handyman,
newsboy, Postal Clerk & instructor at Kerouac School of Poetics, he was
discharged from Military after telling government psychiatrist, "An army is an
army against love." Witness of the '50's San Francisco Poetry Renaissance, he
was portrayed by Jack Kerouac as hospital nurse saint Simon Darlovsky among
Desolation Angels, learned driving speech from Neal Cassady & taught heart in
return, partook of psychedelic revolution a pillar of strength with Timothy
Leary & Charles Olson, companioned Kerouac & William Burroughs in Tanger,
was one of the first American poets to make modern passage to India in early
'60's accompanying Gary Snyder & Allen Ginsberg, studied Sarod, Banjo &
Guitar, read poetry in Chicago & at Harvard Columbia Princeton Yale & New
York's St. Marks Poetry Project, survived Speed & Junk Hells, sang in jail at
anti-war protest & political convention occasions, was published in historic
Beatitude & Don Allen Anthologies of *New American Poetry,* played Self in early
underground Robert Frank Movies, travelled with Dylan's *Rolling Thunder
Review,* farmed solitary upstate New York ten years organic & herculean, fed
and nursed decades of poetry families. An experienced Buddhist sitter & Vajra-
yana meditation practitioner, his Dharma name is "Ocean of Generosity."

Books

Dear Allen: Ship will land Jan 23, 58. Beau Fleuve Series No. 5, Intrepid Press,
     Buffalo, 1971.
Lepers Cry, Phoenix Book Shop, NY, 1972.
Clean Asshole Poems & Smiling Vegetable Songs. City Lights Books, SF, 1978.

236

Index of Names

(Chronology, Interview, Letters)

Parkinson, Thomas, 134,
137-138, 140n
Parra, Nicanor, 189, 220
Patchen, Kenneth, 135-
136n
Peret, Benjamen, 175
Philippe, Gerard, 162n
Pivano, Nanda, 218
Plato, 156
Portman, Michael, 204-
206, 208n

Quendo de Amat, Carlos,
194-195n

Ray, Man, 175
Reed, Ishmael, 230
Rimbaud, Arthur, 201
Rivers, Larry, 111, 185
Romanova, Ylena, 211-
212n
Rosen, Dr. J., 163
Rosenthal, Irving, 158,
192n, 194-195n, 210-
211, 218, 221
Rubin, Barbara, 229, 231
Rumaker, Michael, 138,
157, 162n

S., Lois, 218
Sanders, Ed, 219, 230-231
Sansher, 215-216
Santamaria, Haydee, 221-
223n
Schlachtner, Henry, 138,
140n, 148, 159, 196,
216
Schoen, Steve, 179

Schulman, Howie, 211,
219
Selby, Hubert, 220
Sever, Richard, 230
Shakespeare, William, 136,
139
Shastri, Trilochan, 214
Sheila, 111
Shelley, Percy Bysshe,
139, 167
Shields, Karena, 124n
Shinder, Jason, 12
Shulman, Howard, 221
Singh, Namwar, 215
Singh, Samsher Bahadur,
214
Sitwell, Edith, 169
Smith, Harry, 231
Smith, Linda, 221
Snyder, Gary, 11, 157,
196-197n, 210-211,
215, 217, 220
Snyder, Joanne, 11, 210
Sokolsky, George, 197
Solomon, Carl, 143, 159,
175, 178
Somerville, Ian, 204-205n
Soutine, Chaim, 147
Spellman, Francis Cardinal,
162n
Sqvorecky, Josef, 223
Stern, Jacques, 175, 177-
178
Stevenson, Pamela, 203-
204
Sutherland, Alistair, 169

Taylor, Simon W., 137,
140n, 169

Trungpa, Chögyam, 162n
Turnbull, Gael, 136
Turner, J. M. W., 136
Tzara, Tristan, 175

Valentine, 181
Vial, Ron, 215
Vijyashankar, 212-213n
Villon, François, 123, 146
Vinkenoog, Simon, 225
Vosnosensky, Andrei, 215,
223, 225n

W., Billy, 171, 173
Wakefield, Dan, 159
Wallace, Mike, 135, 141,
152
Whalen, Philip, 128n, 136,
148, 152, 157, 160,
196-197n, 213, 220
White, J. Richard, 218n
Whitman, George, 134-
135n, 176
Wieners, John, 188, 192n,
194-196, 200-201,
203n
Wilentz, Ted, 220
Williams, Jonathan, 161
Wilson, Colin, 211
Wisdom, Ignaz, 155
Wyse, Seymour, 137

Yacoubi, Achmed, 203,
205n

Zak, Nathan, 217
Zambelli, Hugo, 190, 192
Zebrann, Jan, 223